D0380347

Why People Don't Trust Government

Why People Don't Trust Government

Edited by
Joseph S. Nye, Jr.
Philip D. Zelikow
David C. King

Harvard University Press
Cambridge, Massachusetts
London, England

Library of Congress Cataloging-in-Publication Data

Why people don't trust government / edited by Joseph S. Nye, Jr.,
  Philip D. Zelikow, David C. King.
      p.   cm.
   Includes bibliographical references and index.
    ISBN 0-674-94056-3 (cloth).—ISBN 0-674-94057-1 (paper)
     1. Political participation—United States.   2. Political
alienation—United States.   3. Political culture—United States.
4. Public opinion—United States.   5. Allegiance—United States.
I. Nye, Joseph S.   II. Zelikow, Philip, 1954–   .   III. King, David C.
JK1764.W59   1997
306.2'0973'09049—dc21   97-20363

Third printing, 1998

9/98

Contents

Preface

The idea for this book began with the bombing of the Alfred P. Murrah Federal Building in Oklahoma City in April 1995. The shock of the terrorist attack was followed by a troubled and confusing debate about the role of government in the United States. Americans have always had a healthy skepticism about concentrated power, but at the time of the bombing the levels of trust seemed to be at a new low. The founding fathers created checks and balances and divided power between the states and the federal government because they cared about preserving individual liberties. But they also knew that effective government was essential to the new republic's promise of life, liberty, and the pursuit of happiness.

What will effective government mean in the next century? We have been told that the era of big government is over, but no one has yet articulated what will take its place. Clearly change is needed. We are witnessing a widespread loss of confidence in and a dissatisfaction with government as it is currently functioning. While the possible reasons for this situation are many, the simple fact that the world itself is changing rapidly stands as the primary cause. Mid–twentieth-century visions of government must yield to new conceptions consistent with an information-based economy and society.

In an effort to understand the changes needed, the Kennedy School of Government has inaugurated a multiyear research and outreach project that will consider and articulate Visions of Governance for the Twenty-first Century. The project will explore what people and communities want from government, from the private sector, and from nonprofit organizations. Participants will consider the areas in which government, both in the United States and abroad, is currently succeeding and failing. Scholars will work with civic leaders and citizens to study the balance between individual liberty and the needs of the community and how societal trends are affecting that balance. The project will address issues such as the relationship between markets and governments, the distribution of public power, the emergence of mediating institutions, and the processes of public decision-making.

Understanding governance is central to the mission of the Kennedy School. Our multidisciplinary faculty is involved in research, teaching, and public outreach, all of which contribute to better public service in democracies. The Kennedy School does not stand for large or small government but for clarity in thinking about the role of the public, private, and nonprofit sectors in managing the common aspects of the lives of citizens—in other words, governance. This book, which focuses on why confidence in government has plummeted, does not provide solutions. It is a first step in our new project and a continuation of our mission to foster better understanding and improved public service in our democracy.

Many have contributed to this volume and this project. We are grateful to members of the Senior Study Group, many of whom participated in our special meeting at Bretton Woods, New Hampshire: Graham Allison, Alan Altshuler, Francis Bator, Robert Blendon, Derek Bok, George Borjas, John Donahue, former congressman Mickey Edwards, David Ellwood, Henry Louis Gates, Mary Ann Glendon, Stanley Hoffmann, Samuel Huntington, Christopher Jencks, Marvin Kalb, Joseph Kalt, Robert Lawrence, Jane Mansbridge, Harvey Mansfield, Theodore Marmor, Ernest May, Thomas McCraw, Mark Moore, Richard Neustadt, Joseph Newhouse, Katherine Newman, Gary Orren, Thomas Patterson, Paul Peterson, Susan Pharr, Roger Porter, Robert Putnam, former governor Barbara Roberts, Michael Sandel, Fred Schauer, former congressman Phil Sharp, Theda Skocpol, Raymond Vernon, Shirley Williams, William Julius Wilson, and Richard Zeckhauser. We are also grateful for the comments and criticisms of numerous colleagues, including Robert Keohane, Pippa Norris, Richard Parker, Daniel Yankelovich, and Jane Wales. Careful readers will note frequent citations to papers written for the Bretton Woods meeting. Scholars who wish to examine these more closely may do so by referring to our web site, http://www.ksg.harvard.edu/visions.

We thank the Carnegie Corporation of New York, Parker G. Montgomery, the Daniel and Joanna S. Rose Fund, and the Henry J. Kaiser Family Foundation for their support.

Last but not least, we are grateful to the able staff efforts of Lori Carr Treviño, Cathy Coyle, Robin Worth, Sara Porter, Zach Karabell, Janet Fletcher Hauswirth, and Sarah Peterson.

Joseph S. Nye, Jr.
Philip D. Zelikow
David C. King

Introduction: The Decline of Confidence in Government

Joseph S. Nye, Jr.

Confidence in government has declined. In 1964, three-quarters of the American public said that they trusted the federal government to do the right thing most of the time. Today only a quarter of Americans admit to such trust. The numbers are only slightly better—35 percent—for state government. Some polls show even lower levels. A 1995 poll showed a confidence rate of 15 percent at the federal level, 23 percent at the state level, and 31 percent at the local level. In 1997, the same poll showed a slight improvement to 22, 32, and 38 percent at the federal, state, and local levels, still far behind the numbers three decades ago. The top reasons given for distrusting government are that it is inefficient, wastes money, and spends on the wrong things.[1]

Government is not alone. Over the past three decades public confidence has dropped in half for many major institutions: 61 percent to 30 percent for universities; 55 percent to 21 percent for major companies; 73 percent to 29 percent for medicine; and 29 percent to 14 percent for journalism. In a 1996 poll, 30 percent of the public said that they had hardly any confidence in the leaders of the press—about the same as for Congress.[2] Nor is the United States alone. Canada,

Britain, Italy, Spain, Belgium, the Netherlands, Norway, Sweden, and Ireland have also seen some decline of trust in government.[3] In Japan, mistrust of politics has been high for several decades, but more recently it has spread to include the bureaucracy as well.[4]

If the decline of confidence affected only government or only the United States, the issue might seem rather straightforward. Perhaps the federal government has outgrown its public support. In 1929, before the Great Depression and World War II, the size of the federal budget relative to the gross national product was under 3 percent; today it is 19 percent. (State and local governments account for another 14 percent.) Public spending at all levels of government increased from 18 percent of GNP in 1947 to 30 percent in 1973, but only slightly thereafter.[5] Although this is one of the lowest levels among advanced countries, it represents a considerable departure from the American past. Moreover, the composition of what the government does has changed dramatically. In 1954, 70 percent of federal expenditure was for national defense; today it is closer to 17 percent.

For the past decade the overall size of the federal budget relative to the GNP has not increased. And within that total, the areas of growth have been transfer payments—Social Security and health care—that are popular with the public. Another reason to be suspicious of simple explanations such as the idea that government has outgrown its support is the drop in confidence in many other major institutions. Have companies, churches, universities, and medicine also grown too fast, or are there broader causes? The best explanations should tell us something about government, but in a larger context.

Does It Matter?

Whatever the symptoms, we should not overly worry about causes if the consequences do not matter. The "So what?" question comes first. One possibility is that the current symptoms are a sign of health. The United States was founded with a mistrust of government. The American Constitution was deliberately set up in such a way that a King George could never rule over us again. And some might add, "Nor anybody else." In the federalist debates that divided the early republic, there was clearly a difference between the Thomas Jefferson side and the Alexander Hamilton side. Hamilton believed that the United States needed a strong central government, whereas Jefferson felt that the less government the better. A long Jeffersonian tradition says we should not worry too much about the level of confidence in government. If the polls reflect wariness rather than cynicism, the result may be healthy.

Second, if you look not at the way government works day to day but at the underlying constitutional framework, the public opinion polls are still positive. If you ask Americans what is the best place in the world to live, 80 percent say the United States. If you ask them whether they like their democratic system of government, 90 percent say yes. If one looks at the Eurobarometer polls in Europe, even in those countries where there is a decline in confidence in government, 90 percent are "satisfied with a democratic form of government."[6] At the constitutional regime level, the current situation is not like France in 1968—much less 1789! Most people do not feel that the system is rotten and has to be overthrown. Oklahoma City was an aberration. Militias are not the norm. Something is steady, even though there is less confidence in governmental institutions than there was three or four decades ago.

Some aspects of the current mood are probably cyclical, while others represent discontent with gridlock and bickering in the political process rather than deep disillusion with government. Part of what we see is a cyclical swing in the pendulum of public attitudes. For example, 1900 also saw a prevailing mood of nationwide irritation. Compared with the recent past, party politics has become more polarized, but nasty politics is nothing new. In the 1884 presidential campaign between James G. Blaine and Grover Cleveland, the two prevailing slogans were "Blaine, Blaine, James G. Blaine, the continental liar from the State of Maine" and "Ma, Ma, where's my Pa? Gone to the White House, ha, ha, ha"—referring to Cleveland's illegitimate child. Perhaps the current problem is that expectations of government became too high after World War II.[7] In that case, the anomaly would be the 1950s, and the solution would be to reduce expectations to a more "normal" historical level. Then the mood may improve.

Nonetheless, there remains a case for concern. Differences of degree exist between loss of confidence, dissatisfaction, cynicism, and hatred. But what is the connection between them? Does low confidence tend to become cumulative? If politicians and the press repeat as conventional wisdom that government cannot do anything right, does that breed cynicism? Business experts talk of "demarketing campaigns" in which consumers are urged not to buy certain products. Since Jimmy Carter's campaign of 1976, presidential candidates have tended to "run against Washington." Now most politicians do. Studies show that over the past three decades the media have tended to report on politics and the government with a much more negative slant.[8] This might not matter if the only casualty were the vanity of politicians, but over time such devaluation of government and politics could affect the strength of democratic institutions. Social scientists do not fully understand the relationship between satisfaction with day-to-day government and support for democracy as a regime, but one thing is clear: the future of democratic governance matters very much.

Three ways in which institutional confidence and regime stability might be connected are through the willingness of the public to provide such crucial resources as tax dollars, the willingness of bright young people to go into government, and voluntary compliance with laws.[9] If people believe that government is incompetent and cannot be trusted, they are less likely to provide these resources. Without critical resources, government cannot perform well, and if government cannot perform, people will become more dissatisfied and distrustful of it. Such a cumulative downward spiral could erode support for democracy as a form of governance. Even if government were cut back significantly from its current one-third of our GNP to something like a quarter, that is still a large part of our common life to be poorly administered.

In the next century, the information and biotechnology revolutions and the increasing importance of the global economy will pose new challenges. Some argue that the best thing for government to do is to get out of the way and leave the responses to the private sector. Certainly government needs to adapt to new conceptions consistent with an information-based economy and society in which private and nonprofit actors are likely to play a larger role but a weak and ineffective government performance could be costly. For example, in a global economy, political stability attracts capital; education provides crucial skills; basic research in science and technology enhances competitiveness and living standards; and protection of intellectual property rights becomes more important. Provision of such public goods depends on effective government. In the defense domain, while the end of the cold war seems to have reduced the traditional sense of external threat, the rise of transnational terrorism and the proliferation of weapons of mass destruction are new types of threat that will require effective government responses.

In addition to the costs of ineffective government performance, the decline of trust may have a cost in terms of democratic values. The U.S. Constitution created institutions that encouraged deliberative democracy. The American system was not designed to be efficient in producing action. As James Madison wrote in *The Federalist Papers,* it was designed to encourage extensive debate and the protection of liberties. If the political process becomes merely political consultants using polls and focus groups to learn what politicians should tell the public via thirty-second advertisements, Madison's deliberative democracy will shrink to a "thin" democracy. Except for writing checks and pulling a lever in a voting booth, the citizen's role will wither. Cynicism about the political process and the elected government may reduce participation and the quality of our democracy. Despite some signs of the "thinning of democracy," recent studies indicate that several areas of participation remain strong. The question is whether a continuing decline in confidence would seriously erode Madison's deliberative democracy.[10]

The polls showing a loss of confidence in government and other institutions over the past three decades must be taken with a grain of salt. Survey research has its limits. Polls are snapshots of moving targets. Responses vary with the phrasing and context of the questions that are asked. The data are incomplete. And even if the questions and sampling procedures were perfect, a degree of wariness and skepticism about government is healthy for a democracy. But if the sky is not falling, neither is all well with the world. A clear assessment lies somewhere between Chicken Little and Pollyanna. The purpose of this book is not to provide solutions, but to clear the ground so that we have a better understanding of where we are in the evolution of democratic governance. We do this by asking three questions: What does government do? (its "scope"); How is it doing? (its performance); and How is it seen by its citizens? (its perceived performance). Then we ask why things have changed over the past three decades by examining a series of political, economic, and social-cultural hypotheses about causes.

Scope of Government

The scope of government has not expanded constantly throughout history. On the contrary, the Enlightenment in the eighteenth century removed government from many of the religious and moral aspects of daily life and left those to privileged private life. The U.S. Constitution was a product of Enlightenment thinking. Government was to (1) establish justice, (2) ensure domestic tranquillity, (3) provide for the common defense, (4) promote the general welfare, and (5) secure the blessings of liberty. This is a limited but potentially expansive list that can (and has) been used to justify a broad range of issues. While nineteenth-century government was limited, it played a significant role in education, public works, and the allocation of new lands as well as defense, justice, and order. At the turn of the twentieth century, in response to the rise of large corporations that accompanied the second industrial revolution, government became a counterbalance to private power through antitrust and regulatory roles. Even before the Great Depression, the American political system turned Civil War pensions and laws protecting women and children into an extensive redistribution system.[11] The largest expansion of government's scope, however, was in response to the depression, World War II, the cold war, and the accompanying rise of the welfare state.

A possible explanation of the current dissatisfaction with government in the United States is that its scope has expanded too much, that it has intruded into areas best left to private life. At first glance, responses to poll questions only partly support this view. When asked why they distrust the federal government, respondents to polls tend to stress poor performance more than ambitious scope. Eighty-one percent say government is wasteful and inefficient, and 79 percent say it spends too much money on the wrong things, but only half that number say that it is interfering too much in people's lives or that the problems that it is trying to solve cannot be solved by the federal government.[12] If 40 percent feel that government scope is too broad, that is an important fact for politicians to consider, but in a democracy one might expect a roughly even split between those who want more and less government. For much of the period of its greatest growth (from the mid-1930s to the mid-1960s), government remained popular, and the areas of most rapid growth in the federal budget—Social Security and Medicare—enjoy broad support. And despite their lack of confidence in government, a majority of Americans believe government should regulate business on matters of environment, product safety, unsafe working conditions, discriminatory hiring, and failed pension funds.[13]

It is also possible that the American public holds inconsistent views about what it wants from government. Majorities want the federal budget balanced, but not at the cost of cutting large programs like Social Security or Medicare. This lack of consensus on what to cut makes it difficult for any party to fulfill what people say they want of government. It is also possible that public concern about the scope of the federal government has less to do with its greater share of GNP (which has not grown significantly in the past two decades) than with its regulatory role in environmental and safety matters, or its role in promoting racial and gender change. Whatever the substantive gains in safety or justice, a sense of intrusiveness accompanies such roles. Federal actions promoting racial integration of schools, for example, created resentments in segments of the public both in South Boston as well as the South.

If one looks at the question of what government *should* do, one can identify at least three different normative models that Americans use. One is the microeconomist's model that can be traced back to Adam Smith. Government plays a limited but crucial role in providing defense, establishing property rights, maintaining justice, and creating public works and institutions that make commerce possible. A second is a more macroeconomic view that has arisen in this century and argues that the government should also dampen business cycles and pay attention to distributional effects of markets. Certainly management of the economy now seems to be part of what the public wants, for electoral studies show that the strongest predictor of presidential elections is the condition of the economy.[14] A third approach, the civic virtue model, holds that government should go beyond economic concerns and become involved in promoting the public and private virtues of the republic.[15] Purely neutral government is impossible, because citizens want some discussion of what is good. But how far the government should go in determining the content of the good and enforcing it in the private lives of its citizens is a matter of considerable current contention. Ernest May explores these and other issues of scope in Chapter 1.

Performance

People say they are dissatisfied with the performance of government, and in a democracy that is one important measure. But performance is more complicated than it first appears. Performance compared with what? Expectations? The past? Other countries? Other institutions such as businesses or nonprofit organizations? And what are people willing to pay for government efficiency, either in dollars or other values? The founding fathers designed a governmental system that protected liberties at the price of efficiency. A federal system with separated institutions sharing powers is not designed to optimize performance. Do people want this changed? Probably not. Would they if new problems like terrorism produced a "domestic Pearl Harbor"? Perhaps.

Another problem with measuring performance is distinguishing general outcomes from specific outputs of government. People may be properly unhappy with poor social outcomes even though the quality of government outputs does not change. For example, American test scores in science and mathematics compare poorly with those of a number of other nations, but the role of schools may be less important than the role of family values and the general culture in explaining those differences.[16] Or as Theodore Marmor points out, the Canadian, Dutch, British, and American publics all express dissatisfaction with their national health care systems, although the role of government differs. (The U.S. public expresses greater dissatisfaction, and there is less governmental involvement in America than in other countries.)[17] Further complications arise from the unevenness of public knowledge. For example, Americans express more dissatisfaction with foreign aid than almost any other aspect of foreign policy, but they overestimate the amount of foreign aid given by an order of magnitude.[18]

In their chapters that follow, Derek Bok and Gary Orren try to sort out real changes in governmental performance from perceived (including misperceived) changes. One important step is to unbundle the cluster of activities that we call "government and politics." Performance differs by fields and by institutions. For example, over the past few decades, security for the elderly and the quality of air and water have improved in the United States. In a 1995 poll, 44 percent of the public credited the federal government with improving the quality of air, and 23 percent gave it credit for reducing poverty over age 65.[19] And some government institutions rate higher than others. While only 10 percent of the public reported in 1996 that they had a great deal of confidence in Congress, 31 percent had a great deal of confidence in the Supreme Court, and 47 percent in the military.[20] The latter case reflects a recovery from a 27 percent level during the Vietnam War, and may reflect not only good performance during the Gulf War but also the relative success of the military in dealing with the drug, race, and education issues that have plagued modern American society. (We discuss this further in the concluding chapter.)

A major puzzle in the relationship between dissatisfaction and government performance is understanding how distant people feel from government. For instance, while polls show a low rating for Congress, they also show a higher rating for the local U.S. representative. Although there is criticism of the school system, people express higher satisfaction with their local school. As noted earlier, there is a somewhat higher level of satisfaction with state and local compared with the federal government.[21] Values may play a role here. Even if government makes mistakes, there may be greater willingness to tolerate mistakes that are made by "people like us." On the other hand, in a 1995 poll, only 37 percent responded that their mistrust of the federal government was because the policies did not reflect their own beliefs and values.[22]

If mistrust is not closely related to personal values and experience, then explanations may lie in generalized beliefs or moods. Understanding this relationship between distance and perceived performance bears on the issue of devolution. Some observers believe that more devolution to the state and local level will restore confidence in government; others believe that devolution will merely shift the spotlight of criticism to the local level. If the public reaction to government had a clear, one-to-one relationship with performance, there would be little to explain why attitudes have changed over the past three decades. But the ambiguities in the relationship between real and perceived performance, along with the decline of confidence in other major institutions besides government, suggest that larger causes are also involved.

Economic Causes of Dissatisfaction

In 1965, at the peak of confidence in government, Robert Lane discerned an increase in trust since the 1930s, which he attributed to economic improvement. His prediction that an age of affluence would also be one of trust and a "rapprochement between men and their government" did not prove accurate, however.[23]

Robert Lawrence's chapter takes an economic cut at this puzzle. Perhaps the decline in confidence is the result of the economic slowdown. That could explain why it is happening across so many rich countries. The rate of growth during the first two and a half decades after World War II was much higher in all advanced economies than after 1974. Even though Japan's growth was high in the 1980s, it was lower than it was in the 1960s. As for the United States, the annual growth rate was 3.5 percent during the first postwar decades and then about 2.3 percent in the period after 1975, a 50 percent decline in growth rate. Over 20 years, that would be about $2.5 trillion—enough to mean no government deficit or enough to give government the wherewithal to do some of the things it now cannot afford to do.[24]

The slowdown of economic growth, we might hypothesize, has led to public dissatisfaction, which in turn has led to a search for political scapegoats. From 1979 to 1995, real hourly wages in the United States rose by about 5.5 percent, or one-third of a percent per year.[25] That contrast to the earlier postwar period is a possible reason that people would say something is not as good as it used to be and to blame it on government. A major problem with this hypothesis, however, is that it fits poorly with the timing of when confidence in government began to decline. In the United States (although not in Europe), the greatest drop in confidence occurred from 1964 to 1974, when growth was fastest, and the recession of the early 1980s was accompanied by a rise of confidence in government.

Another related economic explanation is global competition. This argument says that it is not just the economic slowdown that matters but the popular view that the economic slowdown has been caused by global markets and competition. As some people put it, what is really at issue is the enormous rise of the East Asian economies that provide almost an infinite source of low-priced labor that is bound to lead to a depression of wages in the advanced countries. This particularly depresses the wages of the unskilled and leads to increased inequality, which in turn burdens the political system.

This explanation solves the timing problem of the larger "slowdown" explanation, but it faces another difficulty. Trade accounts for only about one-tenth of the American economy. And the slowdown and the depression of wages has occurred in the other 90 percent as much as it occurs in the part that deals with traded goods. Of course, there are spillover effects from wages in traded to nontraded goods, and the fact that multinational corporations can threaten to move jobs overseas can also depress wages. Still, trade may be too small a tail to wag such a large dog. In addition, 70 percent of American trade has been with other rich countries, where wages are just as high as ours. So while global competition has an important effect, it may not be sufficient to explain what's happening in the depression of wages.

Robert Lawrence and other economists think that international trade can explain only a part of what's going on. The real culprit is changes in technology and particularly what he calls skill-biased technologies that are depressing wages.[26] But even if the economists are right, global competitiveness and interdependence produce a political dimension worth noting. If people sense a loss of control of their lives because of larger competition in the world, that becomes a political reality in and of itself. So when Pat Buchanan campaigns on the theme that foreigners are causing people's problems, it may not be good economics, but it becomes a political reality.

Another hypothesis is that there is something still deeper going on in the economic area—the third industrial revolution. This revolution, an information revolution, means that computers and communications are to the end of the twentieth century what the introduction of steam was to the end of the eighteenth century or the introduction of electricity was to the end of the nineteenth century. We are seeing a tremendous wave of technological innovation that takes twenty to forty years to work itself through the system. And in this dimension, according to Joseph Schumpeter, capitalism is a process of "creative destruction."[27] It has a positive and a negative effect at the same time. When the Rust Belt factories close, somebody suffers. When plants open in Silicon Valley, somebody else benefits.

This creative destruction is happening in almost all advanced countries. The Americans have responded to it by creating jobs, albeit often at low wages. The Europeans have responded to it by supporting incomes and thereby causing unemployment rates of 10 to 12 percent—and in some countries, a youth unemployment rate of 20 percent.[28] The ways in which different societies respond to this economic process can take different forms, but each creates a certain amount of turmoil, either with low wages or high unemployment. In addition, the development of information technology is increasing inequality. The people who win are those who are informationally advantaged, and those who lose are those without the education to cope. Thirty years ago a high school drop-out could go to an auto factory and get a good wage. Today he or she would be out of luck, as such jobs now require a high school diploma and perhaps more technical training so as to operate a numerically controlled machine tool.

In addition to those problems of creating a gap between the informationally advantaged and disadvantaged, creative destruction and restructuring often means downsizing. Firms lay off workers. This can be one way that productivity rises. But many of the people being laid off today are middle-class holders of white-collar jobs—something that was not as prevalent in the past. We are seeing the "democratization of insecurity." This produces a "politics of the anxious middle."[29] In the long run the country may profit from this creative destruction, but in the interim people feel insecure and anxious and then blame the government rather than the deeper economic and historical forces. But even here the causation is complicated. If the economy was the primary cause, one would expect to see the greatest decline in trust among the economic losers. Yet as Lawrence points out in his chapter, the decline of confidence in government is virtually the same for both winners and losers. Like the absence of a close connection between confidence and personal experience or values mentioned earlier, this lack of connection between economic and expressed attitudes suggests the need for explanations that are more general, ideological, or reflective of the broad public mood.

Social and Cultural Causes of Dissatisfaction

Jane Mansbridge's chapter looks at social and cultural hypotheses about the causes of the decline of confidence in government. One is the alleged decline of social capital. "Social capital" is a commonsense concept, the ability of people to work together. It is the trust, norms, and networks that facilitate coordinated action. Social scientists believe that such skills are developed in part through citizens working together in voluntary organizations.[30] While not all such organizations have a positive effect, most probably do, and their decline would be a source of concern. Robert Putnam has focused on the decline in voluntary groups such as the Parent-Teacher Association, the YMCA, or the Girl Scouts of America since the 1960s.[31] Of course, participation in some other groups—for instance, the American Association of Retired Persons—is rising, but while such new groups have large memberships, the members rarely see one another. People send a check in the mail for dues, and that's about it. Members of the Parent-Teacher Association are more likely to see one another and to learn to work together. The argument here is that the decline in participatory groups removes the kind of intermediary institution that Alexis de Tocqueville believed essential to the structure of civil society that undergirds our democratic government. Putnam's thesis has been challenged, but to the extent that his data hold up, the hypothesis about contributing to decline of confidence in government is worth exploring.[32]

Another aspect of decline in social capital is a longer-term dimension of cultural change. As Ronald Inglehart shows in Chapter 9, developed societies have experienced a long-term decline of trust in institutions, not just governments. Inglehart argues that the declining respect for authority is part of modern and postmodern values as people switch from survival to quality-of-life values.[33] The "youth revolts" of the 1960s saw a rapid increase in challenges to authority and institutions, not only in the United States but in many other developed countries as well.

Western culture has seen a change in the balance between the individual and the community in the favor of greater individualism. This is a long-term secular trend. Divorce, for example, has increased in almost all advanced societies. One aspect of divorce is that some women have been liberated from abusive and unequal marriages. Women used to be trapped economically in unhappy marriages because there was virtually no way out. Men have also benefited from easier divorce. So one thing that divorce represents is a libertarian trend. The other thing divorce represents, however, is the decline of the family. It means less attention to the children, less attention to the basic unit of community. Divorce illustrates two sides of the same coin, as the ratio changes in the libertarian rather than the communitarian direction.

The decline of the family has important implications for both actual and perceived performance of government. Of the tasks for government, public education and preventing youth violence come high on the list of what people care most about. Both rest heavily on the family. Government can run schools, but if parents cannot run families well, government is not going to do very well on schools. Yet government is going to get much of the blame. People are not going to say, "I did a pretty lousy job as a parent, so I will not blame the schools or the government." They are more likely to say that the government is letting us down. Or many are likely to demand that government "do something" about family values even though government may be unable to reverse larger social causes.

Another dimension of this cultural change is our public political philosophy and its current emphasis on rights. Everybody has a right. There used to be a set of basic human rights about which people were in broad agreement. Now people seem to be claiming a right to everything, from a pension to a vacation. We have created a society of entitlements. The net effect is extraordinarily constraining on government. As government is constrained by court interpretations of entitlements, its effectiveness is reduced, and confidence is further diminished. Moreover, as Fred Schauer points out, rights have costs, and some people pay a price for the expansion of the rights of others. Losers are likely to blame this cost on government.[34] For example, the expansion of civil rights in the 1960s and 1970s benefited African-

Americans, but it angered many whites and helped cause the defection of the South from the Democratic to the Republican coalition.
Social changes have had large political effects, and these include a
weakening of our confidence in government.[35] As Mansbridge argues,
some of these effects are indirect as well as direct.

Political Causes of Dissatisfaction

David King's and Richard Neustadt's chapters examine a number
of political explanations about the causes of the decline of confidence
in government. None of the political hypotheses is vacuous, but some
do more of the heavy lifting as explanations. One hypothesis is that
the decline of confidence in government is due to the end of the cold
war. Common defense is a public good, and willingness to sacrifice
is higher in wartime. The cold war was the glue that held public
opinion together. With the end of the cold war, people have come to
differ more about government purposes. The cold war ends, and
things fall apart. The trouble with this hypothesis is that the decline
of confidence in government starts in the mid-1960s. So unless one
wants to date the end of the cold war from the mid- to late 1960s, the
hypothesis does not fit very well.

A second political hypothesis is that the decline in confidence is
the fault of poor leaders—in particular Lyndon Johnson and Richard
Nixon. As the Orren and Blendon, et al. chapters describe, the sharpest dips in the curve of confidence occur after America's involvement
in Vietnam and the Watergate incident in 1972. Johnson and Nixon
are blamed for both misleading the public and becoming involved in
episodes that reduced respect for government. The more hostile tenor
of press coverage dates back to these events. Yet while Vietnam and
Watergate help to explain the onset of the decline, they do not explain
the duration. Why is it still going on? When Ronald Reagan came to
office, confidence in government actually made an uptick from 25
percent to 44 percent in the early 1980s. But then it went down again
in Reagan's second term and after.[36] This type of anomaly requires a
deeper explanation. It is not sufficient to blame everything on Johnson
and Nixon.

A related explanation for rising mistrust would be the growth of
corruption and dishonesty in American politics. Many close observers,

however, doubt that such behavior has increased.[37] What *has* increased is media attention to scandal and public belief that politicians
have become more corrupt. Certainly we have witnessed enough
deceptive and dishonest behavior to fuel this belief, but it is difficult
to make the case that increased corruption is the cause.

A fourth political explanation is "the World War II effect." World
War II was a success story for government. At the end of World War
II, growth was high. The prevalent view was that government works.
It had accomplished what we wanted. Then we tried a "war on
poverty" and a "war on drugs." The wartime success of government
led to too much confidence in government, overexpectations, and
misapplication of the war analogy to other issues. What needs explaining is not why confidence is low today but why it was so high after
World War II. Maybe the postwar generation was unique because of
the effect of the war. There is probably a good deal of truth in this
hypothesis, but again it is not sufficient. For example, it does not help
to explain why confidence would also decline in Italy or Japan.
Something more than just the World War II effect is going on.

Another political hypothesis is that we are seeing a realignment
of political parties not only in the United States but in Italy, Japan, and
other countries. That process of realignment, when the old coalitions
fall apart, produces a loss of confidence not just in the parties but in
government more generally. The Roosevelt coalition, which governed
in the United States after 1932, gradually eroded, and with it went the
faith in liberal big government that held the coalition together. The
defection of the South over race and blue-collar Democrats over
cultural issues brought Nixon to power in 1968. That defection under-
pins the current conservative movement. With this realignment of
political parties, one would expect a decline of trust in government
that went along with a particular view of government. But again, the
hypothesis does not explain everything. Why did confidence go up
when Reagan came into office and go down again during his later
years as president? And maybe what is happening in the United States
is not party realignment but *de*alignment—not one party replacing
another as much as voters moving toward independent status. Party
realignment may be part of an explanation, but again, it does not tell
us everything.[38]

A final political hypothesis attributes the decline in confidence to the changing role of the media. Thomas Patterson reports three major trends in news coverage since the 1960s not only in the United States but also in Britain, Sweden, and Italy. In all of these countries, press and television news have become more negative, more journalist-centered, and more focused on conflict than substance. In its new interpretive role, the press has become an unaccountable part of the political process.[39]

Television may have added a special dimension. The public now gets its political information more from television than from newspapers. Television has had at least two major effects. First, it changed the political process. Politicians can appeal over the heads of the political parties directly to the public, and that may have something to do with the dealignment mentioned earlier. Parties are less effective in connecting politicians with the public, and the negative ads on television and the costs of broadcast time create a greater sense of distance between politicians and the public.

Second, television has created what is sometimes called "the mean world effect." Television likes dramatic pictures. Information is conveyed by what people see, not just by what they hear. The result is that messages are often confused by the public. For example, in a poll conducted in Levittown, New York, a middle American suburb, people were asked, "What is the biggest problem in Levittown?" They answered, "The rising crime rate." In fact, crime had been falling in Levittown.[40] But the mean world effect means that it's a lot easier to remember somebody spread-eagled against a police cruiser with a blue light flashing than to remember a table of statistics about how crime is going down. These arguments suggest that the way we now get our information about politics has had an effect on the political process which is likely to reduce confidence in government.

Conclusion

These are some of the things that we need to understand and to study. Many of the hypotheses suggest pessimism. But the future is open. Creative destruction may work in the polity as well as the economy. The information revolution may bring opportunities or causes for hope. The third industrial revolution may mean the industrial countries are on the verge of a rise in productivity that will end the slow growth. We do not yet know. The information technology revolution may also help government get closer to people, and when people feel a closer connection to government, confidence tends to be higher. It may be possible to have more devolution with information technology. It may also be possible to do more outsourcing and to cut bureaucracy in government. Perhaps the nonprofit sector will provide more intermediary institutions that will work with government, both in helping to provide services and in providing the new ideas that make democracy flourish.[41]

The end of the last century saw a sense of unease and discontent much like what we are seeing at the end of this century. The American economy was shifting from one in which 30 percent of the employment was in agriculture to one that was industrial and urban. The era's unease and unhappiness led to a number of creative changes in the U.S. government, including the Sherman and Clayton antitrust acts, the creation of the Food and Drug Administration, and the establishment of the Federal Reserve system. A wave of creativity ran through both political parties. But the first step before searching for remedies is to understand how we arrived where we are. Many people are proposing a wide variety of remedies for the current discontent with government. But some remedies may prove feckless or even counterproductive unless we have a better understanding of causes. That is the task of the chapters that follow.

PART One

The Scope and Performance of Government

One

The Evolving Scope of Government

Ernest R. May

Among explanations for a seeming decline of confidence in government, one favorite has to do with its scope. Some allege that government has taken too much on itself, assuming responsibilities it should not assume and promising what it cannot deliver. President Ronald Reagan said famously that government was the problem, not the solution. To illustrate, he said, "We declared war on poverty. And poverty won." Others argue the opposite. The economist and statesman John Kenneth Galbraith ridicules the Reagan presidency as having achieved primarily "tax relief for the very affluent." Its theory, he says, was "that if the horse is fed amply with oats, some will pass through to the road for the sparrows."[1] And the dispute can be shrill. Reagan also said, "Runaway government threatens . . . the very preservation of freedom itself." Galbraith closed his book by asserting that the Reagan administration's neglect of the "underclass" threatened America's "long-run peace and civility."[2]

This essay sketches the history of changes in the scope of government. It makes three points:

1. The terms of debate about government have changed over time and have varied by locale. Before the seventeenth century, hardly anyone anywhere would have understood either Reagan

or Galbraith. In some parts of the present-day world, the issue would have to be framed differently. Iran and Afghanistan are two examples among many.

2. Change in thinking about government has accompanied enormous changes in the human condition. Especially during the past two centuries, every aspect of life has changed—birth, childhood, family, learning, work, leisure. Each of the seven ages ticked off by Jaques in *As You Like It*—from mewling infant to second childhood "sans everything"—has changed in degrees that earlier generations could scarcely have imagined, let alone foreseen.

3. The rate of change has accelerated, but our thinking has not kept pace. Disputes such as those between Reagan and Galbraith may be as out of date as disputes over mercantilism or the gold standard.

The Scope of Government before Modern Times

Until the seventeenth century in Europe, the scope of government was theoretically almost without limit. In most societies of which we have knowledge, the roles of law-giver, high priest, code enforcer, currency-creator, and lord protector were intertwined. Often rulers were presumed to own as well as control the tribal or national domain. God had given it to them. This remained the organizing presumption of czarist Russia down to the nineteenth century (and was part of its legacy to the Bolsheviks).

In practice, individuals and families almost always had a sphere of their own. In classical Greece, where rulership was sometimes shared among residents of a city, a distinction was drawn between the *polis* and the *oikos*—in a sense, the public and the private. But the *oikos* was essentially the circle around the family's hearth or private altar. Hannah Arendt makes a persuasive case that, for the Greeks, the *polis* was the realm in which individual freedom became possible. That was where individuals could exercise some choice. In the *oikos*, by contrast, tradition and superstition controlled.[3]

In Rome, although the legal code protected private property, choice beyond the reach of rulers remained limited. In Justinian's

Digest (L, iv), one finds the Roman equivalent of a family-assistance plan and old-age assistance: fathers with five living children and men over seventy were exempted from compulsory work on road gangs.

In almost every part of the world for which we have evidence, conflict between individuals and families on the one hand and rulers on the other was a constant fact of life. In *Pre-Industrial Societies,* Islamicist Patricia Crone writes,

> Though we still complain of the tax-burden, the Inland Revenue Service does not normally have to call upon the army to make us pay, nor do we normally engage in prolonged haggling with the tax-collectors, weeping, crying, tearing our clothes or grovelling in the dust to convince them that we have not got a penny left. . . . Such procedures were however commonplace in most pre-industrial societies. For the peasants, tax-collectors were like swarms of locusts descending to strip them of everything they possessed; for the tax-collectors, peasants were like recalcitrant cattle which had to be milked however much they might protest. The sheer fact that yields were so low accustomed the authorities to take everything they could without destroying agriculture altogether. "The tax-payers should keep only as much of their cultivated produce as suffices for their subsistence and the cultivation of their lands," a third-century Persian emperor is supposed to have decreed. "Every care should be taken that there should not remain with the villagers more food supplies than required for one-year's consumption, nor more oxen than wanted for [the tillage of] their fields," an eighth-century king of Kashmir is said to have ruled. "The peasants are the foundation of the state," a seventeenth-century Japanese document declares, "each man must have the boundaries of his fields clearly marked, and an estimate must be made of the amount needed for his consumption. The rest must be paid as tax."[4]

Until after the religious wars of the sixteenth and seventeenth centuries, it remained true in Europe that government in one form or another was the individual's only source of hope for protection against government. From almost the top of society to almost the bottom, degrees of freedom and control depended chiefly on exploiting differences among authorities higher up—dynasty versus dynasty or noble versus noble, as in the histories of Magna Carta or of charters granting privileges to towns or families. But in seventeenth-century England, for Francis Bacon and Thomas Hobbes, as for Nicolò Machiavelli in Italy a century and more earlier, the precondition for individual liberty was subservience to some protector or protectors—a prince or an oligarchy. Hobbes wrote of such a protector as the "*Mortall God,* to which wee owe under the *Immortall God,* our peace and defence."[5]

The terrible religious wars erupting after Martin Luther's break with Rome in 1519 led eventually to separation, not just competition, between ecclesiastical and secular authority. Priests, monarchs, and oligarchs all lost power. Except in a few limited areas, such as the Papal States, priests became less able to call in the headsman. Even where priests *were* the secular authority, as in France under Cardinals Richelieu and Mazarin, the state became less able to invoke eternal damnation as the penalty for not paying taxes.

One result was that citizens began to ask questions about the legitimate scope of government. If belief and worship were off limits for kings and princes, what else might not be? The practical separation of ecclesiastical and secular authority proceeded differently in different parts of Europe. In much of Southern and Eastern Europe, it awaited the French Revolution or even the nineteenth century. Nevertheless, one can see quite early the wide circulation of the idea that, in addition to things of Caesar's and things of God, there could be things of the citizen equally sacrosanct and equally important.

One indication was the sudden entry into common usage of the term "interests." Previously signifying only "objects of curiosity" or "fruits of usury," it suddenly acquired a new sense during the 1640s. A book by the Huguenot soldier Henri, Duc de Rohan, became the equivalent of a best-seller. The first English edition, which appeared in 1640, had the title *Treatise of the Interests of the Princes and States of Christendom.* A second edition appeared in 1641. Immediately translated into several languages and circulated all over Western Europe, it permitted discourse about princes and governments based on an assumption that they acted for themselves or their subjects rather than for God. It eventually became common to distinguish between types of interests, with those of individuals gradually being differentiated from a broader "public interest" and those in turn from interests guided by *raison d'état.*[6]

In the meantime, an equally fundamental change occurred in common understanding of the substantive content of "interest." Until roughly the period of Europe's religious wars, the assumption had prevailed that the world's wealth was finite and fixed in quantity. The relationship between wealth and political power had become increasingly evident as European princes became more and more dependent on mercenary soldiers. (Among the best were the Swiss, of whom the saying ran, *"Pas d'argent, pas des Suisses"*—No money, no Swiss.) The assumption that contests among princes were necessarily what we would now call zero-sum games pervades the writings of Machiavelli. It persisted into the seventeenth century, as evidenced in Francis Bacon's assertion that "the increase of any estate must be upon the foreigner (for whatsoever is somewhere gotten is somewhere lost)."[7] But Columbus's voyages, followed in the sixteenth century by the exploits of Hernán Cortés and Francisco Pizarro, multiplied by a significant margin the wealth of the monarchs of Spain. The subsequent success of the Dutch and English in adding to their wealth and power primarily by maritime trade made the error of the previous assumption increasingly apparent. A best-seller of the 1660s, not only in England but elsewhere, was *England's Treasure by Forraign Trade* by Thomas Mun.[8] By the early eighteenth century, the new belief had become so strong as to make possible get-rich schemes such as John Law's Mississippi Bubble and Britain's South Sea Bubble.

Writing in 1776, Adam Smith described the discovery of America and the subsequent opening of the East Indies as "the two greatest and most important events in the history of mankind." Saying that the full consequences of these events had yet to unfold, Smith explained: "One of the principal effects of those discoveries has been to raise the mercantile system to a degree of splendor and glory which it could never otherwise have attained to. It is the object of that system to enrich a great nation rather by trade and manufactures than by the improvement and cultivation of land."[9] Karl Marx put the same point more mordantly, writing, "The discovery of gold and silver in America, the extirpation, enslavement and entombment in mines of the aboriginal population, the beginning of the conquest and looting of the East Indies, the turning of Africa into a warren for the commercial hunting of black-skins, signalised the rosy dawn of the era of capitalist production."[10] Smith and Marx alike made the point that both rulers and ruled had come to see that increase in estate did not have to be "upon the foreigner."

For most of the two centuries after Cortés and Pizarro stole the treasures of the Aztecs and Incas, European rulers took the lead in trying to expand wealth as well as to take it from other rulers. They adopted mercantilist policies, attempting to monopolize for their realms whatever could be obtained either from exploiting colonies or from converting raw materials into manufactures or from transporting goods to markets or from usury. They found, however, that success was difficult if not impossible without cooperation from individual citizens who wanted to expand their own wealth. In France, kings ended up creating whole new strata of nobility, distinguished primarily by their ability to enrich themselves at the same time that they helped to enrich the state. Something similar occurred in most other parts of Europe.

By the mid-eighteenth century, the separation of state from church, combined with the burgeoning of capitalism, had created two important bodies of ideas concerning the scope of government. One was the idea of "inalienable rights," broached by Hobbes, further developed by John Locke, and codified by the American and French revolutions. William Pitt, the Earl of Chatham, caught the essence of this idea in the often-quoted lines attributed to him by Lord Brougham: "The poorest man may in his cottage bid defiance to all the forces of the Crown. It may be frail—its roof may shake—the wind may blow through it—the storm may enter—the rain may enter—but the King of England cannot enter!"[11]

The second body of ideas is that associated with the phrase of the early eighteenth-century French thinker, François Quesnay. Prescribing how government could best promote expansion in the nation's wealth, Quesnay said, *"Laissez faire, laissez passer"*—let producers, merchants, and capitalists alone, and let them trade freely. The logic was worked out in detail by figures of the Scottish Enlightenment, particularly David Hume, James Steuart, and Adam Smith. The most famous exposition was Smith's *Inquiry into the Nature and Causes of the Wealth of Nations,* published in 1776. Rejecting mercantilism root and branch, Smith asserted that no government could ever have the wisdom or knowledge needed for the tasks of "superintending the industry of private people, and of directing it towards the employments most suitable to the interests of society." In a system of "natural liberty," wrote Smith, the sovereign has only three duties to attend to . . . : first, the duty of protecting the society from the violence and invasion of other independent societies; secondly, the duty of protecting, as far as possible, every member of the society from the injustice or oppression of every other member of it, or the duty of establishing an exact administration of justice; and thirdly, the duty of erecting and maintaining certain public works and certain public institutions, which it can never be for the interest of any individual, or small number of individuals, to erect and maintain, because the profit could never repay the expense.[12]

The Wealth of Nations, it is often forgotten, was Smith's second book. The first, published in 1759, was *The Theory of Moral Sentiments.* And *The Wealth of Nations* is best understood as in part a sequel—the effort of a professor of moral philosophy at the University of Glasgow to pursue further the theme of "practical virtue," for it was one of Smith's essential contentions in *The Wealth of Nations* that humans are most likely to do good for others if—within limits—they pursue their own self-interest. The underlying theory was captured nowhere more succinctly than in Bernard de Mandeville's "The Fable of the Bees," which concludes: "There every Part was full of Vice / Yet the whole Mass a Paradise."

The ever-rising bourgeoisie embraced Smith's arguments as if they had come from heaven on stone tablets. For the most part, as historian W. L. Burn argues, the bourgeoisie became attached not so much to a laissez-faire theory as to "a well-used set of laissez-faire clichés."[13] The attachment was nonetheless strong and enduring. Witness the testimony of Peggy Noonan, a speechwriter for President Reagan, who recalls that at White House staff conferences all the men wore Adam Smith ties. (She adds that the ties were usually "slightly stained from the mayonnaise that fell from the sandwich that was wolfed down at the working lunch.")[14]

The twin propositions—that individuals had inalienable rights on which government should never trespass and that wealth increased most efficiently if government left the economic activities of individuals alone—figured in shaping government for the newly independent United States. The first proposition was especially powerful. The Declaration of Independence, the Articles of Confederation, and most constitutions for the new states embodied some form of language about inalienable rights. Not satisfied that the original Constitution had enough such language, Thomas Jefferson and some of his friends conditioned their approval of it on the ten amendments known as the Bill of Rights, which identified domains on which the new federal government should not encroach.

Americans divided, however, over laissez-faire. In *Federalist* 23, Alexander Hamilton stated a position close to Adam Smith's: "The principal purposes to be answered by union are these—the common defence of the members; the preservation of the public peace, as well against internal convulsions as external attacks; the regulation of commerce with other nations and between the States; the superintendence of our intercourse, political and commercial, with foreign countries." Hamilton went on, however, to stress the importance of government's having adequate power to execute the functions reserved for it. Hamilton described as "axioms as simple as they are universal" that "the *means* ought to be proportioned to the *end;* the persons, from whose agency the attainment of any *end* is expected, ought to possess the *means* by which it is to be attained." He continued, "Not to confer in each case a degree of power commensurate to the end, would be to violate the most obvious rules of prudence and propriety, and improvidently to trust the great interests of the nation to hands which are disabled from managing them with vigor and success."

Hamilton's successful rival, Thomas Jefferson, had misgivings about government's having any powers at all. In his first inaugural address in 1800, he spoke of government in terms more narrow than even those of Adam Smith. He called for "a wise and frugal Government, which shall restrain men from injuring one another [but] shall leave them otherwise free to regulate their own pursuits of industry and improvement." He declared, "This is the sum of good government." In private, Jefferson expressed almost as much fear of capitalist greed as of governmental power. He would have preferred that America remain a pastoral society.

Future history would be significantly affected by the fact that Western Europe alone experienced both the separation of ecclesiastical and secular authority and the discovery that wealth could expand. The future would also be much affected by the fact that Western Europe spawned a new American republic that shared Europe's history (or at least England's) but was less encumbered by intellectual and social residue from centuries when government had been all-encompassing and one person became rich only by some other person's becoming poor.

The First Technological-Economic-Social Revolution, ca. 1760–ca. 1850

Historian Thomas McCraw provides a concise summary of the first *industrial* revolution:

> Agricultural productivity increased. Manufacturing, which for thousands of years had been based on human and animal energy, was powered more and more by water and steam. New canals facilitated water transport. Machine tools came into wider use. The factory system spread rapidly, and an industrial proletariat began to gather in cities. People started to work by the clock. The corporate form of business organization began to spread. Some companies employed several hundred persons each, and a few employed more than one thousand.
>
> Typical new products were steam engines and factory-produced items such as cotton textiles, ironware, and pottery.[15]

This revolution was preceded by what another historian, Jan de Vries, has labeled an "industrious revolution."[16] For reasons probably rooted in the changes discussed earlier, output from farmers and artisans had increased during the eighteenth century, especially in England, to an extent not adequately appreciated at the time or long afterward. The industrial revolution proper then allowed this increased industriousness to result in hugely increased output.

In the nascent discipline of economics (the science of the *oikos*), savants debated how to measure the changes in progress. The monetary unit was not everyone's favorite. Holding it too subject to changes that owed to either new discoveries of precious metals or vagaries in government finance, some early nineteenth-century economists argued for substituting an energy metric. An example rated a mechanical pump as equivalent to forty men because it would have taken between thirteen and fourteen men, in three eight-hour shifts, to lift the same quantity of water in a twenty-four-hour period.[17] Perhaps unfortunately, the energy metric lost out to the money metric. (Had it won, we might have understood sooner the concepts eventually bundled as "transaction costs" and might today be better able to take account of the impact of information technologies that steadily increase in output but decline in dollar value.) The example, however, suggests how enormously mechanical power could multiply industriousness.

The lives of workers caught up in industrialization changed in two important ways. First, they gained access to a much more abundant supply of commodities. The best evidence collected by economic historians indicates that individual earnings did not rise much, if at all.[18] Because of the immensely greater output of textiles, ironware, pottery, and such, workers could, however, buy articles previously beyond their reach. The second change, which probably had more important effects, occurred in households. Theretofore, most workers, whether farmers or artisans, had worked at home or very close by (one implication of the phrase "cottage industry"). Now many workers went to factories or mines, often at considerable distances from their homes. Family members spent increasingly less time in one another's company.

Another change, perhaps driven by technological and economic change but at least in part independent of it, was a general expansion in population. This expansion was dramatic. Prior to the mid-eighteenth century, population in Europe had been comparatively stable. The years 1760 to 1800 saw an overall increase of about 30 percent. The years from 1800 to 1850 then saw another jump, exceeding 40 percent. In the latter period, while the population of France increased by less than 40 percent, that of the United Kingdom more than doubled, and that of the states that would eventually unite as Germany went up by 80 percent. And rates of increase for urban populations far outstripped nationwide rates. In the single decade of the 1830s, Paris gained 120,000 inhabitants; London, 130,000; Manchester, 70,000; and Birmingham, 40,000. Vienna and Berlin, neither of which had had 200,000 inhabitants at the turn of the century, had 400,000 by the end of the 1840s.

Yet another change, this more psychological than social or demographic, was the rise of nationalism. Throughout Europe, individuals manifested emotional identification with a nation. The core identification could be—in almost any combination—with a place or a language or a culture or a history, real or imagined. The phenomenon antedated the industrial revolution. It had been manifest in Britain at least in the eighteenth century, perhaps earlier. It was strong in France during the Revolution, and it showed itself in almost every area reached by the armies of Revolutionary or Napoleonic France—sometimes in imitation of France, sometimes in reaction against France. It is arguable that this was in part a result of the earlier secularization. It reflected popular desire for a new object of worship. It is also arguable that nationalism was primarily a product of economic change. Ernest Gellner argues forcefully that nationalism has to be understood in terms of need for identity on the part of dislocated persons, particularly peasants separated from their native farms and villages.[19]

In response to these immense changes, governments both narrowed and widened their scope of action. It is not easy to generalize, for the governments in question included those of many different nations and often of differing localities within those nations. Distinctive cultures and traditions influenced what governments did and how they did it. In many instances, there was imitation or competition between or within nations. Hence, one sees a lead taken first here, then there, and action that begins the same in one place as in another turns out to evolve very differently.

Because this period figures as a golden age in some present-day mythologies, it is worthwhile to look at some of its details. And because Britain was unquestionably the leader in industrialization (Table 1-1 suggests the margin by which it led), it is useful to summarize how, in that country, the scope of government both contracted and expanded, and then to comment on how the American experience differed.

Britain shifted slowly but resolutely from mercantilism to laissez-faire capitalism. After prolonged political debate, Britain committed itself to free trade. The action came in the 1840s, when Parliament repealed the Corn Laws, which provided tariff protection to British-grown grain. Laissez-faire theory said that free trade would eventually work to everyone's advantage. The immediate effect of repeal of the Corn Laws was to lower the price of bread. Humanitarian reformers cheered no less loudly than businessmen and manufacturers. But repeal of the Corn Laws meant also that the government relinquished its ancient responsibility for protecting the population from dearth and famine.

Another important step away from mercantilism was the Bank Charter Act of 1844. This act gave the quasi-independent Bank of

Table 1-1. Cotton, Coal, and Iron Production in the Nineteenth Century

	Great Britain	Germany	United States
Spun cotton (million pounds)			
1830	250	16	77
1850	588	46	288
1870	1,101	147	400
Coal (million tons)			
1830	16	1.7	n.a.
1850	49	6.7	7
1870	110	26.0	30
Cast iron (thousand tons)			
1820	400	90	20
1840	1,400	170	180
1870	3,800	500	900

Source: Michel Beaud, *A History of Capitalism, 1500-1980* (London: Macmillan, 1984), 86.

England sole power to issue notes, which meant that, for all practical purposes, the government renounced its right to increase or decrease the amount of currency in circulation. By assuring capitalists that they could count on the gold standard, or at least on a stable currency, the government bound its own hands and guaranteed price stability in ways that nowadays require ironclad contracts with the International Monetary Fund.

Equally indicative of Britain's new commitment to laissez-faire capitalism was Parliament's enactment in 1834 of the New Poor Law, replacing the Poor Law that dated back to Elizabeth I. Harsh by design, the New Poor Law removed from localities their traditional responsibility to care for their own poor and thus created state-run almshouses where conditions were *supposed* to be so bad that no able-bodied person would prefer them to employment of any kind. (It was in one of these almshouses that Oliver Twist begged for "more.") As economic historian Peter Mathias explains, the legislation was based on the assumptions "that unemployment was voluntary for the able-bodied poor, that work was available for the willing. Hence the justification for the principle of 'less eligibility' or deterrence in the workhouses. The idea was that, if conditions inside were worse than those prevailing outside, then the able-bodied poor would take the rational decision to stay out of the workhouse and work."[20] (This rationale has eerie contemporaneity.)

At the same time that the British government was removing restraints on business activity, it was promoting the fortunes of individual firms. In particular, Parliament provided charters for railroad companies and passed legislation to allow them to obtain rights of way. All told, measures such as repeal of the Corn Laws, the Bank Charter Act, and the New Poor Law reflected a significant change in the relationship between government and the citizenry. Through almost all of known history, government had been a taker of wealth. The laissez-faire doctrine made it a redistributor, transferring wealth to capitalists on a theory somewhat like that captured by the later shibboleth that a rising tide raises all boats.

But that is only part of what happened, for government in Britain also began to provide new services for the citizenry at large. In 1829 the British government created for London a uniformed Metropolitan Police Force, which soon numbered more than 3,000. Parliament prescribed that boroughs and counties all over England follow suit. Few obeyed. In the 1850s, however, as a result of additional legislation, uniformed police forces became common throughout the realm. Reform of the criminal justice system meanwhile spawned a network of prisons (earlier, most criminals had either been executed, transported, or released).

American's response to the first industrial revolution differed from Britain's in important ways. Although Americans had protested British mercantilism in the eighteenth century, they adopted mercantilist policies of their own once they were independent. Also, although they were slow to imitate the British in establishing police forces and building prisons, they, too, began providing new public services, particularly for health and education.

The American national government can hardly be said to have had any policies, either mercantilist or laissez-faire. Hamilton had favored laissez-faire capitalism much as it was to develop in Britain. Although he was not doctrinaire about free trade, he attached high importance to having money on which merchants and manufacturers could rely. His Bank of the United States had been intended to be a counterpart to the Bank of England as it was before the Bank Charter Act and hence a bank that could enable the national government to raise money for wars or great public works. After Andrew Jackson dismantled this bank, there existed no national-level governmental institution (the post office excepted) that was able to play much of a role in American economic life. Congress did impose tariffs to assist some industries, particularly textiles and iron, but the tendency from Jackson's time was toward lower tariffs. Jacksonians also successfully resisted proposals that the national government back road-building or other "internal improvements." For all practical purposes, this rendered the national government a passive actor, doing little besides handing out public land according to set formulas. The District of Columbia was a locale in which ambassadors from the states negotiated publicly about touchy questions, particularly the future of slavery. But most of what happened there was theater, not governance. The most influential national body was the Supreme Court, led and energized until 1836 by Chief Justice John Marshall, but the effect of its decisions was mainly to force uniform practices upon the separate states.

Effective government in America, not only during the first industrial revolution but for a long time afterward, was state and local government. At that level, mercantilism was strong. The colonists had revolted against the British monarchy. Many of their protests had been on behalf of their colonial governments. When the colonies became independent states, their constitutions made provision for separating executive and legislative powers and otherwise creating checks and balances. For the most part, however, these constitutions did not impose strict limitations on the scope of governmental activity. Quite the contrary. Immediately after independence, the New England states passed parallel "regulatory acts" that set wages for most types of wage earners and fixed the prices of farm products, manufactures, and many services. The Continental Congress recommended that all states follow suit.[21] The constitution of the Commonwealth of Massachusetts enjoined the state government to provide "rewards and immunities, for the promotion of agriculture, arts, sciences, commerce, trades, manufactures."[22] During the first half of the nineteenth century, the state legislature voted money to assist construction, in particular places, of paper mills, textile mills, and other factories. It sometimes did this by authorizing lotteries. The state also gave charters and grants to assist construction of toll roads and canals. At the same time, it imposed such tight regulations that most such companies ended up bankrupt, with roads and canals becoming direct responsibilities of government.

Some of what was done by Massachusetts and other states

amounted to redistribution of wealth in favor of capitalists. While Britain and most European nations were loath to create corporations, American states did so eagerly. After 1810, Massachusetts was chartering more than one hundred a year. This permitted mobilization of capital without the risks involved in entrepreneurship by individuals or partnerships. Initially, it was common for states also to invest money in corporations and to claim seats on their boards of directors. Pennsylvania owned $100 million in stock and had representatives on 150 boards.[23] Nor was this true only in the North. South Carolina poured money into roads, canals, and, eventually, railroads. In 1818 alone, the state appropriated $1 million for such purposes.

Nowhere perhaps was the difference between America and Britain more evident than in social policy. Down through the 1840s, the view prevailed in Massachusetts that it was society's duty to see that the able-bodied not only had work but also were comparatively well-paid. Writing in criticism of Britain's New Poor Law, Massachusetts jurist Theodore Sedgwick protested that a man condemned to a British almshouse "must regard the . . . society, which holds him in this condition, as an inhabitant of a conquered territory looks upon a citadel of the conquerors. He is naturally, and . . . almost . . . justifiably, an enemy of the government."[24] As the urban population grew, especially after German, Irish, and other European immigrants began arriving in large numbers in the 1850s, local governments assumed increasing responsibility for feeding, housing, and caring for the poor. Some cities created municipal hospitals.

State and local governments in America began not only to offer education but to require it. All through the colonial era, communities had had schools. As a rule, they were church-run. Often, however, they received public money in one form or another. But it was not assumed that all children would go to school. Indeed, some questioned whether children of the poor *ought* to receive schooling. By the second quarter of the nineteenth century, however, champions of mass education had succeeded in selling the argument that compulsory public schooling was desirable not only as a matter of charity but also as a way of occupying idle youth, preparing them for productive work, and "Americanizing" the immigrant. Pre–Civil War Massachusetts, with its concern for the poor, its leadership in the public school movement, and its lively concern for temperance and other forms of moral uplift, is characterized by its most distinguished historians, Oscar and Mary Handlin, as "a humanitarian police state."[25]

Over time, as American corporations prospered, their managers came to think of themselves as having interests separate from those of the public at large. Attitudes toward the poor such as those expressed by Judge Sedgwick became less common. The justification for public schools, hospitals, and the like came to be put increasingly in terms of these institutions' potential contribution to social order and an increase in wealth. As one disillusioned Massachusetts reformer put it "education is merely a branch of general police, and schoolmasters are only a better sort of constable."[26] Through most of the first industrial revolution, however, it is fair to say that government in the United States was much more mercantilist, much more paternalist, and much less laissez-faire than in Britain.

The Second Technological-Economic-Social Revolution, ca. 1850–ca. 1950

Sometime in the nineteenth century, a second industrial revolution succeeded the first. To quote Thomas McCraw again:

> Communication and transportation were revolutionized, first by the telegraph and railroad, then by the telephone, automobile, truck, and airplane. Production was increasingly powered by electric motors and by the internal combustion engine. Corporations proliferated, becoming commonplace in all capitalist countries. Mass marketing arose. "Big business" as we know it first appeared, and some companies built complex organizations with semi-autonomous divisions and many layers of management. A few very large firms, clustered in a small number of industries, employed several hundred thousand persons each. In most industries, traditional small shops and medium-sized factories persisted alongside the new industrial giants. . . .
>
> Typical products included "producers' goods" such as steel, turbines, and chemicals, plus a profuse array of new consumer goods, which were now mass-produced, branded, and individually packaged. Consumer durables such as automobiles, radios, home appliances, and ultimately television sets became focal points of daily life. . . . The continuous introduction of new products of all kinds became the hallmark of modern capitalism.[27]

Accompanying these immense changes in technology, industry, and business came both continuing and new change in the social environment and in the lives of individuals. Population growth and urbanization accelerated. Between the mid-nineteenth century and World War I, the population of Western Europe increased by another 60 percent. This occurred even though tens of millions sailed across the Atlantic, making the United States by 1900 more populous than any European country other than Russia. With rural areas emptying, cities experienced a genuine population explosion. By the second decade of the twentieth century, Western Europe had sixteen cities with populations of over one million.

The advent of mass production, as in automobile assembly lines, meant that more and more workers performed monotonous mechanical tasks. In compensation, however, industrial workers received higher pay, for their productivity increased. It took fewer men to match the water-lifting capacity of the machine, and they could be paid more. In combination with rural depopulation and migration, this also made labor markets less completely buyer's markets for employers. Labor unions formed for collective bargaining. World War I increased demand for manufactures while at the same time curtailing the labor supply. (New machine guns were needed to mow down men who, if not conscripted, might have been making machine guns.) Wages skyrocketed and never quite returned to pre-1914 earth. Even in parts of defeated Germany, Austria, and Hungary, working-class families attained standards of living that, before the war, would have required middle-class status. Contrast scenes in Gerhart Hauptmann's nineteenth-century plays with those in Alfred Döblin's twentieth-century epic, *Berlin: Alexanderplatz*. Hauptmann's characters wear rags and scrabble for food; Döblin's wear machine-made working clothes and frequent beer halls.

To an extraordinary extent, people in the industrialized world became members of a single society. The spread and standardization of manufactures meant that people on almost all economic and social levels used many of the same goods. Even in countries slow to develop systems of public education, literacy became the rule. Mass production of books, magazines, and newspapers put immense varieties of reading matter within the reach of almost everyone. The mass-circulation penny press made public affairs—and the private affairs of the great—common topics of conversation.

At the same time, people in the industrialized world became increasingly differentiated. Between the top and bottom levels of societies, layer on layer developed. Blue-collar and white-collar workers separated, with hierarchies on each side of the line. Under owners of companies (or sometimes over them) were managers, and under upper managers were middle managers and so on. Specialties developed within corporations. Professions developed. In each profession, specialties and hierarchies multiplied. Schools provide an example, with higher, secondary, and primary education separating; teachers dividing by subject specialty; and school administration becoming a career line all its own. Universities provide an extreme example, becoming colonies populated by scores of tribes, each with its own languages and customs, often incomprehensible even to others in the tribe, let alone to members of other tribes.

The psychological changes evident during the first industrial revolution accelerated during the second. Nationalism exploded very much as did the population of cities, though with largely different causes. Nationalism showed itself in two new forms. Especially among late-uprooted peasants and artisans dislocated by the emergence of factories, nationalism turned into murderous hatred of other nationalities. There were many examples in the multiethnic Austro-Hungarian empire. Among them were South Slavs who joined the Black Hand and the anti-Slav, anti-Semitic German Austrians, among whom was the adolescent Adolf Hitler. Another example was Sinn Féin, founded in Ireland in 1905.

The other new form of nationalism was chauvinist patriotism, especially manifest among old aristocracies being elbowed aside by newly rich capitalists—Eastern European landowners who became Pan-Slav or Pan-German; French officers with particules who wanted to send Captain Alfred Dreyfus to the guillotine, even if he was innocent; members of the Primrose League; the Theodore Roosevelt who spoke about how war purified the master races. These diseased varieties of nationalism would form the boils that burst in 1914, with World War I.

During this second period of revolution, as during the first, governments used their powers, especially the power of taxation, to redistribute wealth for the benefit of enterprising capitalists. In at least two major respects, however, the activities of government broadened. First of all, government came increasingly to attempt to solve problems resulting from industrialization, urbanization, and social change. That is, instead of just helping capitalists, government began to help the larger public cope with conditions created by capitalists. Second, governments increasingly exerted shaping influence within nations by virtue of their responsibility for national defense. During the previous revolution, the demands of possible war had produced little strain. The eighteenth century in Europe had been not only the heyday of limited government but also practically the only period in the history of humankind when war or preparation for war was not a dominating fact of life. The artifacts in Europe of earlier eras are the remains of castles and forts. Those of the eighteenth century are mansions and country houses. After the French Revolution and Napoleonic Wars, conditions of the eighteenth century returned. Armies were hidden away in remote garrisons, to be called in case of revolution but not otherwise to be seen—as in Stendhal's *Lucien Leuwen*.

In Europe, Germany was the leader in this second revolution as Britain had been in the first. In the Atlantic world, the United States gained a lead over both Germany and Britain. Germany, of course, had not become Germany until 1871. Earlier, however, the majority of German-speaking states had formed a customs union. Led by Prussia, they had marched toward economic unity long before the Franco-Prussian War gave birth to the German empire. Statistics dating from mid-century told the tale of Germany's comparative economic success (and America's).

The basis for Germany's economic growth was very similar to that of America's. The separate German states had pursued essentially mercantilist policies, using governmental power to develop communications and manufactures and to provide education. Statistics on schooling show the extent to which Germany and the United States led nations that also lagged behind them in economic indices.

Government continued to play a very large role in the German economy. After unification, German capitalists looked to the new national government for the kind of support they had previously obtained from Prussia, Saxony, Bavaria, and other states. They did so with particular anxiety because of a twenty-year recession that settled

Table 1-2. Population and Gross National Product, 1840 and 1910

	1840	1910
Population (millions)		
Germany	31.2	64.6
United Kingdom	26.5	44.9
United States	17.1	92.4
GNP ($ billion U.S. 1960)		
Germany	8.3	47.7
United Kingdom	10.8	43.3
United States	10.6	117.8

Source: *Cambridge Economic History of Europe*, vol. 8 (Cambridge: Cambridge University Press, 1989).

over Europe very soon after German unification. And they got what they asked for. Chancellor Otto von Bismarck and his successors obliged business leaders by subsidizing industries such as steel and chemicals, by aiding formation of cartels, and by providing tariff protection for manufactures as well as for agricultural products. Continuing competition among the various German states led to Germany's outdoing all other European states not only in schooling but in railway construction and in the formation of corporations and banks. Laissez-faire principles made some headway, the most important example being reduced government control over the coal industry. A boom in coal production in the Prussian-controlled Ruhr Valley occurred in part because of increased competition, and this boom was a crucial element in Germany's economic growth. But even in the early twentieth century, government dictated to business to a greater extent than was ever the case in Britain or the United States.

One reason for government's having a heavy hand in Germany was, of course, concern about preparation for war. Prussia had been described as an army with a state rather than a state with an army. Given the enmity of France and the continual risk of conflict with Russia, Germany had reason to maintain high levels of land armament. This became increasingly expensive and costly as technology progressed. Then, in the 1890s, after Bismarck's retirement, Germany began to build a large navy and to acquire overseas colonies. By 1911 the strain of maintaining a powerful army *and* a powerful navy had become almost insupportable. Meanwhile, the scope of government had expanded to include virtual dictation to large armaments and

Table 1-3. Primary School Enrollment Rates (per 10,000 population)

	1830	1850	1900
Germany	1,700	1,600	1,576
United Kingdom	900	1,045	1,407
United States	1,500	1,800	1,969

Source: Rondo Cameron, *A Concise Economic History of the World,* 2d ed. (New York: Oxford University Press, 1993), 220.

shipbuilding concerns and, by extension, to the steel industry and many allied industries.

Germany set the pace in using governmental powers to ameliorate conditions created by industrialization. Although great variations existed from place to place, German cities and towns were generally ahead of those elsewhere in Europe and in America in their attention to sanitation, crime control, and public health. In the 1880s, Bismarck created national programs providing sickness, accident, and old-age insurance for industrial workers. Although Bismarck has been accused of simply trying to neutralize socialism (and there is no doubt that this figured in his calculations), there is also ample evidence that such paternalism had precedents in preunification Prussia and that Bismarck himself had a sense of social responsibility not entirely unlike that of Judge Sedgwick.[28]

The extent and importance of Bismarck's programs have also been debated. Benefit levels were not generous, the proportion financed by employee contributions was large, and fine print worked to the disadvantage of men or women who changed jobs or could be accused of negligence or malingering. Nevertheless, Bismarck's programs impressed contemporaries as almost revolutionary. David Lloyd George, who engineered counterpart programs for Britain when chancellor of the exchequer in the first decade of the twentieth century, declared after a visit to Germany that "I never realised before on what a gigantic scale the German pension system is conducted. . . . It touches the great mass of German people in well-nigh every walk of life. . . . Does the German worker fall ill? State insurance comes to his aid. Is he permanently invalided . . . ? Again he gets a regular grant whether he has reached the pension age or not."[29]

In the United States, in contrast to Germany, the active role of government lessened. The Civil War of 1861–65 saw the national government (indeed, two national governments) assume and exercise unprecedented powers. Afterward, however, it relinquished nearly all of those powers. It continued to transfer public resources to private interests, now on an immensely larger scale, but it did little to guide how those resources should be used. The federal government subsidized business to a degree not matched anywhere else in the world. The subsidies were provided partly via tariffs, which enabled both manufacturers and producers of raw materials to charge Americans prices well above those in world markets. The largest subsidies took the form of donations of public land, primarily to companies building transcontinental railroads. Federal land grants to railroads amounted to almost 7 percent of the continental United States. As Marc Allan Eisner comments, this was more than the combined area of Indiana, Illinois, Michigan, and Wisconsin.[30] State and local governments also contributed land and, in addition, purchased railroad securities.

Government, however, regulated the economy to a lesser degree than had been the case before the Civil War. As earlier, most regulation took place at the state or local level. Until the 1930s, the most powerful regulatory body in the nation was probably the Texas Railroad Commission, which, by setting ceilings on crude oil production from Texas wells, significantly influenced supply worldwide. At the state and local level, however, the mercantilist tradition weakened, partly because of the advertised success of British laissez-faire policies and partly because of the decline in the sense of community.[31] Also, it should be remembered that the states exercised power by ordinance rather than by administration. As James Leiby writes,

> state governments were not, in the nineteenth century, conceived as administrative agencies. The main organ of government was the legislature, which met for a few weeks every second year. The governor was a caretaker. Some of his really important powers applied to the state militia. He and other high executives—the state treasurer, for example—worked one day a week in the weeks when they worked at all. The state prison and lunatic asylum were the principal continuing expenditures of state government until the rise of the state universities. Some special committee of managers, trustees, or inspectors was necessary if there was to be any one at all prepared to check on the institutional executive.[32]

Even within states, in any case, business concerns were rapidly becoming too large, too complicated, and too rich to be controlled. There developed what has been called, at the international level, "competition in laxity," with states and localities vying as to which could offer corporations the least regulation.

One result of the lessened government regulation of business was a proliferation of cartels and monopolies. In the first years of the twentieth century, seventy-one industries in the United States were so organized as to be virtually free of competition. This included not only the well-known examples of steel and oil but also lead, rubber, paper, chemicals, tobacco products, bricks, and leather.[33] Aggrieved consumers, frustrated in their efforts to obtain relief at the state level, pressed increasingly for action at the national level. Congress responded by creating an Interstate Commerce Commission to regulate railroad rates and by passing antitrust legislation. The ICC proved comparatively impotent, however, and although the Justice Department achieved dissolution of a few monopolies (notably of John D. Rockefeller's Standard Oil Company), the essential condition persisted.

The U.S. government also lagged in moving to ameliorate conditions created by or accompanying the second wave of industrialization. That problems existed, no one could doubt. Cities were becoming more crowded. So were factory towns. In the industrial Northeast, the countryside emptied. Municipal and state governments responded primarily by continuing or increasing support for private charitable organizations and by creating agencies to set standards for those organizations. And this occurred in the face of considerable resistance. Even in the 1930s, Roman Catholic charities would protest government welfare programs, with one bishop declaring, "The poor belong to us. We will not let them be taken from us."[34] While the federal government maintained one large welfare agency—indeed, as of the 1890s, the largest such agency in the world—to provide pensions for Civil War veterans and their widows, this agency was so much an instrument of the reigning Republican party and so ridden with scandal that its example long served as an argument against government-administered welfare programs.[35]

Given America's isolationist tradition, preparation for possible war had less effect on the scope of government than in Germany, or even in Britain. The argument for a strong navy, made by the American captain Alfred Thayer Mahan, in *The Influence of Sea Power on History* had contributed to the naval arms race in Europe. In Mahan's own country, this argument helped to induce a naval construction program designed to stabilize the iron and steel industries and the railroads that served them. At the beginning of the twentieth century, the United States had the second largest navy in the world. The British-German dreadnaught race, however, left America behind. As of 1910, U.S. defense expenditures totaled less than 2 percent of the gross national product (GNP).

World War I changed all of these conditions dramatically but temporarily. When an active belligerent in 1917–18, the United States had a command economy. The federal government took control of all railroads. The War Industries Board dictated industrial production quotas and timetables and fixed prices and wages. Other government agencies controlled agriculture and shipping. After the war, however, the apparatus of state control was dismantled even more rapidly than it had been constructed. The experience remained only as a memory of the national government's latent capabilities for action. President Calvin Coolidge exaggerated only a bit when he said in the 1920s, "If the Federal Government should go out of existence, the common run of people would not detect the difference in the affairs of their daily life for a considerable length of time."[36]

It took the Great Depression to change lastingly the economic and social role of the national government. World War II and the cold war then changed, at least for the remainder of the century, the extent to which preparation for possible war would influence the character of both the economy and society. States and cities proved helpless to deal with the massive unemployment and hunger of the early 1930s. With Franklin Roosevelt's New Deal, the national government began to become employer of last resort, backer of unions against management, and the place to which Americans looked when seeking any counterweight to business enterprise or the solution to any social problem.

Evidence that the transition was less than abrupt can be found in the fact that the Social Security Act of 1935 made the national government the funder but not the administrator of programs to aid the unemployed and the poor. As Edward Berkowitz writes, "Rather than a national unemployment compensation system, the states ran a series of 50-odd systems, each with its own rules, regulations, and level of benefits. Efforts to unite these state systems under federal control, meeting stiff resistance from the states and from unemployment compensation administrators, invariably failed."[37]

As the Civil War had seen a shift in identity, leading Americans no longer to speak of Virginia or Massachusetts as their "country" and to use "United States" as a singular, not a plural, noun, so World War II produced a comparable change in what Americans meant when they spoke of "the government." Previously, the term had been at least as likely to apply to a local or state government. "The capital" had usually been the state capital. The popular American version of the British legal dictum "The king can do no wrong" was "You can't fight city hall." After World War II, "the government" meant Washington, D.C.

The United States did briefly show some sign of turning backward. The election of 1946 produced a seemingly revolutionary turnover in Congress, with Republicans acquiring large majorities in both houses. (The turnover was more extensive, and the majorities larger, than those of 1994.) Many in the new majorities talked of returning the national government to its status under Coolidge. But seniority rules gave veteran members control, and those veterans remembered too sharply the experience of the depression. Not much was undone. The election of 1948, keeping Harry Truman in the White House and restoring Democratic majorities in both houses, decreased the likelihood of the New Deal's being repealed. The Republican president who succeeded Truman, Dwight Eisenhower, talked of smaller government, but in practice kept the New Deal intact and, in addition, put the federal government for the first time in the position of providing large-scale subsidies to higher education.

After being elected president in his own right in 1964, Lyndon Johnson promised legislation to make America "a Great Society." His presidency, with some of its momentum carrying through that of his successor, Richard Nixon, saw the scope of government widen more than at any period in the past. The pace and character of change is suggested in a summary by political scientist David Vogel:

> From 1900 through 1965, only one regulatory agency was established at the federal level whose primary responsibility was to protect either consumers, employees, or the public from physical harm due to corporate activities: the Food and Drug Administration. Between

1964 and 1977, ten federal regulatory agencies were created with this as their mandate: the Equal Employment Opportunity Commission (1964), the National Transportation Safety Board (1966), the Council on Environmental Quality (1969), the Environmental Protection Agency (1970), the National Highway Traffic Safety Administration (1970), the Consumer Product Safety Commission (1972), the Mining Enforcement and Safety Administration (1973), the Materials Transportation Bureau (1975), and the Office of Strip Mining Regulation and Enforcement (1977).[38]

The extent of change is perhaps best indicated by testimony from contemporaries who seek to ameliorate it. Bill Clinton's vice president, Al Gore, became executive agent for a program to "reinvent government" in the United States. Reporting on his accomplishments, Gore boasted in 1996 that *two hundred* federal agencies had been forced to publish their service standards and 16,000 out of 86,000 pages of federal regulations had been scrapped. He cited the elimination of one layer of management in the Department of Health and Human Services, the merger of an Agency for Toxic Substances and Disease Registry with the Centers for Disease Control, termination of the Clean Coal Technology Program, and the privatization of the College Construction Loan Insurance Association.[39]

Almost by coincidence, the human mind had, by the time of the Great Depression, begun to understand some of the mechanisms driving the ups and downs of the industrial era business cycle. Economists—students of the *oikos*—had made discoveries comparable, if not to those of physicists, at least to those of botanists. One of their most important discoveries was that fiscal and financial levers could be manipulated by governments to reduce, if not completely to smooth, the volatility of the business cycle.

In one way or another, governments could thus moderate ups and downs in consumption, production, and employment by making imaginative use of one of their oldest prerogatives—the power to coin money. The recovery and prosperity attributable to government spending during World War II made at least closet converts out of almost everyone. President Dwight Eisenhower offset his cuts in domestic welfare programs by sponsoring a hugely expensive interstate highway system. President Reagan did likewise by greatly increasing outlays for defense. The business cycle almost flattened. (See Figure 1-1.)

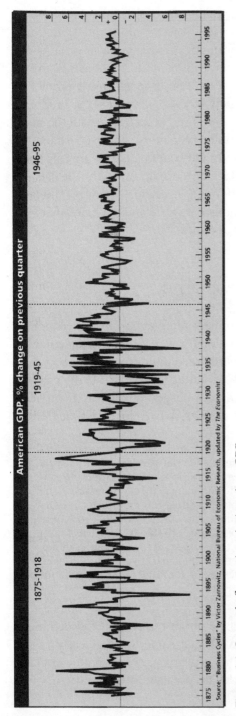

Figure 1-1. Quarterly fluctuations in American GDP

Source: "Business Cycles" by Victor Zarnowitz, National Bureau of Economic Research, updated by *The Economist.*

Meanwhile, because of requirements first for combatting the Axis powers and then for containing the Soviet Union and China and deterring nuclear war, the American government guided and in some respects forced the evolution of the national industrial base. As Anne Markusen and her collaborators write (with a touch of hyperbole) in *The Rise of the Gunbelt,* "Whole new industries, and a set of predominantly defense-dependent firms, were bred in lock step with the new, permanent bureau in charge of military matters—the Department of Defense. Pentagon dollars created industrial complexes in California orchards, in Arizona and New Mexico deserts, on Utah salt flats, in the Rocky Mountains of Colorado, and in Florida swamps. The lack of these dollars helped create industrial wastelands in cities that had once been the industrial core of America."[40]

A Third Industrial Revolution, ca. 1950–?

Although the surge in government intervention in the economy, apart from that relating to preparation for war, represented a continuing reaction to the second industrial revolution, that revolution may long since have run its course. Around the middle of this century commenced what many label a third industrial revolution. Economist Philip Cerny characterizes it as consisting of five closely linked trends:

> The first is the development of flexible manufacturing systems, and their spread not only to new industries but to older ones as well. The second is the changing hierarchical form of firms (and bureaucracies) to what has been called "lean management." The third is the growing capacity of decision-making structures to monitor the actions of all levels of management and of the labour force more closely through the use of information technology. . . . The fourth . . . is the increasing segmentation of markets in a more complex consumer society. Finally, the third industrial revolution has been profoundly shaped by the emergence of more and more autonomous financial markets and institutions.[41]

Despite these changes, most debate about the scope of government still takes place within a framework that came together early in the second industrial revolution. Although varying somewhat from place to place and time to time, this debate oscillated between two poles.

One can label them "cooperation" versus "control" or, more polemically, "corporatism" versus "socialism."

"Cooperation" supposes that the public interest is best served if government and private interests work in tandem. Where it was actually called "corporatism" or something equivalent (as in Fascist Italy), it became control, with private interests ending up inside the state, much like the lady riding the tiger. In Anglo-American versions, called "corporatism" only by critics, the reality has usually been cooperation subject to strong restraints from other affected interests and citizens. Elsewhere, particularly in European states under Christian Democratic governments, cooperation has often involved government's acting as broker to encourage concessions by business and labor to one another and to the public at large.

The alternative of "control" supposes that private interests, whether business or labor, will serve the public interest only if compelled to do so. The extreme version was Soviet-style socialism. Much milder versions appeared occasionally in Europe, when Socialist or Social Democratic parties came to power. Labour's welfare state in post–World War II Britain is one example. Scandinavian countries offer others.

In the United States, the extremes were never approached. The national-level Progressivism of the early twentieth century, whether Theodore Roosevelt's or Woodrow Wilson's, played variations on the theme of cooperation. Advocacy of any form of control was confined to minority parties or to local leaders, some of whom successfully championed limited versions of public ownership, mostly for utilities and street railways. Only after the Great Depression did there develop in America much constituency for national-level control, and that manifested itself chiefly in statutes chartering regulatory agencies on a premise that the business concerns to be regulated were predisposed to criminality. In practice, most such agencies ended up implementing cooperation more than control. They were then accused of having been captured. The truth was usually some variant of the proverb "to understand everything is to pardon everything."[42]

In any case, deep into the third industrial revolution, debate about the scope of government continues mostly to run within the confines of this traditional framework. It was President Reagan's basic thesis that business served the public interest best if government confined itself to an occasional nudge or chiding word. It is Professor Galbraith's thesis that business concerns are not apt to serve the public's interests unless compelled to act contrary to their perceptions of their own interests.

It seems unlikely that continued debate within this traditional framework will get us far in coping with the third industrial revolution. The economist Richard Zeckhauser suggests that we may have to go back to approximately the point where political philosophers were when they began to analyze the hypothetical social contract. Perhaps, says Zeckhauser, some principles could be deduced concerning the proper spheres of government and private enterprise if we began by distinguishing three classes of goods produced or at least affected by government. The first are "public goods," such as national defense, which provide common or widely shared benefits. The second are "directed goods," such as industrial subsidies or public housing, which benefit certain groups at the expense of others. The third, sometimes overlapping with the second and even with the first, are "clash goods," the very approach to which generates conflict that carries costs of its own. Obvious examples are abortion rules and affirmative action.

Others see Zeckhauser's formulation as neoclassical economics with catchy new labels. There is a question, for example, whether the *Sea Wolf* submarine is a "public good," given that part of its rationale is to provide employment in Connecticut. And there is a question whether the category of "clash goods," and the point that such goods carry both opportunity and transaction costs, is not implicitly another way of arguing what Adam Smith argued.

Looking back at the record of how human thinking responded to the first and second industrial revolutions, Thomas McCraw voices skepticism as to whether a new framework for thinking about the government's role in the economy is likely to develop at any foreseeable time. He points to the fact that one hundred years intervened between the first bruising downturns in production, prices, and unemployment—in the Atlantic-wide Panics of the 1820s and 1830s—and the discovery by John Maynard Keynes and others that the ancient prerogative of coinage could be reworked to provide a remedy. How much longer may it take, he asks, when we deal with near-instantaneous, planet-spanning transactions practically beyond the reach of any traditional element of the *polis?*

Meanwhile, alongside debate about the role of government in economic affairs, we see renewed discussion of whether government has not evolved too far in the direction of concerning itself only with the material interests of citizens. When state and church separated in Europe, churches retained not only the function of educating children but also that more generally of setting moral standards. Civil authority often enforced these standards, as we see most obviously in laws against adultery and sodomy. Sometimes churches and high-minded lay persons joined to insist that government act as an instrument of conscience. The movement to abolish slavery is the outstanding example. Some of these movements were successful but short-lived, as, most notably, was the case of Prohibition. In most cases, however, moral standards were expected to be sustained less by the power of government than by the simple force of example and of public opinion. As Alexis de Tocqueville wrote in the 1830s,

> while the law permits the Americans to do what they please, religion prevents them from conceiving, and forbids them to commit, what is rash or unjust.
>
> Religion in America takes no direct part in the government of society, but it must be regarded as the first of their political institutions.[43]

Over time, however, religion lost more and more of its authority. Education became primarily public education. Resistance to sectarian laws, such as those in England that limited the civil rights of Roman Catholics, gradually merged into attacks on all laws and rules relating to belief or related behavior. In the meantime, increased physical and social mobility, together with broadening intra- and international communication, dissolved many traditional constraints. Marshall McLuhan may have been right about the rise of a "global village," but it was not a village with any of the characteristics of the village where Hester Prynne got her scarlet letter.

The question of whether government should or should not assert itself as a shaper of morality is increasingly debated, but confusingly so. On the one hand are people who protest "government in the bedroom" yet call for government to crack down on action or even speech that offends some identity group, ethnic or other. On the other hand are people who protest permissiveness and pornography yet in most respects oppose all government exercise of power. Feminist antipornography crusaders are an example of the former; Evangelical Christian militia groups are an extreme example of the latter.

This debate has many ramifications, for the successive industrial revolutions eventually affected the entire world. Much of the non-European world, however, has never had Europe's particular experience of conflict between church and state. In the Islamic world, priests remained politically powerful to a degree true almost nowhere in Europe after the seventeenth century. In imperial China, secular authority absorbed ecclesiastical authority, with imperial mandarins serving as setters of norms for all compartments of life.[44] This makes for no end of conflict as non-European societies increasingly achieve parity with Western societies in wealth and power.

Partly because changes in global communications affect private life as well as life in the marketplace, the third industrial revolution poses challenges for thinking about the scope of government that are both different from and larger than the challenges posed by previous industrial revolutions. And this chapter closes with a caution similar to McCraw's.

The most important task before us, as we think about the scope of government in the future, is to identify the questions that need answering. In all probability, few, if any, of the important questions are ones formulated in response to the earlier industrial revolutions. The whole framework of cooperation versus control may be irrelevant or nearly so. How can we employ this framework, for example, to contemplate questions surrounding intellectual property rights or pornography or sedition carried via the Internet?

Indeed, even within its limited sphere, the great discovery of the mid-twentieth century may be meaningless for the twenty-first century. If financial transactions are global and essentially uncontrollable, it may not matter what princes do with their traditional power to coin money. Philip Cerny singles this out as the most important feature of the third industrial revolution, writing, "This new global transformation has gravely challenged the capacity of the state to provide effective governance not only of financial markets themselves but of economic affairs generally."[45] Sir Samuel Brittan, the shrewd columnist for London's *Financial Times,* makes the point that, if all governments were simultaneously to adopt policies of "fiscal responsibility," the consequences could be catastrophic. "All countries cannot run higher current account surpluses or lower deficits," he writes, "for . . . these imbalances would sum to zero. So it is still possible to have a Keynesian-type slump in a global economy."[46]

Questions relevant for thinking about nationalistic great powers with propensities for war may also be anachronistic. The passionate nationalism manifest in the former Yugoslavia, parts of the former Soviet Union, and ex-colonial areas may be residual phenomena, like the religious warfare that continued in isolated parts of Europe and still goes on in Northern Ireland. The European Union, the North American Free Trade Agreement, and other such innovations suggest that the nation-state may become a less and less significant factor shaping personal identities. And it is at least arguable that, whether this is true or not, advances in military technology have made preparation for large-scale warfare much less central in the lives of nations.

At the same time, we see arising new challenges to the safety of society and individuals that even Adam Smith saw as essential responsibilities of government. Terrorists not sponsored by states attack innocent government workers in Oklahoma City and subway riders in Tokyo, and at present we understand only dimly, if at all, how to limit the risk that their like will strike large populations with chemical, biological, or nuclear weapons. "Safety" in the twenty-first century may mean something quite different from what it has meant in the past, with powerful implications for the possibility of preserving the cottager's rights that the Earl of Chatham celebrated. To put our minds around the possibilities of the future, we may need entirely new ways of thinking about the *polis* and the *oikos*.

Although the proposition is unlikely to command universal assent, a case can be made that humankind has not done much serious thinking, for a very long time, about the nature of the *polis*. This was a preoccupation of the foremost minds in Europe and America from the Renaissance through the Enlightenment. As it became clearer what could be done with the intellectual tools devised by Descartes, Bacon, Newton, and Leibnitz, most of the best minds in the Atlantic world turned away from human affairs and toward nature. The great economist Simon Kuznets argued that this was the driving force in the industrial revolutions; they represented, he wrote, "the extended application of science to problems of economic production."[47]

Because quantified exchanges of goods and services were growing in volume, and because they lent themselves to comparison, at least superficially, with forces in nature (supply and demand, for example, equated with gravity), the greatly expanded *oikos* became one of the foci of this new thinking.[48] (The science of the *oikos* would earlier have been understood as relating to husbandry.) Now economics effectively displaced political philosophy.

After John Stuart Mill, who wrote as much about economics as about politics, not a single thinker brought forth a new idea about the *polis* as distinct from the *oikos*. (If there is an exception, it may be Lenin's concept of "the dictatorship of the proletariat.") The creative minds that focused on the topic usually ended up looking backward. Unlike the American founding fathers or Rousseau or Locke or even Hobbes, these thinkers did not develop conceptions of a future *polis*. Instead, they idealized something from the past and regretted its disappearance. For Max Weber it was preindustrial Europe; for Hannah Arendt, Periclean Athens; for Jürgen Habermas, the Enlightenment, when "the public sphere" had been occupied by ideas, not by interest groups.[49] And the other focus of classical thinking—*ethos* or character—virtually disappeared from view except to the extent that it figured in one version or another of utilitarian economics.

Recent stirrings faintly reminiscent of those in early modern Europe have been heard, however. Amartya Sen has revived the original Adam Smith by pressing questions about economics *and* ethics. Building on suggestions from philosophers as diverse as John Rawls, Thomas Nagel, and Ronald Dworkin, Michael Sandel has urged fundamental rethinking of how politics and ethics might intertwine.[50] McCraw may well be right that it takes a century or more to find a workable version even of an old idea. If so, we may be a very long distance from having a body of new political ideas that can be translated into reality. Still, it may be a small and essential step forward to recognize that we do not now have any such ideas and that, if we are to obtain manageable understanding of what should be the scope of government in the approaching century, we need to start building a stock of such ideas, not just polishing the surfaces of ideas appropriate for times past.

CHAPTER TWO

Measuring the Performance
of Government

Derek Bok

If one thing has become clear about the federal government, it is that Americans have little regard for its performance. Through much of the last decade, most people have felt that the country is headed in the wrong direction and that Washington deserves much of the blame. A majority of the public believes that Washington's efforts to regulate the economy usually make matters worse, and considerably larger majorities feel that federal officials waste huge amounts of money and that Congress frequently spends public funds on the wrong things. When asked what constitutes the greatest single threat facing this country, more people currently point to the federal government than the combined total of those identifying the other perennial scapegoats, big labor and big business.

These harsh judgments are now well known. But are they true? Is there any hard evidence that can either justify the public's views or discredit them as malicious, misguided, and without merit?[1]

Alternative Means of Evaluation

Some observers might say that the best index of the government's performance *is* the verdict of public opinion. In a democracy, after all, the ultimate aim of the government is to satisfy its citizens. According to this view, a democratic regime that has so completely lost the confidence and trust of the people must, ipso facto, be doing a bad job.

There are several problems, however, with simply relying on public opinion to evaluate the performance of the state. For one thing, citizens may lose confidence in government for reasons having no relation to the quality of its policies or the work of its officials. The very fact that trust and confidence have dropped substantially in the past thirty years for almost all major institutions in our society suggests that something more far reaching than poor performance in Washington must be responsible.

Further consideration suggests that confidence in or satisfaction with the work of any institution is not simply a reflection of its record but depends on a relationship between expectations and performance. Hence, confidence could erode because expectations have increased even if performance has remained the same. In much the same way, confidence might decline, not because the government is performing worse than before but because it has decided, quite possibly with strong public support, to perform more difficult, more controversial tasks.

Finally, the public may have a jaundiced view of government because many people are in error about the facts. This possibility seems more plausible in light of several well-known findings from public opinion polls. One of these findings is that people tend to evaluate the work of government officials and agencies much more highly if they have direct contact with them than if they know about them only secondhand. For example, more than 60 percent of Americans have a favorable impression of their own representative in Congress even though confidence in Congress as a whole has dropped below 25 percent. Other surveys cast doubt on whether the public is well enough informed to make reliable judgments about the government's performance. For example, large majorities believe that air pollution and violent crime have grown worse over the past twenty years even though there is good evidence that the reverse is true. Most people estimate that more than fifty cents of every dollar in the Social Security program is eaten up in overhead. The true figure is less than two cents. If the public can be so wrong about basic facts relating to government performance, its evaluations based on such facts may likewise be incorrect.

Another way of assessing the work of the government is to measure the outcomes of specific programs to determine how well they have done in achieving their objectives. Such data may accumulate rapidly now that Congress has passed the Government Performance and Results Act, requiring every agency to specify its objectives and document its success in attaining them. Further evidence may come from examining the experience of privatizing services such as garbage collection, street repairs, and even public education to see whether private organizations consistently outperform government officials. As data of this kind become available, might it not be possible to assemble all the information and arrive at a solid estimate of government performance?

Alas, several reasons lead one to doubt how reliable an evaluation we will be able to make by this procedure. To begin with, it is impossible to privatize the work of many important agencies or to measure their results in any meaningful way. For example, the Defense Department cannot calculate the amount of national security it has provided, nor can the Justice Department easily estimate the impact of its efforts. Of course, both Justice and Defense can set certain targets and measure their success in achieving them. Nevertheless, such targets will at best be intermediate goals that fall far short of telling us how well laws have been enforced or whether we have gained enough security to justify the vast amounts expended on our armed forces. At the same time, it is probably neither wise nor feasible to contract out the most important functions of the military or the system of justice and law enforcement. As a result, comparisons with private firms performing the same functions are not a practical possibility.

Another problem with measuring the results of specific programs is that it is often impossible to know how much would have been achieved had the program not existed. For example, evaluators may be able to calculate how many people were trained through a particular job program, how many of them received jobs following their training, and how their wages compare with what they previously earned. Still, no one is likely to demonstrate convincingly whether the new jobs and extra earnings were brought about by the training program or whether the trainees merely took jobs from others who would have gotten them at the same enhanced wages had no trainees been available. Similarly, if test scores rise in a neighborhood school, it is generally hard to tell whether they rose because of improved teaching and administration or because drugs, crime, and other neighborhood distractions diminished for extraneous reasons.

A third problem with assessing program results is that it is often difficult to look at such records and decide how good or bad a job the government actually did. In some instances, it may be possible to answer such questions by comparing certain public services with those of private suppliers to determine whether the government is performing better or worse. Where no such comparisons are possible, however, there is often no frame of reference with which to estimate how well or badly the government has functioned.

Finally, even if all the preceding difficulties can be overcome, the problem remains of aggregating the records of countless individual programs into a single overall estimate of performance by the federal, state, or local government. How can we assign appropriate weights to many different program results? What is the common metric with which to combine school test scores, crime rates, air pollution trends, new jobs, industrial accidents, and countless more in a single evaluation of performance?

A slightly different method of proceeding would be to select a limited number of important policy areas with widely shared goals— such as health care, housing, and the environment—and then determine how much progress has been made over a period of years. Once again, of course, it will be impossible to aggregate the records in such different fields to arrive at a single composite measure of progress. Nevertheless, one should at least come away from such a study with a rough sense of whether a nation, overall, has been gaining or losing ground in its efforts to achieve the goals that matter most to its citizens. In addition, an assessment of this kind may also help in making an informed judgment about whether government programs and policies have succeeded, on the whole, in helping the society progress toward generally accepted goals and whether such progress has been accelerating or declining over time.

While studies of this kind can be useful, they, too, have significant limitations. To begin with, if the rate of progress has increased or decreased in recent years, such changes may not have come about from improving or deteriorating policies and programs but from external conditions over which the government has little control. For example, a drop in violent crime may not result from better policing but from demographic trends, such as a decline in the number of teenage males. Similarly, productivity may rise at a slower rate not because of changes in economic policy but as a result of shifts in the mix of manufacturing and services. Considerable skill is often required to estimate how much progress is attributable to government programs, and, in some cases, the results may be inconclusive.

Historical trends, moreover, do not readily yield *evaluative* judgments. The nation may be moving ahead on a wide number of fronts—education, productivity, environmental conditions, and the like—but how do we know whether it is progressing as fast as it should? After all, even the most backward countries often make *some* headway toward basic goals. Unless we have a way of estimating how much progress is possible through effective public policies, we have no means of judging how well our government has performed.

One way of attacking this last problem is to compare the performance of the United States with that of other advanced democratic nations in a series of fields in which (a) public policy plays an important role and (b) the nations involved share similar goals. By comparing how much each nation has progressed toward common objectives over the past several decades, one may be able to arrive at a rough overall judgment as to which of these countries has been most successful. With varying degrees of difficulty, one can also judge how important a role the government has played in contributing to whatever advances or setbacks the society has experienced in each policy area considered. Conceivably, therefore, it may be possible to draw from these comparisons some tentative conclusions about the performance of our government during the past thirty to forty years.

Two difficulties arise in using comparative analysis to decide how well or badly our government has functioned. To begin with, estimating the government's contribution to the nation's performance is extremely difficult in some fields. The effect of law enforcement on crime is one prominent example; the impact of schools on student achievement is another. The second problem is that conditions vary substantially from one nation to another so that one cannot help but wonder whether variations in the amount of progress made in various fields of endeavor are due to the performance of government or to differences in the external conditions in which individual governments have to operate. For example, if the United States has made less progress than other countries in eradicating poverty, reducing pollution, or achieving higher test scores, it is at least conceivable that our record reflects such factors as the country's larger size, its greater population diversity, its heavier defense burdens carried during the cold war, or its unfortunate legacy of race.

In summary, it is clear that no method of evaluating the progress of a nation or the record of its government will be free of difficulty. Still, historical and comparative assessments can be of some limited help. What conclusions, then, can we draw from examining the experience of the United States and other leading democracies over the past several decades?

Results of Historical and Comparative Performance

Large majorities of Americans share a number of basic goals for their society: steady economic growth and prosperity (with low inflation and unemployment); a quality of life that includes such matters as a clean environment, pleasant neighborhoods, and vibrant programs in the arts; reasonable opportunities for everyone to succeed according to his or her abilities and efforts; protection from the major hazards of violence, poverty, sickness and disease, and indigence in old age; and respect for basic values, notably individual freedom and concern for the legitimate interests of others. Fortunately, the same fundamental aims are also shared by large majorities in other leading democracies as well. With these goals in mind, it is possible to chart the progress of the United States both historically and comparatively in a wide variety of fields, such as health care, the economy, education, poverty, old age pensions, housing, and crime. In all these areas, the specific objectives of advanced democracies are very similar, and one can generally obtain fairly reliable information to compare the progress made in each nation during the past thirty to forty years. For example, with respect to the broad goal of economic prosperity, all nations share the objectives of growth in per capita income, rising productivity, full employment, and low inflation. For each objective, reasonably good data exist for each country covering the last several decades.

Having spent considerable time collecting and analyzing such information in some eighteen of these fields of activity, I believe that it is possible to offer the following tentative judgments regarding several current complaints about our government.[2]

1. On the basis of some sixty to seventy specific objectives of importance to most Americans, the United States has made definite progress over the past few decades in the vast majority of cases. With respect to the economy, for example, the gross domestic product has almost tripled in real dollars since 1960 and unemployment and inflation have come down to levels only slightly above those of the early 1960s. Opportunities for Americans have increased as rates of college attendance have grown and discrimination against women and minorities has diminished. Americans have become more secure through wider coverage of Social Security, the advent of Medicare and Medicaid, and stricter safeguards for consumers. The quality of life has risen through higher rates of home ownership, cleaner air and water, and the rapid growth of the arts. Finally, the federal courts have greatly expanded the scope of individual freedom by guaranteeing to black citizens the right to vote; to newspapers the right to comment more freely about public figures; to women the right to have an abortion; to black children the right to attend white schools, just to mention a few examples. All of these developments are summarized in Table 2-1 at the end of this chapter.

2. Of the few instances in which the society's performance has actually declined (for example, crime, teenage births out-of-wedlock, and other cases of personal irresponsibility), most are situations in which the ability of the government to affect the desired results is especially tenuous and uncertain. Overall, therefore, the historical record gives little evidence to support the opinion of a majority of Americans that the country is "headed in the wrong direction." Nor does it afford support for the view that when our government addresses a problem it generally makes matters worse.

3. The evidence is mixed on whether the record of progress in

the United States has declined during the past twenty years. Forward movement has definitely slowed in a number of fields, such as racial integration, the elimination of poverty, access to health care, and growth of gross domestic product. Nevertheless, crime has probably diminished since 1980; student test scores have stopped declining and have begun to rise; unemployment has dropped; and the environment has definitely become less polluted. Examining the sixty to seventy specific goals that matter to Americans, progress has speeded up or stayed the same more often than it has slowed since the mid-1970s. These findings are summarized in Table 2-2, at the end of the chapter. Of course, to someone who feels that economic growth or poverty and social justice matter more than anything else, it may appear that the country has gone into decline since 1970. Conversely, to those who feel especially strongly about the environment, crime, or personal responsibility, America will seem to be doing somewhat better than it did in the 1960s and early 1970s, although not as well as it should. All things considered, it would therefore be difficult to assert categorically that America or its government has performed less well in the past fifteen to twenty years than during the preceding two decades.

4. There is also little evidence to support the widespread impression that government inefficiency squanders huge amounts of money (forty-eight cents of every tax dollar, according to one public opinion poll). Many reports by outside groups, notably the General Accounting Office, affirm that "waste, fraud, and abuse" exist in many government programs. At the same time, GAO reports do not suggest that waste occurs on nearly the scale suspected by most Americans. Moreover, a series of blue-ribbon commissions has studied the operations of our national government intensively without finding waste totaling more than a small fraction of the amount estimated by the public. For example, Vice President Al Gore's recent National Performance Review examined federal agencies in great detail and issued scores of specific recommendations, yet the total amount of estimated savings from this review was less than two cents per dollar of tax revenue, far below the forty-eight-cent figure just mentioned.

5. If large-scale waste exists, it probably results not so much from inefficient administration, as the public seems to believe, as from poorly designed programs. Poor design can embody a multitude of sins. Examples would include classic pork-barrel projects authorizing spending for projects of questionable value, programs that receive inadequate funds to achieve their objective, programs embodying a strategy poorly conceived to achieve the desired ends, and programs in which expenditures to protect human lives are distributed with little relation to what is scientifically known about relative risk. A prime example of deficient program design would be the American health care system, which produces in expenditures (private and public) that are more than $250 billion per year greater than those of the country with the next highest costs and with no demonstrable improvements over other nations in the health or longevity of the people. Another example involves government programs to protect human lives where experts have concluded that federal agencies could spend $30 billion per year less and still save as many lives if the legislature reallocated funds to correspond more closely to known risks. Such examples are not meant to imply that there is little government waste of the conventional kind or that efforts to improve bureaucratic efficiency, such as Vice President Gore's National Performance Review, are not worth making. Still, if one is after truly major savings, the place to begin is almost certainly Congress much more than the executive branch.

6. The disappointing news comes chiefly from comparisons between America's performance and that of other nations (specifically, Britain, Canada, France, Germany, Japan, and Sweden). These countries have been experiencing serious problems of their own, especially with the performance of their economies. Even so, observing the progress of all of these countries toward more than sixty commonly shared objectives, one finds that *in roughly two-thirds of these cases, the United States has performed less well than most of the other nations since 1960. In roughly half of the cases, our record is actually at or near the bottom of the list.* America continues to have the most productive economy, the highest standard of living, and the best scientific research in the world. But poverty rates are

higher, health care costs are greater, and programs for children more restricted than in the other countries surveyed. The United States also provides its citizens less personal security; more of its people lack health insurance, the risk of violent crime is higher, the workplace tends to be less safe, and the safeguards from layoffs and arbitrary firing are less effective. Finally, efforts to regulate the economy often seem to produce fewer results and lead to more litigation, delay, and expense than in other leading democracies. These comparisons appear in Table 2-3, at the end of the chapter. None of the obvious distinguishing characteristics of this country or the special burdens that we have carried (for instance, in the cold war) can explain more than a small part of this performance, especially when one remembers that other leading democracies have special problems of their own.

7. Close analysis suggests that government practices and programs have played an important part in our performance in almost all of the cases listed in Table 2-3. In many instances, such as health care, old-age pensions, environmental quality, and affordable housing, the role of government has been decisive. In other fields, such as research, educational achievement, technological progress, and the arts, the government's part has been less important but still substantial. Even in accounting for America's superior wealth and productivity, recent massive studies by the McKinsey Global Institute credit America's pro-competitive policies as being the most important element in our success—more important than such factors as entrepreneurial skill, quality of the labor force, or levels of investment. Because government policies appear to have so much to do with our record as a society, and because America has lagged behind other leading nations in most important fields of endeavor, there are grounds for suspecting that our government's performance over the past several decades does leave much to be desired.

8. The verdict just reached does not mean that America's politicians or civil servants are necessarily responsible for our modest comparative record. In a democracy, interest groups, the media, and elites (not to mention ordinary citizens) all play a

part in the government's performance. Rather than blame public officials, the fairest conclusion to draw from the evidence is simply that, since 1960, America's policies and programs do not appear to have been conceived or executed as well as those of other leading democracies in addressing a wide range of concerns common to large majorities of citizens.

Conclusion

Attempts to measure the effectiveness of American government are necessarily crude. In certain cases, to be sure, one can measure the progress of particular programs with clearly defined goals and even compare the government's record with that of private firms performing similar tasks. But scattered examples of this kind hardly add up to a complete picture of the government's performance. And even if the examples could be multiplied, there is no way of aggregating the results into a reliable overall measure of effectiveness.

By studying progress over time in various important policy fields, however, and by comparing America's results with those of other advanced democracies, one can arrive at crude but nonetheless useful judgments about the performance of our government during the past thirty to forty years. By and large, although the results do not justify the overwhelmingly negative impressions that most Americans currently hold about their government, they do paint a disappointing picture. In most important fields of endeavor, the United States has not progressed as far or as fast as other advanced democracies toward goals commonly shared by people everywhere. In almost all these fields, official policies and programs play an important part, often the decisive part, in accounting for our lagging performance. As a result, it is hard to look carefully at the overall record without agreeing with the majority of Americans that something is seriously amiss with the way in which our government goes about creating and executing public policy.

Table 2-1. The 1990s Compared with the Early 1960s

Policy Area	Improved	About the Same	Worse
A. *Prosperity*			
1. *The Economy*			
a. Per capita income	x		
b. Productivity per worker	x		
c. Controlling inflation		x	
d. Minimizing unemployment			x
e. Net investment in plant and equipment as percent of GDP	x		
2. *Research and Technology*			
a. Number of scientists and engineers per 100,000 people	x		
b. Number of articles in refereed journals	x		
c. Number of patents issued to Americans	x		
d. Share of GDP devoted to civilian R&D	x		
e. Share of worldwide high-tech exports			x
3. *Education*			
a. Percent graduating high school	x		
b. Percent graduating college	x		
c. Student achievement (reading)		x	
d. Student achievement (math and science)		x	
4. *Labor Market Policy*			
a. Percent of work force trained by employer	x		
b. Range of vocational courses available in high school and college	x		
c. Amount of government-sponsored training	x		
B. *Quality of Life*			
1. *Housing*			
a. Percentage of dwellings with serious defects	x		
b. Percentage of population owning home	x		
c. Affordability for renters[1]			x
2. *Neighborhoods*			
a. Concentration of poverty in urban neighborhoods			x
b. Degree of segregation by race	x		
c. Percent of population living in a neighborhood of choice (city, suburb, exurb)	x		
d. Fear of crime			x
3. *Environment*			
a. Amount of air pollution	x		
b. Amount of water pollution	x		
c. Percentage of drinking water purified	x		
4. *The Arts*			
a. Number of arts organizations	x		
b. Size of audience for plays, concerts, etc.	x		
c. Public and private funding for arts (other than ticket sales)	x		

Table 2-1. (continued)

Policy Area	Improved	About the Same	Worse
d. Consumer spending on arts (as percent of disposable income)	x		
C. *Opportunity*			
1. *Children's Well-Being*			
a. Rate of infant mortality	x		
b. Availability of day care	x		
c. Extent of prenatal care	x		
d. Percent of children in poverty	x		
e. Parental leave policy	x		
f. Percent of infants vaccinated	x		
2. *Racial Equality*			
a. Voting rights	x		
b. Housing discrimination	x		
c. Segregation in schools	x		
d. Quality of education for blacks	x		
3. *Equality of Opportunity*			
a. Access to preschool	x		
b. Access to universities	x		
c. Extent of racial discrimination in employment	x		
d. Extent of gender discrimination in employment	x		
e. Overall equality of opportunity	x		
D. *Personal Security*			
1. *Health Care*			
a. Technical quality	x		
b. Life expectancy	x		
c. Percentage of population covered by health insurance	x		
d. Cost (percent of GDP)			x
2. *Job Security*			
a. Percent of work force with some form of legally sanctioned representation			x
b. Protection from arbitrary[2] discharge		?	
c. Retraining and other help in case of layoffs	x		
d. Unemployment insurance (percent of unemployed receiving)			x
e. Incidence of job-related illness and injury		x	
3. *Violent Crime*			
a. Incidence (per 100,000 people)			x
b. Success in solving crime (clearance rate)			x
c. Fear for personal safety			x
4. *Old Age*			
a. Retirement income (as percent of prior wages)	x		
b. Percent living in poverty	x		
c. Percent covered by insurance	x		
d. Financial assistance for long-term care	x		

Table 2-1. (continued)

Policy Area	Improved	About the Same	Worse
E. *Values*			
1. *Personal Freedom*			
a. Degree of freedom guaranteed by law	x		
2. *Personal Responsibility*			
a. Obeying the law (extent of crime)	·		x
b. Percentage of children born out of wedlock			x
c. Percent of income given to charity			x
d. Community service			x
e. Percentage of eligibles voting			x
f. Cheating on exams			x
3. *Providing for Poor and Disadvantaged*			
a. Incidence of poverty	x		
b. Severity of poverty (aggregate poverty gap as percentage of GDP)	x		
c. Effectiveness of government transfer programs	x		

[1] Affordability is used here to indicate the percentage of people paying over 30 percent of their income for housing.

[2] Statutes and court decisions have extended greater protection for certain types of arbitrary discharge, but these gains are offset by declines in the proportion of workers covered by bargaining agreements requiring just cause for discharge. It is not possible to determine which of these conflicting tendencies is the stronger.

Table 2-2. Amount of Progress 1975–90 Compared with 1960–75

Policy Area	Better Record (Faster Progress or Slower Decline)	Record About the Same (Roughly Similar Rate of Progress or Decline)	Worse Record (Slower Progress or Faster Decline)
A. *Prosperity*			
1. *Economy*			
a. Growth rate of per capita income			x
b. Growth rate of productivity			x
c. Unemployment[1]	x		
d. Minimizing inflation[1]	x		
2. *Research and Technology*			
a. Growth in number of scientists and engineers per 100,000 people	x		
b. Citation of scientific articles worldwide		x	
c. Number of U.S. patents		x	
d. Share of global market for high-tech products		x	
e. Share of GDP devoted to R&D			x
3. *Education*			
a. Growth in percent graduating from high school			x
b. Growth in percent graduating from college			x
c. Student achievement (math, science, and reading)	x		
4. *Job Training*			
a. Increase in formal company training	x		
b. Increase in federal job training	x		
B. *Quality of Life*			
1. *Housing*			
a. Improvement in quality of housing			x
b. Increase in percentage of population owning home			x
c. Affordability of rental housing			x
d. Affordability of owning home			x
2. *Neighborhoods*			
a. Degree of segregation by income in large cities		x	
b. Degree of segregation by race in large cities		x	
3. *The Environment*			
a. Reduction in air pollution	x		
b. Reduction in water pollution	x		
c. Percent of water supply treated			x
d. Recycling of waste	x		

Table 2-2. (continued)

Policy Area	Better Record (Faster Progress or Slower Decline)	Record About the Same (Roughly Similar Rate of Progress or Decline)	Worse Record (Slower Progress or Faster Decline)
4. *The Arts*			
a. Number of arts organizations		x	
b. Total government support for the arts			x
c. Consumer expenditures on the arts (as percent of disposable income)	x		
d. Total audience for the arts		x	
C. *Opportunity*			
1. *Children's Well-Being*			
a. Reducing infant mortality		x	
b. Increasing access to preschool	x		
c. Reducing poverty			x
2. *Racial Equality*			
a. Increasing black voting rates			x
b. Reducing housing discrimination	x		
c. Increasing school integration			x
d. Equalizing years of schooling			x
3. *Equal Opportunity*			
a. Racial discrimination in employment[1]			x
b. Racial wage gap			x
c. Access of poor to universities			x
d. Gender wage gap	x		
e. Overall mobility (structural and circulation)			x
D. *Personal Security*			
1. *Health Care*			
a. Increasing life expectancy		x	
b. Increasing insurance coverage (public and private)			x
c. Restraining costs[2]		x	
2. *Security at Work*			
a. Percentage of employees with representation			x
b. Protection from arbitrary discharge[3]		?	
c. Training and relocation assistance in case of layoff	x		
d. Likelihood of receiving unemployment insurance			x
e. Protection from job-related illness and injury	x		
3. *Violent Crime*			
a. Incidence (per 100,000 people)	x		
b. Success rate in solving crime		x	

Table 2-2. (continued)

Policy Area	Better Record (Faster Progress or Slower Decline)	Record About the Same (Roughly Similar Rate of Progress or Decline)	Worse Record (Slower Progress or Faster Decline)
c. Reducing fear for personal safety	x		
4. *Old Age*			
a. Elderly poverty rate			x
b. Health care coverage			x
E. *Values*			
1. *Individual Freedom*			
a. Extent of freedom protected by courts[4]		?	
2. *Personal Responsibility*			
a. Obeying the law	x		
b. Children born out of wedlock			x
c. Cheating on exams	x		
d. Charitable contributions	x		
e. Voting		x	
3. *Providing for Poor and Disadvantaged*			
a. Reducing rate of poverty (under 65)			x
b. Reducing aggregate poverty gap (under 65)			x

[1] In fact, the average rates of inflation and unemployment were lower from 1960 to 1975 than they were from 1975 to 1990. But the record of combating inflation and unemployment can be considered better from 1975 to 1990 in the sense that rates went *up* from 1960 to 1975 whereas they went *down* from 1975 to 1990.

[2] Measured by extent to which increases in health care costs exceeded cost-of-living increases.

[3] The period 1975 to 1990 shows a sharper decline in union representation together with an increased willingness by courts to adjudicate the appropriateness of discharges. It is not possible to combine these trends to develop a reliable overall result.

[4] Although personal freedoms as defined by the courts probably expanded more rapidly from 1960 to 1975 than they did thereafter, it would be rash to conclude that this represented a "worse" record or a slowdown in progress, as many would argue that there was little room for further movement in the direction of expanding judicially protected freedom after the mid-1970s and that some retrenchment may have been desirable.

Table 2-3. U.S. Record Compared with Six Other Industrial Democracies (Britain, Canada, France, Germany, Japan, and Sweden)

Policy Area	At or Near the Top	Better than Average	Average	Below Average	At or Near the Bottom
A. *Prosperity*					
1. *The Economy*					
a. Per capita income	x				
b. Per capita productivity[1]	x				
c. Growth rate of per capita income (1960–90)					x
d. Growth rate of productivity (1960–90)					x
e. Controlling inflation (1960–90)		x			
f. Minimizing unemployment (1960–90)				x	
g. Minimizing unemployment (1980–95)		x			
h. Net investment in plant and equipment as percent of GDP (1960–90)					x
2. *Research and Technology*					
a. Number of scientists and engineers (per 100,000 people)	x				
b. Percentage of articles in refereed journals	x				
c. Number of citations per scientific article	x				
d. Percentage of patents issued	x				
e. Share of world trade in high-tech goods	x				
3. *Education*					
a. Percentage graduating high school			x		
b. Percentage graduating college	x				
c. Student achievement (reading)		x			
d. Student achievement (math)					x
e. Student achievement (science)					x
4. *Labor Market Policy*					
a. Percent of GDP spent on training (public and private)					x
b. Percent of work force receiving training					x
c. Effectiveness of employment service				x	
d. Effectiveness of school-to-work programs				x	

Table 2-3. (continued)

Policy Area	At or Near the Top	Better than Average	Average	Below Average	At or Near the Bottom
B. *Quality of Life*					
1. *Housing*					
a. Quality of housing	x				
b. Percentage of population owning home	x				
c. Affordability for entire population					x
2. *Neighborhoods*					
a. Degree of segregation by income					x
b. Degree of segregation by race				.	x
c. Fear of crime					x
d. Variety of choice in neighborhoods	x				
3. *Environment*					
a. Reduction in air pollution (1970–90)				x	
b. Reduction in water pollution (1970–90)			Impossible to compare		
c. Percentage of population with waste-water treatment				x	
d. Percentage of waste recycled					x
4. *The Arts*					
a. Total audience for performances and exhibitions				x	
b. Total support (public and private) other than ticket sales				x	
c. Rate of growth in total support for the arts (1960–90)	x				
C. *Opportunity*					
1. *Children's Well-Being*					
a. Infant mortality					x
b. Percent of children vaccinated				x	
c. Percent enrolled in preschool				x	
d. Percent in poverty					x
e. Parental leave policy					x
2. *Race*			Impossible to compare		
3. *Career Opportunities*					
a. Rate of upward mobility[2]			x		
b. Gender earnings gap				x	
c. Women in high-status jobs		x			

Table 2-3. (continued)

Policy Area	At or Near the Top	Better than Average	Average	Below Average	At or Near the Bottom
D. *Personal Security*					
1. *Health Care*					
a. Technical quality	x				
b. Life expectancy					x
c. Patient's evaluation of his/her own care			x		
d. Cost as percentage of GDP					x
e. Coverage by health insurance					x
f. Public evaluation of system					x
2. *Job Security*					
a. Percent of work force with some form of representation					x
b. Protection from arbitrary discharge					x
c. Assistance in case of layoffs					x
d. Reduction in job-related illness and injury				x	
3. *Violent Crime*					
a. Incidence (per 100,000 people)					x
b. Success in solving crime					x
c. Fear for personal safety					x
4. *Old Age*					
a. Level of average retirement income after taxes (as percent of previous wages)	x				
b. Percent in poverty					x
c. Percent covered by health care insurance					x
d. Access to affordable long-term care					x
E. *Values*					
1. *Individual Freedom*					
a. Extent of freedom under law[3]			x		
2. *Personal Responsibility*					
a. Violations of criminal laws					x
b. Percent of children born out of wedlock			x		
c. Incidence of teenage pregnancy					x
d. Voting rates					x
e. Charitable contributions	x				
f. Community service	x				

Table 2-3. (continued)

Policy Area	At or Near the Top	Better than Average	Average	Below Average	At or Near the Bottom
3. *Providing for Poor and Disadvantaged*					
a. Incidence of poverty					x
b. Severity of poverty (aggregate poverty gap as percent of GDP)					x
c. Effectiveness of government transfer programs					x

[1] The proper rating depends on whether one relies on hourly productivity or annual productivity. Hourly productivity reflects the skills of the work force and the methods of production, while annual productivity also includes the number of hours worked. American workers still lead the world in annual productivity but only because they work longer hours and receive shorter vacations than their counterparts in Germany and France.

[2] There is dispute among scholars over whether mobility in the United States is above average or only average. It is fair to say that there is not a preponderance of expert opinion that the United States has unusually high rates of mobility for the countries herein compared.

[3] This is admittedly an arbitrary judgment, but it is consistent with evaluations made annually by Freedom House.

Fall from Grace: The Public's Loss of Faith in Government

Gary Orren

> With public sentiment nothing can fail; without it, nothing can succeed. Consequently, he who molds public sentiment goes deeper than he who enacts statutes or pronounces decisions.
> —Abraham Lincoln, Lincoln–Douglas debate, July 31, 1858

In 1965 I telephoned my parents from college to tell them that I planned a change of direction. "Dad, I've decided to switch my major to government." The silence on the other end of the line seemed interminable. Then I heard my father say to my mother, "Dorothy, Gary has decided to open up his own government."

My father's unenthusiastic and somewhat derisive reaction fit the prevailing mood toward government and politics at the time. Over the next thirty years, such mild public skepticism would deteriorate into a much harsher cynicism.

Today's electorate has had to reconcile itself to the following reality: in the early days of the American republic, citizens were offered the choice between George Washington and John Adams, John Adams and Thomas Jefferson, Thomas Jefferson and Aaron Burr. In recent years the voters have been offered the choice between Michael Dukakis and George Bush, George Bush and Bill Clinton, Bill

Clinton and Bob Dole. No wonder so many people think Darwin was wrong.

A belief that government is getting worse instead of better, and that today's public officials simply do not measure up, has become one of the hallmarks of contemporary politics.[1] For three decades, administrations have come and gone, and polling charts have bounced up and down in response to this leader or that policy, yet public trust has tumbled ever downward, regardless of which party has been in power. The comedians on late-night talk shows have no more reliable target of ridicule than the government and its leaders. In some circles, "government" itself has become anathema. The Democratic county executive of Montgomery County, Maryland—home to large numbers of federal bureaucrats—banished the word "government" from official letterheads, cars, and business cards on the grounds that it was "arrogant" and "off-putting."[2]

Should anybody care? Some observers believe that the decline of trust in government is nothing to worry about: public disillusionment makes little fundamental difference in public affairs, they argue. In this line of reasoning, suspicion of government is a time-honored strain of American political culture, and civic trust, taken to extremes, produces abominations like the Third Reich.[3] Surveys suggest, after all, that public dissatisfaction with government has not been matched by a general unhappiness in people's lives or eroded support for the legitimacy of the underlying constitutional order.[4] Some have argued that political mistrust is only a ritualistic negativism, or a temporary swing of the pendulum rather than an enduring estrangement.[5] A more extreme variant of this view holds that what really matters is the actual objective performance of government, and that public opinion is irrelevant.

Still other observers go as far as to applaud public mistrust. Wariness or skepticism toward government and its leaders, they argue, bodes well for democracy; it provides a necessary check on government action and centralized authority, it strengthens individual freedom, and it reasserts the Madisonian tradition.[6]

In contrast to this sanguine view of public mistrust, I contend that today's discontent is neither transient nor shallow and that it holds profound (and negative) consequences for governance. Several streams of public sentiment have flowed together to produce the churning river of disenchantment in which politicians now swim. These streams range from the age-old suspicion of authority dating from the founding of the republic to the more recent and rapidly growing sense that politicians have lost their dignity. Today's cynicism, however, is not just the latest manifestation of traditional skepticism toward government, nor is it simply a response to the unpopularity of particular incumbents or parties. Today's cynicism is fueled by a deeper set of accumulated grievances with political authority, institutions, and processes in general—grievances that cut across party and ideology. Not just a temporary slump, the ensuing cynicism has lasted for three decades, during which time mild discontent has for many citizens turned to outrage and loathing.

Public dissatisfaction also harms democracy. It hampers governing in a constitutional structure that intentionally makes action difficult without strong popular approval. It is the oxygen that fuels the incendiary tone and negativity of today's political discourse. It hinders the task of recruiting and retaining capable public servants. From the left, right, and center it invites quick fixes to complex problems—term limits, tax revolts, third-party panaceas, extremist appeals both inside and outside the major parties—and it discourages steady and pragmatic solutions.

Popular hostility toward government deserves to be taken seriously, and if we are to discover a solution we must carefully analyze the components of public perceptions and expectations. Accordingly, I begin by reviewing the evidence on trends in public confidence. This will lead me to consider several commonly cited causes of political mistrust. My conclusion that most of these have minimal effects will lead back to political mistrust itself, and an effort to specify its component parts. These components will yield an overall framework that helps to illuminate the causes of public cynicism and its possible remedies.

What Has Happened to Public Confidence

Americans' growing alienation from government is captured poignantly in Calvin Trillin's memoir *Remembering Denny*. Trillin draws a portrait of one of his 1950s college classmates who was so accomplished and talented that his friends often speculated, half in jest, that he was destined to become president of the United States. According to Trillin,

> Having such conversations even as a joke seems, in retrospect, an activity peculiarly suited to the fifties. There was an assumption that the society was ours to lead and that preparing what amounted to a leadership class made sense. There was also an assumption that the society was worth leading. When I went back to New Haven in 1970 to write about changes at Yale—1970 was, depending on your point of view, the high point or the low point in undergraduate disaffection and rebelliousness—I asked a group of seniors whether they had anyone in their class who was going to be President. After a puzzled silence, one young man said, "President of what?" In the fifties, the what was assumed.[7]

Bearing out Trillin's observations, public faith in government reached its high-water mark in the two decades following World War II.[8] In the late 1950s and early 1960s—according to the most popular and reliable indicator of political confidence—about 75 percent of Americans trusted the government in Washington "just about always" or "most of the time," and fewer than 25 percent "only some" or "none of the time" (see Figure 3-1). After 1964, confidence waned almost uninterruptedly. By 1994, public sentiment had completely reversed itself in comparison with the halcyon 1950s: from three out of four Americans trusting the government to three out of four mistrusting the government, a turnaround rarely seen in public opinion.

Public disenchantment has not grown uniformly over time. Trust fell by a full 15 percentage points from 1964 to 1968, years of intense racial turbulence and turmoil over Vietnam during Lyndon Johnson's administration, and then another 8 percent in the first two years of Richard Nixon's presidency. Between 1972 and 1974, in the wake of Watergate and Gerald Ford's pardon of Nixon, trust fell another 17 points. All told, the level of mistrust nearly tripled in the decade after 1964. Trust continued to fall during the years of Jimmy Carter's presidency, followed by a partial recovery after 1980 during Ronald Reagan's first term. This resurgence in confidence to pre-Watergate levels was short-lived. Trust began to fall again in Reagan's second administration. By George Bush's second year in office, the level of trust in government had nearly returned to its pre-Reagan low point, and it

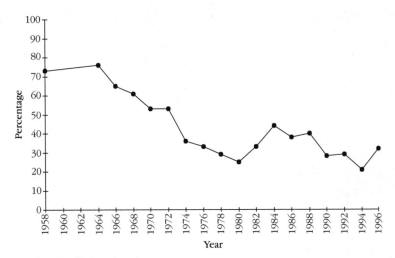

Figure 3-1. *Declining trust in government*

Respondents were asked "How much of the time do you think you can trust the government in Washington to do what is right—just about always, most of the time, or only some of the time?" The above figure traces the percentage who said that they trust the government "always" or "most of the time."

Source: American National Election Studies, 1958–1996, University of Michigan.

continued to decline in the first years of Bill Clinton's presidency. Despite a rebound in the latter half of Clinton's first term, during which trust in government rose 11 points, public confidence stood only slightly higher than it had at the end of the Bush years. The overall downturn in trust since 1964 occurred about equally under Democrats and Republicans.

This trend of mounting disillusionment is mirrored in a host of survey questions that track opinions on other aspects of political trust, confidence in government, and government responsiveness (see Figure 3-2).[9] Since 1964, for example, the number of Americans who feel that the government is run by a few big interests looking out only for themselves has more than doubled (to 76 percent), and the number who believe that public officials don't care about what people think has grown from 36 percent to 66 percent. The number saying that quite a few people running the government are crooked increased from 29 percent to 51 percent. The public has not only lost faith in the ability of government to solve problems, but it has actually come to believe that government involvement will just make matters worse.

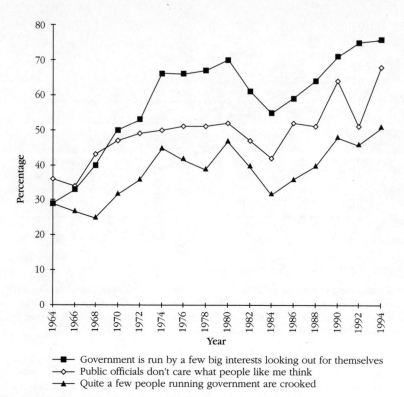

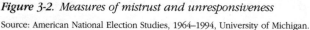

──■── Government is run by a few big interests looking out for themselves
──◇── Public officials don't care what people like me think
──▲── Quite a few people running government are crooked

Figure 3-2. *Measures of mistrust and unresponsiveness*

Source: American National Election Studies, 1964–1994, University of Michigan.

These attitudes have found expression in politics through the tools of direct democracy. In the tax revolt of the late 1970s and the term-limits movement of the 1990s, disgruntled citizens used state referenda and initiatives to take matters into their own hands. So far, some twenty-five states have passed ballot measures, generally by lopsided margins, limiting the number of terms that elected officials can serve.

Confidence in the executive branch, the Congress, and the Supreme Court dropped sharply between 1966 and 1971, and since then it has moved slightly downward and remained fairly low (except for a small rebound around 1984). Among these three branches of government, Americans have the highest regard for the Supreme Court, far less for the presidency (which, not surprisingly, undergoes the widest swings in esteem), and even less for Congress.[10]

State and local governments have fared only somewhat better. In 1972, when Americans were asked which level of government gave them the most for their money, they said the federal government. Twenty years later, the public puts more (if only modest) faith in local government (see Figure 3-3).[11] One possible reason for this switch is that people have much less direct experience with the federal government and are therefore more reliant on the news media—and the increasingly negative coverage of government—for their impressions. Nevertheless, faith in state and local government has slipped over the past thirty years as well.

Government is not alone in its fall from grace. As noted in the Introduction, since the late 1960s, it has been difficult to find any major institution that gets high marks. Americans have lost faith in banks, corporations, labor unions, lawyers, doctors, universities, public schools, and the media.[12] And this is not a peculiarly American phenomenon either. Declining respect for hierarchical authority in general, and government in particular, is a global trend, as Ronald Inglehart spells out in Chapter 9.[13]

As we begin the search for causes of declining political trust, it is important to keep in mind that these trends are both general and

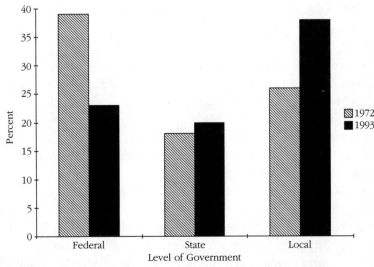

Figure 3-3. Which level of government gives the most for the money?

Source: *Changing Public Attitudes on Governments and Taxes,* U.S. Advisory Commission on Intergovernmental Relations, Washington, D.C., 1993.

specific. The generality of the trend toward mistrust is impressive: a widespread loss of faith occurred in most major institutions in the United States and abroad at roughly the same time. Yet the trend also has been specific. Confidence in government has not declined continuously and uniformly over time. It has fluctuated in response to specific conditions and events in the United States and other countries. And the public has differentiated its attitudes toward different branches and levels of government and different institutions.

The Search for Causes

Why do Americans trust government less today than they did thirty years ago? In investigating this question, it is tempting to seek out concentrations of cynicism among certain groups—to search for some disgruntled population segment that is skewing the results. Alternatively, one might look for large-scale psychological or economic trends on which to peg declining faith in government. Invariably, however, such lines of investigation turn up only weak and inconclusive correlations. Americans from all backgrounds have lost faith in government. Today's public cynicism cuts across all categories—black and white, male and female, rich and poor (see Table 3-1). Loss of faith in government has attached itself to every population group.[14]

Is age a factor? It is not unreasonable to suspect that the elderly might be more supportive of the government. After all, they grew up during the peak of popular faith in the government, they display stronger partisan allegiance, and many are the beneficiaries of major entitlement programs. This suspicion, however, is not correct. Since 1964 the oldest cohort of citizens has been the least trusting, and the youngest cohort the most.

A popular psychological explanation for declining trust in government is that it is connected to interpersonal trust, which has fallen twenty percentage points since the 1960s. In fact, social scientists have been suggesting such a link since the 1950s.[15] And as recently as 1995, a *Washington Post* survey showed that people who did not trust other people were also less likely to trust the federal government and other institutions. According to the *Post,* "Mistrust of each other is a major reason Americans have lost confidence in the federal government and virtually every other major national institution. . . . This collapse of trust in human nature has fueled the erosion of trust in government. . . . An environment in which a majority of Americans believe that most people can't be trusted breeds attitudes that hold all politicians as corrupt, venal, and self-serving, and government action as doomed to failure."[16] Despite these strong claims, most academic studies have found only a modest relationship between interpersonal trust and trust in government.[17] Interpersonal trust is closely tied to the era in which people grew up: studies indicate that people born before 1945 tend to trust their fellow citizens much more than those born after 1945. In contrast, the decline in political trust cuts across generations.[18] So although heightened social mistrust may make the restoration of governmental trust more difficult, it does not appear to have fueled the three-decade decline in political trust. The most one can say is that a final verdict on the alleged connection has yet to come in.

As the following chapters show, it is unlikely that dwindling social capital (the web of associational and civic life) has directly undermined public trust in government, nor can we assign too much weight to the economy or personal financial circumstances in explaining shifts in political trust over time.[19] All the usual suspects—those demographic, psychological, social, and economic factors that at first seem to offer convenient explanations for declining trust in government—can be dismissed or at least deferred until a more conclusive correlation is proved. Perhaps we will learn more by examining political mistrust itself more carefully.

"Unpacking" Public Satisfaction

Public satisfaction with government, as Robert Putnam has noted, is "a compound of expectations and actual performance" that might be loosely expressed as the ratio of actual government performance to citizens' expectations. A drop in satisfaction might reflect diminished government performance or rising expectations, or some combination of the two.[20]

Table 3-1. Average Score on Trust in Government Index for Selected Population Groups, 1964 and 1994

	1964	1994
Male	52	26
Female	51	26
White	51	26
Black	57	29
South	50	29
Non-South	52	25
Grade School/Some High School	51	29
High School Graduate	54	25
Some College	50	25
College Degree/Postgrad	52	27
Family Income		
0–16 percentile	50	30
17–33 percentile	51	27
34–67 percentile	53	25
68–95 percentile	52	25
96–100 percentile	54	27
Occupation		
Professional	51	27
White-collar	52	25
Blue-collar	52	25
Unskilled	60*	28*
Farmers	52	26*
Housewives	51	25
Union Household	54	26
Nonunion Household	51	26
Generation		
Born 1975 or later	—	27
Born 1959–74	—	27
Born 1943–58	51	25
Born 1927–42	54	25
Born 1911–26	51	29
Born 1895–1910	49	30*
Born before 1895	50	—

This formulation will help to guide our analysis, but we must make two important amendments. First, it is the correspondence between citizens' expectations and citizens' *perceptions* of government (which may or may not match the actual performance of government) that is most relevant. Second, we shall reserve the word "performance" to designate one of three types of government action (more about that later). Our amended formulation, then, is

$$\text{Satisfaction} = \frac{\text{Perceptions of Government}}{\text{Citizens' Expectations}}$$

Table 3-1. (continued)

	1964	1994
Age		
17–25	52	27
26–35	55	26
36–45	52	24
46–55	50	25
56–65	49	24
Over 65	49	27
Protestant	50	25
Catholic	56	27
Jewish	47*	29*
Ideological Self-Identification		
Liberal	—	28
Moderate	—	26
Conservative	—	25
Democrat	55	28
Independent	46	23
Republican	46	25

*Average score based on 50 or fewer respondents.
— Indicates no cases within group or that the question was not asked.
Note: The Trust in Government Index combines the answers to four questions. It is constructed as follows: "How much of the time do you think you can trust the government in Washington to do what is right—just about always, most of the time or only some of the time?" (None of the time [volunteered] = 0, some of the time = 33, most of the time = 67, and just about always = 100); "Would you say the government is pretty much run by a few big interests looking out for themselves or that it is run for the benefit of all the people?" (A few big interests = 0 and benefit of all = 100); "Do you think that people in the government waste a lot of money we pay in taxes, waste some of it, or don't waste very much of it?" (A lot = 0, some = 50, and not much = 100); and "Do you think that quite a few of the people running the government are [in 1964: "a little"] crooked, not very many are, or do you think hardly any of them are crooked [in 1964: "at all"]?" (Quite a few = 0, not many = 50, and hardly any = 100). The respondents' scores on each of these four questions are totaled, and the sum is divided by the number of valid responses (the result is rounded to the nearest integer). An average is then computed for each population group. The maximum score is 100 and the minimum is 0.
Source: American National Election Studies, 1964 and 1994, University of Michigan.

This simple yet illuminating formulation has been the explicit or implicit model underlying most scholarship on trust in government over the past thirty years. But if we are to get a better idea of what causes satisfaction and dissatisfaction with government, we must define more precisely the two terms in the model—perceptions of government and citizens' expectations. We can begin differentiating the components of perceptions of government by identifying six streams or sources of attitudes toward government (see Table 3-2).

First, there are two long-term factors that shape people's views toward government: the traditional antipathy toward government that has been part of American political culture since colonial times and the relatively new postmaterial values challenging hierarchical author-

Table 3-2. Components of Public Satisfaction

Perceptions
  Long-term
    Traditional skepticism
      Suspicion of government and concentrated power since colonial times
    Postmaterial values
      Challenge to hierarchical authority in advanced industrialized societies

  Short-term
    Performance
      Evaluation of the effectiveness of government action
    Policy
      Disagreement over specific policy alternatives
    Probity
      Assessment of the integrity of political leaders and political process
    Denunciation of government
      Criticism of government by political leaders and the press

Expectations
  Wants
    Desire for government programs and services
  Anticipation
    Prediction of what government is likely to accomplish

ity that have arisen since the 1960s. These two represent a basso continuo that has droned persistently beneath the din of daily politics.

Four more immediate, short-term processes also affect views toward government. Three of them—the public's appraisal of government performance, the public's ideological views on certain policies, and the public's assessment of the ethics and integrity of the people and processes of government—correspond to the different ways people think about the question "Do you trust the government to do what is 'right'?" The term "right" means "effective" to some people, "ideologically correct" to others, and "moral" to still others. These three sources of public dissatisfaction also correspond to the three fundamental types of political issues: performance issues (retrospective judgments of how good a job the government is doing), position issues (those revealing the policy alternatives that people favor or oppose), and valence issues (questions on which everyone agrees about the goals— such as honesty, peace, and reducing crime).[21] The fourth factor is the denunciation of government by political leaders and the press.

Citizens' Perceptions

Traditional Skepticism.   The American republic was born in a climate of suspicion that persists to this day. "Distrust of government," writes Samuel Huntington, "is as American as apple pie. It has historically been a central, continuing, and distinctive element of the American political tradition and the idea that people *should* trust their government is a radical departure from that tradition."[22]

Postmaterial Values.   The second long-term source of public disillusionment with governmental and other institutions emerged in the mid- to late 1960s. A number of scholars have found that with technological advancement and economic development, public support for political authority around the world has eroded.[23] Successful industrialization, according to this view, has eased citizens' worries about economic and physical security and has given rise to a preoccupation with self-expression and self-realization. As a result, the populations of advanced industrial states have become more and more challenging to the leaders of established institutions.

It might be helpful to think of these two long-term sources of public discontent—traditional skepticism and postmaterial values—in the way that political scientists think of the "normal vote." The normal vote is a baseline or expected vote that reflects long-term patterns of partisan allegiance and turnout, all else being equal. By calculating departures from this norm owing to the immediate circumstances of a particular election (for instance, public opinion on a burning campaign issue), one can identify the long-term and short-term components of voting.[24] Similarly, we should be able to separate the long-term component of the public's disaffection from the public's more immediate views on performance, policy, and probity.

Performance.   Perhaps the most obvious influence on public satisfaction is how people rate the government's competence. This subjective assessment does not necessarily square with the actual or "objective" performance of government. Derek Bok argued in the previous chapter that the U.S. federal government has performed reasonably well on a long list of domestic issues of paramount importance to most Americans—economic prosperity, quality of life, opportunity, personal security, and societal values among them. Although the United States has performed poorly, even dismally, in some fields compared with other nations, Americans are better off today in most areas of government activity than they were in 1960, and progress in many domains has quickened since the mid-1970s.[25] Significantly, however, this fairly rosy reality does not impress the public. In fact, the period from 1964 to 1976—a time of great federal accomplishment on many of the key performance indicators—witnessed the greatest decline in public trust in government. The same gap between perception and reality plagues state and local politics as well.[26] Nor is the pattern unique to the United States. The most striking contrast of all may be in Japan, where Susan Pharr describes political disillusionment and personal dissatisfaction coexisting for years with a spectacular reality (see Chapter 10).

What is going on here? There may be several factors at work. First, the most telling comparison for citizens may not be how government performance today compares with government performance fifteen or thirty years ago but how government performance today stacks up against current expectations. Another consideration is that not all indicators of government performance weigh equally in the minds of citizens. Gains in research and technology or funding for the arts are far less compelling than deterioration in crime, poverty, and reading and math scores. Similarly, negative news about any of these issues tends to stick much more than positive news.[27] Finally, the government's role is often equivocal. Even the most seasoned policy analyst has trouble isolating the government's effect on social problems from the myriad of other forces at play. So it is no wonder that the public fails to recognize government's contribution to winning the battle against polio yet blames the government unduly for losing battles against crime, drugs, and urban decay.

Still, the best explanation for the stunning disparity between actual and perceived performance lies elsewhere. Bad reviews of government performance are largely a response to a litany of dramatic and highly visible international misadventures and domestic shocks that do not appear on the performance inventory in Chapter 2: several years of escalation and stalemate in Vietnam and turmoil at home, race riots in most large cities, crisis after crisis—Watergate, the hostages in Iran, Iran-Contra, energy, savings and loan, and so forth. These episodes were punctuated by spells of double-digit inflation, stagflation, and recession.

Regardless of their ideology and policy preferences—whether hawks or doves, liberals or conservatives—large masses of people shared the conclusion that government was handling problems poorly and failing to deliver on its promises. Here the public was operating in its most traditional and comfortable role: not as debaters arguing about specific policy alternatives but as judges evaluating the ability of government to competently and effectively solve problems.[28] From 1964 to 1994, the public judges handed down a long string of "thumbs down" verdicts.

Policy.   A modest portion of declining trust in government stems from disagreements over policy direction and alternatives. In contrast to citizens who lost faith because they concluded that government was doing a lousy job, some lost faith because they felt that government was doing too good a job in advancing the wrong mission. Government policies, actual or contemplated, may have clashed with these citizens' policy preferences and ideological principles. Or perhaps neither political party, the ins or the outs, represented their policy views.

Strong liberals and strong conservatives, divided over such polarizing issues as race and Vietnam, were the defecting vanguard who led the downturn in political trust in the mid- to late 1960s. In these early years, political cynicism was highest among people whose policy preferences were either very liberal or very conservative and who disapproved of the centrist choices offered by the two parties. Political scientist Arthur Miller has dubbed them "cynics of the left" and "cynics of the right."[29] Rather quickly, however, the across-the-board-pattern described earlier settled in as people of all ideological stripes became disaffected. As late as 1988, there were still traces of greater cynicism on the far left and far right—a pattern that has persisted to varying degrees depending on how ideologically polarizing the messages of political leaders have been.

The decline in trust that took place after 1984, following a partial recovery in Ronald Reagan's inaugural term, had similar beginnings to the first. It was, as Arthur Miller and Stephen Borrelli have written, led by ideologues, "with liberals viewing Reagan's policies as uncaring and inequitable, and conservatives thinking they did not yet go far enough in reducing the scope of government and promoting traditional values."[30]

Probity.   The third short-term source of citizen mistrust is public opinion on ethical issues. The English historian Walter Bagehot once argued that the government's most important attribute for sustaining public trust was not efficiency but dignity.[31] The dignity of government, as measured by the integrity of both leaders and the political process, has sharply deteriorated in the public's mind.

The ethical image of political leaders is shaped by incidents ranging from professional duplicity and impropriety to personal indiscretions and character weaknesses to outright corruption. Since the 1960s, citizens have witnessed jarring conflicts between rhetoric and reality ("light at the end of the tunnel;" "I am not a crook;" "I'll never negotiate with terrorists;" "read my lips . . . no new taxes"), political scandals, unsavory influence peddling, and tales of fraud and favoritism. In the months following the 1996 election, the public braced itself for yet another winter of political discontent as the parties hurled charges of ethical transgression and hypocrisy at each other: illegal foreign campaign contributions to the Democratic party, improper use of tax-exempt organizations for political purposes by the Republican Speaker of the House.

Trust in political and other institutions is closely correlated with the public's perception of the ethics and morality of those institutions' leaders. On both scales, government officials rank low.[32] Americans rate their representatives and senators near the bottom of professions on honesty and ethics—above used-car salesmen but below lawyers.[33]

Recently, the principal reason the public gave for not trusting the government was the lack of honesty and integrity of public officials. Close behind, they said that politicians serve their own interest rather than the public's.[34] Just as perceptions of government performance have curdled despite some objective signs of government success, people probably perceive more corruption than actually exists. Stricter standards, better policing and monitoring, and a more vigilant press have probably uncovered and publicized more violations than in the past, contributing to the impression that corruption is on the rise.[35] As noted earlier, the number of Americans reporting that quite a few of the people running the government are crooked and that the government is pretty much run by a few big interests looking out for themselves skyrocketed in the thirty years after 1964.

Dramatic revelations of political corruption and scandal have, of course, fostered this climate of ethical mistrust. But less spectacular evidence also raises doubts about the political and personal authenticity of the nation's leaders. Consider the two protean candidates who ran for president in 1996. As the nominees went about their ideological migrations—one day deploring supply-side economics, the next day championing it, first tacking left (with a massive health care reform) and then tacking right (declaring that "the era of big government is over")—the public couldn't help but wonder what principles, if any, Clinton and Dole were guided by. In stark contrast was the case of Ronald Reagan. People regularly told pollsters that they disagreed with Reagan on the issues but admired and respected his political integrity. He seemed to have ideological consistency, fidelity to a fixed set of convictions. This impression of *political* authenticity probably contributed in no small way to the upsurge in public trust that was recorded during the first Reagan administration.

Doubts about the *personal* authenticity of political leaders also feed public cynicism. Again, consider the 1996 presidential candidates: Senator Dole, with his much-publicized tie removal on the day he resigned from the Senate, as if a change in wardrobe would remake his persona; President Clinton, with his much-spoofed contention from his first presidential campaign, "I didn't inhale." A regular diet of such contrivance undermines the public trust in politicians.

Process—the way the government does things—has become as suspect as personalities. Citizens are frustrated by the obstructionism and bickering they perceive in Washington, and they sense that governance is weighed down by "procedural injustice" and special interests with excessive influence and undeserved privileges.[36]

Some people trace the downward slide in political trust to powerful forces largely beyond the immediate control of public officials: rapid transformations in technology and information, vast changes in family structure and associational life, global economic trends, and a shifting political landscape. Such nongovernmental factors play an important role in the erosion of public trust, but loss of faith in government probably stems as much from the actions of those steering the ship of state as from the roiling seas on which the ship sails. One cannot explain political cynicism without a careful accounting of the performance, policies, and probity of government officials. The argument of this chapter is that the steady descent of trust is intimately tied to the government itself, and not simply a by-product of external trends.

Denunciation of Government.   It is tempting to identify communi-, cations media as the principal culprit behind dwindling political trust. As this argument goes, government performance has been no worse, policy disagreements no more divisive, and official mores no shabbier over the past thirty years than before the onset of deep political disillusionment. What is different, according to this theory, is the advent of sweeping changes in media technology and practice over the past three decades. The intense glare of the modern media spotlight has increased the public's awareness of the government's warts and blemishes.

There is much truth to this line of thinking. In fact, it is one I have argued elsewhere, emphasizing the consequences of the growing volume and speed of news reporting.[37] Yet it seems too easy, too broad a claim. It attributes too much independent influence to the media. To be sure, most people learn about events at home and abroad and about government actions through the media. Today, news organizations, not face-to-face encounters, are the principal sources of public affairs information. However, when the public learns through the news media about setbacks in Vietnam, or the savings and loan crisis, or an economic downturn, and then thinks less of the government, should we conclude that the change in attitude is "due to the media"? If so, virtually every public opinion change is caused by the media. The simple acquisition of information through a media messenger hardly deserves to be labeled a media effect.[38]

The kind of influences that more legitimately can be called media effects are those in which the media (intentionally or unintentionally) shape information by the way they report it. In deciding what events to cover and how to cover them—judgments reporters and editors are obliged to make—news organizations sometimes frame the news in ways that alter, distort, or slant it. Wittingly and unwittingly, the personal prejudices of reporters and the organizational imperatives of news bureaus can bias the coverage. These are essentially matters of interpretation, emphasis, and tone.

Even if we restrict ourselves to the more genuine media effects, the impact of media on public opinion is significant. How have the media, and opinion leaders generally, expressed their messages in a way that has shaped the public's opinion of government?

In his definitive tome, *Public Opinion and American Democracy,*

V. O. Key, Jr., conceived of mass attitudes as a "system of dikes which channel public action or which fix a range of discretion within which government may act or within which debate at official levels may proceed."[39] But a full explanation of what actually shapes those attitudes was difficult for him to assemble. The "missing piece of the puzzle," he emphasized, was the central role played by political elites: "The longer one frets with the puzzle of how democratic regimes manage to function, the more plausible it appears that a substantial part of the explanation is to be found in the motives that actuate the leadership echelon, the values that it holds. . . . The critical element for the health of a democratic order consists in the beliefs, standards, and competence of those who constitute the influentials, the opinion leaders, the political activists in the order."[40] Over the past thirty years some influential opinion leaders have been swimming against the tide of antigovernment sentiment. But many have been going with the flow, and along the way they have been making waves that reinforce the disillusionment of the populace. The denunciation of government by political leaders and the press has become a familiar and troubling sign of the times.

On the face of it, this appears to be just the latest manifestation of traditional skepticism, or else a healthy exercise in expressing disapproval of particular policies or leaders. In fact, it is neither. Government bashing has become a powerful stream of dissatisfaction in its own right. Indeed, although it has been around for only about thirty years, the denunciation of government by political leaders and the press shares some features with our two long-term trends. Like them, it is now a dependable and constant feature of the contemporary political culture.

At federal, state, and local levels, on the campaign stump and in their official capacity, public officials malign government in terms both abstract and specific. Neither party has a lock on these denunciations. Ronald Reagan is often identified with this point of view because of the rallying cry from his first inaugural address: "Government is not the solution to our problems; government is the problem." But it was Jimmy Carter who ran for office proudly trumpeting that he was not from Washington, and he whose campaign theme condemned the government and praised the people. Carter's campaign manager and chief of staff, Hamilton Jordan, mused out loud before the 1980 reelection campaign that his boss's greatest problem was how to run again as an outsider, having occupied the White House for four years.

Politicians attack one another with even more venom than they unleash at the government. Harsh and uncivil discourse has become a staple of campaigns and governing, sending out negative messages that polarize the electorate while turning off substantial portions of the population.[41] In the process, politicians erase their own credibility. "After all," the public reasons, "it takes one to know one."

Anyone who believes the era of government-bashing has run its course is guilty of wishful thinking. In the fall of 1996, President Clinton proclaimed at a campaign appearance in Portland, Oregon, that "we have ended the era when people could run for office desperate to be in government, by just bad-mouthing government."[42] But a deep-seated trend such as this one cannot be halted by fiat.

It's hard to know which deepens public distrust more—the "demarketing" of government by political leaders or the defaming of government by the press. Again, V. O. Key, Jr., provides an instructive point of departure. Writing about the U.S. media of the 1950s, at the height of trust in government, Key lamented that the press had lost any point of view and no longer interpreted or evaluated politics for its audience:

> In the large, the long-term changes in the treatment of political events have converted the press from a *giver of cues into a common carrier*. When editorial policy, often of a partisan tone, permeated the entire content of the press, the loyal reader had cues of considerable clarity. . . . In a sense, the press has moved from the role of actor to that of narrator. . . . As objective reporter of events, the press fails the one great task of interpretation most likely to arm the people with information on which they could act. . . . The press commits itself to the proposition that its duty is to transmit a dead-pan account of the sayings of statesmen. . . . The so-called American consensus may have its foundations partially in the characteristics of the American media. . . . The content [of the media] . . . tends to reaffirm existing values, to buttress prevailing institutions, and to support ancient ways of doing things.[43]

This description seems quaint alongside the media of today. True, today's press is no more a partisan cue-giver than it was in the 1950s. But the press has shed the role of common carrier reinforcing a pro-government consensus. No longer just a narrator, it is very much an actor in today's political drama, conveying a steady stream of unambiguously negative cues about government and politics. In Key's terms, one might say that the press continues to reinforce the prevailing view, but this view has shifted from trust to mistrust of government.

Only a few years after Key's account, on the eve of the collapse of public confidence, the media underwent two momentous changes. Television, an entertainment medium that had arrived on the scene a decade earlier, became the dominant source of news for most Americans; swiftly, the media, and particularly television, supplanted other institutions to become the main, and in many cases the only, link between citizens and their government.[44] At the same time, the profile of those who worked in the media was changing. For the first time, the ranks of reporting were filled with young men and women who hailed from the upper middle class and had college degrees. They were recruited from the best universities, and they received uncustomarily large salaries. Journalists were becoming an elite professional class. This new generation of reporters ardently embraced the authority-challenging postmaterial values discussed earlier. Journalistic practice became infected with what Lionel Trilling called the "adversary culture."[45]

The authority-challenging attitudes of the press were accentuated by the tenor of the times. The new generation of reporters forged their professional outlooks in the political fires of race riots, Vietnam, and Watergate—events that transformed their professional skepticism into a deep disillusionment with government that would be hard to shake. And they were no more immune from the sour public mood than anyone else.

One could argue endlessly over whether the new media actually created or merely reflected the public's distaste for government. My reading, however, is that the media itself did not cause the initial loss of public faith and affection. Contrary to conventional wisdom, the media did not play a leading role in the collapse of public support for the Vietnam War and the precipitous decline in governmental trust that accompanied it. In fact, media coverage was quite supportive of official policy on Vietnam and shifted toward a more critical view only after the public grew unhappy.[46] In any case, by the late 1960s a new menu of media options and a new set of media chefs converged to

accommodate Americans' appetite for news. The consensual and patriotic tone of the 1950s and early 1960s vanished. Over the next three
decades, the new, more jaundiced style of news coverage magnified
and intensified public estrangement from the government.

Television has set the pace, but the print media have followed
suit, covering politics in an increasingly negative and personalized
way. In the years since Key wrote his account of the press, negative
stories in television, newspapers, and magazines have skyrocketed—
according to one study zooming from about 25 percent to 60 percent
of the news.[47] As coverage has turned from critical to condescending
to contemptuous, candidates and public officials have more often than
not been presented as duplicitous and self-serving. Given the diminished voice of political leaders in news stories—the shrinking amount
of time or space devoted to their own words—public officials have
little defense against this unflattering portrayal.[48] The media have fed
the cynicism of an already cynical public.

Over the years, both print and television have shifted to a more
interpretive, evaluative type of reporting.[49] More and more, news
stories seek to explain the inner workings of political leaders, their
motives and intentions. This type of coverage focuses alternately on
strategy and tactics ("inside baseball"), the leaders' missteps ("gotcha
journalism"), or what the news "really means." Invariably, though, the
interpretation and commentary presumes to lift the curtain on the
wizard and reveal the charlatan behind it. Again, more cynicism.

Today's news coverage also is far more ad hominem than it once
was. Not only does the media intrude more deeply into the private
lives of political leaders, but it shines its spotlight more brightly on
people and their conflicts than on the actions and institutions of
government. Some of this may be inherent to the medium of television. Even when reporters and producers try to emphasize substance
over personality, it is the appearance and demeanor of the person on
the screen that grips the audience. The phenomenologist and social
scientist Hannah Arendt observed this inherently personalizing effect
more than thirty-five years ago. After watching the 1960 Democratic
and Republican conventions on television, she commented that these
institutions had taken on a new role: "The screen brings into view
those imponderables of character and personality which make us

decide, not whether we agree or disagree with somebody, but whether we can *trust* him."[50]

Beyond the intrinsic tendencies of the medium, reporters themselves are drawn to cover people rather than policies, and this predilection, too, has reduced public confidence in government. The media's relative inattention to policy helps account for the public's lack of awareness about actual government performance (noted earlier). Also, the media like to report news events as mini-melodramas, with heroes, villains, and underlying plots; political leaders are rarely cast as the heroes.[51] To compound this problem, the relentless "up close and personal" scrutiny of political leaders, especially on television, is bound to disclose blemishes that will erode respect. "No man," Anne-Marie Bigot de Cornuel once wisely noted, "is a hero to his valet."[52]

Political leaders and members of the press, once strong bulwarks of support for government, have become just the opposite today: in the aggregate, they are a powerful and continuing source of public dissatisfaction.

Although growing disillusionment with government is a product of the six attitude streams I have just outlined, these influences tell only part of the story. Public satisfaction or dissatisfaction also depends on how closely what people see matches what they expect.

Citizens' Expectations

When I was a youngster, my mother would frequently tell me that she *expected* me to clean my room. I came to realize that she used the word "expect" in two different ways. Sometimes she meant "I *want* (or, depending on her tone of voice, order) you to clean your room." At other times she meant "I *anticipate* that you will clean your room." The word "expectations" has the same dual usage in the world of politics. People slip back and forth between one meaning and the other. But in keeping with our goal of specifying more precisely the determinants of public satisfaction, we should carefully differentiate between these two senses. Each holds different implications for the model of public satisfaction.

Wants. The number of Americans wary that the government in Washington is getting too powerful has waxed and waned over the years. Large numbers have yearned for lower taxes and, in the abstract, less government spending. Yet, through it all, most people have had no trouble thinking of things they would like the federal government to do. The wish list of programs and services is long and growing. As one analyst who reviewed the relevant polling data succinctly put it, "Americans have come to expect a great deal from their governments."[53]

There can be little doubt that public expectations in the form of demands have risen over the last half-century. This trend can be traced to post–World War II economic prosperity, the explosion in public entitlements and rights, and an expanding list of pressing social problems.[54] The government has launched a sweeping array of economic and social initiatives (in health, civil rights, education, housing, employment, consumer protection, the environment, energy, and transportation, to name just a few). At the same time, the government has jettisoned its isolationism in the international arena. The widening scope of domestic concerns and greater involvement in world affairs have vastly increased public demands. Some believe that these demands exceed or "overload" the capacity of government.[55] "We've got to fix the budget deficit," says John Q. Public, in a joke making the rounds in Washington. "But the taxpayers shouldn't have to pay. The *government* should have to pay." Excessive or not, citizens' wants are enormous.

Prior to the 1996 elections, House Speaker Newt Gingrich and his fellow Republican revolutionaries failed to appreciate the continuing high expectations (in the sense of "wants") of the public despite its deep cynicism toward the federal government. As a result, they proceeded to cut or proposed to cut programs too aggressively, reducing their own power and enhancing the position of President Clinton as the nation's protector against the indiscriminate budgetary knife.

Anticipation. Before most campaign debates, candidates and their aides work hard to establish what the audience and the news media "expect"—that is, anticipate—the contestants will do, thereby setting the standards against which they will be judged. For example, before the first Dole–Clinton televised debate on October 6, 1996, Bob Dole may have set the all-time record for lowering expectations by referring to Clinton this way: "He's so good [at debating], if I show up, I think I win."[56]

The promises and claims that government officials make about their programs create expectations as well. Political leaders are notorious for making grandiose, extravagant promises that raise citizens' anticipations. Even if the leaders' performance remains steady, the public is disappointed, and its level of satisfaction is bound to drop.

Today, however, we live in an era of "diminished expectations." At the same time that expectations in the sense of "wants" are rising, expectations in the sense of anticipating government accomplishments are probably falling. According to Wilson Carey McWilliams, both kinds of expectations were at play in the elections of 1992: "The clearest message of 1992 was the majority's *demand* for active government, engaged to relieve America's discontents and reclaim the future." However, "along with some hope, the electorate harbored an abiding *doubt that government can succeed.*" That doubt is even greater today than it was in 1992.[57] Unquestionably, the long cumulative history of negative perceptions of government has dampened people's anticipation of future government accomplishments.

In 1996, the Democrats and President Clinton deliberately tried to lower such expectations by promising less. They billed their congressional agenda, "Families First," as modest and achievable. "It's incremental by design," Senate Minority Leader Thomas Daschle told reporters. "We want it to be something that people can understand and believe can happen."[58] In the same vein, President Clinton's campaign promises revolved around a list of relatively small-scale initiatives, including enlisting volunteers to teach young children to read, prohibiting people convicted of domestic violence from owning guns, discouraging children from smoking, requiring businesses to give workers unpaid time off for occasions like parent–teacher conferences, and helping those on welfare find work.

Interestingly, the Democrats' efforts to lower expectations met with scorn from the media, and Clinton was roundly criticized for setting his sights so low. According to the press, Clinton had made "puny, token initiatives." "What about eliminating poverty or improving the economy or making health care affordable to all?" asked one *New York Times* reporter. The editors at the *Times* complained that Clinton's campaign promises were "frankly pedestrian," hardly representing "a ringing endorsement of the kind of broad federal action Mr. Clinton espoused four years ago."[59]

Ironically, it was Republican Bob Dole who tried to raise expectations with a far more ambitious promise: his 15 percent across-the-board tax cut. But this centerpiece proposal never ignited the Dole campaign. Polls showed that it collided with the public's low expectations: the voters simply did not believe that a Dole administration could cut taxes while protecting entitlements and balancing the budget. Dole found himself caught between two kinds of expectations that had moved in opposite directions. He was out of sync with the public's fervent wants—a long list of untouchable domestic services people do not want to see dismantled—and the public's gloomy estimate of what a Dole administration would be able to deliver.

What Can/Should Be Done?

Satisfaction with government depends on both perceptions and expectations. Our perceptions, in turn, reflect both long-term and short-term perspectives. Some of our perceptions have been shaped by forces that arose before and extend beyond the concerns of the day. Such perceptions are relatively constant and predictable features of the climate of opinion. I have argued that American perceptions of government are colored by two principal long-term factors: age-old suspicion of government and postmaterial authority-challenging attitudes.

Perceptions of government also are subject to more volatile forces—the twists and turns of everyday politics. Four main short-term sources of public opinion stand out: citizens' assessment of how well the government is doing its job, their approval or disapproval of specific policy alternatives, their evaluation of the probity of government leaders and the integrity of government processes, and the denunciation of government by influential opinion leaders. These perceptions are matched against people's expectations—both what they want the government to do for them and what they predict the government will do.

These components of public satisfaction—six streams of public perception and two types of expectations—provide a handy framework for understanding the public's disaffection with government, the subject of this volume. But the same framework may also aid in the search for solutions. While the question of how we might address the problem of public cynicism requires further inquiry by scholars, practitioners, and citizens, I conclude by offering some preliminary thoughts.

As with addressing any problem, we must consider what *should* be done and what *can* be done. Should we be more concerned about improving the public's perception of government or about lowering its expectations? Which types of perception or expectation should be emphasized? Is it possible to reduce what people want from government? Can we repair the public's dissatisfaction with the ethical lapses of its leaders? Our answers to these questions embody our visions and theories about the proper role of government.

The first question recalls the opening passages of this chapter. Is declining public satisfaction something we should worry about and try to correct? My analysis has suggested a resounding yes. Today's cynicism is much more than the public's long-standing suspicion of government or its current disfavor with particular leaders or policies. It is a deeper disillusionment with government in general. This mounting tide of popular dissatisfaction colors the content of our politics and influences the behavior of our leaders both in political campaigns and in policy-making.

Where do we begin to solve this mess? One school of thought urges us to concentrate more on public expectations—particularly in the sense of wants—than on perceptions. This view is reflected, for example, in the thinking of many congressional Republicans. It is also found outside Washington. Governor William Weld of Massachusetts expressed this philosophy in the slogan "I'm not saying . . . that government ought to do more with less; I'm saying government ought to do less with less."[60]

Americans certainly want a great deal from the federal government. But what if the problem is not expanding desires—which may be the inevitable result of progress in civilization—but rather an overreliance on one particular level of government, the federal? If so, the goal should not be to provide less but to creatively widen the sources of supply—to state and local governments, the private sector, and nonprofit organizations.

Even if public wants are truly out of line, it may not be politically feasible to reduce them. Recent political history indicates that despite intense public disenchantment with government generally, the public is not prepared to relinquish its favorite government programs.

What about the other type of expectation, in the sense of anticipation? Such expectations appear to be dwindling rapidly, with the public more and more pessimistic about the capacity of government to accomplish its goals. In the past, public officials have been guilty of raising citizens' anticipations through the roof. So one hope is that officials might refrain from making inflated promises. Another is that the media might not greet such moderation with criticism. Yet dumping cold water on public optimism may not be the best way to raise satisfaction—and it seems almost un-American.

What if we concentrate instead on improving the public's perception of government? We probably have little leverage over the two long-term forces: traditional skepticism of government and the challenging of authority that accompanies economic development. Besides, these actually may be healthy sources of government accountability. The denunciation of government by political leaders and the press is an unhealthy but intractable source of discontent; other than imploring political leaders and journalists to refrain from gratuitous attacks, there are few weapons in our arsenal.

Over the long run, public dissatisfaction can grow out of opposition to an administration's policies or policy direction. But squelching dissent and achieving policy consensus is not the goal of a vibrant democracy. As for probity, we certainly do not know how to ensure the integrity of political leaders. We are left grappling with the third source of disaffection—the public's perception of government performance.

Today we are reaping what Madison sowed. It is difficult to get things done in our political system—and recent transformations have only made it more difficult; an amendment here or there in governmental structure and process might update our lumbering "Tudor" democracy for the twenty-first century. But in today's media-dominated world, it is more difficult than ever to be *perceived* to get things done.

Public satisfaction has improved only twice since 1964, and those interludes may yield a clue about what can be done to regain the public's trust in government. During Ronald Reagan's first term, the administration scored well on all four of the short-term factors I have highlighted—performance, policy, probity, and the press. The American public felt that Reagan delivered on his principal 1980 campaign promises. Despite soaring unemployment in his first year in office (the nation's deepest postwar recession), the public was satisfied with the president's action on what they considered the nation's most important problem—inflation. Once the economy began improving after 1982, the public gave Reagan still more credit, and political trust rose even among those bemoaning their own or the nation's economic situation. The increase in trust also reflected public admiration for Reagan's leadership skills, including his image as a decisive and self-confident president.[61]

Citizens looked favorably not only on the Reagan administration's performance, but also on its policies and probity. The upsurge in public confidence stemmed in part from a mood of growing conservatism, especially a widespread preference for smaller government and more assertive foreign policy. Furthermore, whether or not people agreed with Reagan on most issues, they tended to admire his ideological consistency. And they never doubted his personal integrity or character. Finally, Reagan's first administration was spared reflexively negative media coverage, earning the label the "Teflon presidency."

The lesson may be that there are no shortcuts to restoring public trust; good performance, ideological consistency, ethical integrity, and respectful or at least nonderisive news coverage may be necessary for renewal. At the same time, of course, it is sobering to note how difficult it is to sustain this kind of record: public satisfaction plummeted in Reagan's second term, when doubts arose on the same four dimensions where he succeeded in the first term.

The second upturn in public trust occurred in 1996 at the conclusion of President Clinton's first term in office. Like Reagan, Clinton was perceived to have performed well on some important goals over the preceding two years: the economy was growing, inflation was low, the budget deficit had been reduced, and crime rates were dropping. Following the 1994 midterm elections, the administration defied the growing partisanship and polarization of Washington politics by pursuing a policy course of determined centrism.[62] Clinton advocated a series of modest and moderate proposals—including curfews for children, the V-chip for television, community policing, opposition to gay marriages, and welfare reform—designed to seize the political center of gravity. Interestingly, the survey data from 1994 and 1996 suggest that it was moderates—not ideologues, as in the mid to late 1960s— who led the latest change in political trust.

Recognizing that the Republicans, led by House Speaker Gingrich, had pressed their assault on government too far, Clinton established himself as the protector of cherished programs for education, the environment, and the elderly, further reinforcing his centrist credentials. Clinton's eschewal of big promises and defense of popular social programs fit the public mood: dwindling confidence in what government can accomplish, combined with a strong desire to maintain vital services.

On issues of probity, however, Clinton's record was more mixed. On the one hand, his unwavering opposition to Gingrich's proposals bolstered his image of *political* integrity. Countering his image of pliancy on matters of principle, Clinton confronted his foes and stood his (middle) ground. On the other hand, allegations of scandal and ethical abuse raised questions about his *personal* integrity. The highly critical media spotlighted accusations about misuse of confidential FBI files, investigations into the failed Whitewater real-estate deal, and charges of sexual harassment during his tenure as governor of Arkansas. Under the circumstances, one would not expect the public to express greater trust in government.

Yet the public proved forgiving. While most Americans in 1996 believed that Clinton had done something illegal or unethical, more than 60 percent felt that policy issues mattered more than character issues. Only 15 perent of Americans identified Whitewater as very important, one-third the number who rated Watergate as very important in its time.[63] The short-term factors that shape public satisfaction— performance, policy, probity, and the press—do not weigh equally in every case. The first Reagan administration scored high on each measure; the first Clinton administration enjoyed high marks on some but not others.

But what about the future? Will probity continue to take a back seat to other factors? Will government performance measure up? Will that performance meet changing public expectations and survive the scrutiny of a captious and contentious press? Will the government devise pragmatic, middle-of-the-road solutions that address the concerns of average Americans despite an increasingly partisan and ideological political leadership? These are the questions that will determine whether public trust in government will revive over the long run or continue on a downward slide.

The Menu of Explanations

Four

Is It Really the Economy, Stupid?

Robert Z. Lawrence

Governments throughout the world have assumed responsibility for the performance of their economies. They take the credit when performance is strong, and the blame when it is weak. It is certainly plausible, therefore, that economic performance is an important source of the pervasive decline in trust in government in the United States. It is particularly plausible because throughout the developed world, by most measures, economic performance has deteriorated significantly since the early 1970s—the period during which dissatisfaction has increased.

Nevertheless, it is by no means clear that economic performance has actually played a decisive role in generating this decline in trust. The links between economic performance and satisfaction with government are uncertain. First, there is uncertainty about the measures of economic performance. Do measures of productivity, for example, accurately capture improvements in living standards? Do measures of poverty accurately capture distress? Second, there is uncertainty about how performance is perceived and appraised. Do people care about their absolute living standards, their relative living standards, or the rate at which these improve? How are their expectations affected by previous performance and other determinants of their needs? Third, there is uncertainty about the degree to which

government in particular is viewed as responsible for performance—
indeed, trust in government might be higher during times of crisis and
hardship, particularly when these conditions are attributed to forces
beyond government's control. In addition, people could well respond
to poor economic conditions by losing trust in their current government, but not in government per se—the issue with which we are
concerned here.

This chapter reflects these considerations. It is fairly straightforward to document performance with official measures of growth,
employment, and the distribution of income; it is more difficult, however, to ascertain whether these outcomes match people's expectations and the degree to which they actually hold government responsible for shortfalls. On these questions our knowledge seems much
weaker.

My analysis focuses primarily on the United States, but I also
introduce evidence from other developed countries. I begin by suggesting why economic performance could indeed be an important
source of declining trust in government. I describe how, throughout
the developed world, during the first half of the postwar period,
economic performance was stellar and government expanded its obligations and raised expectations about what citizens might anticipate
from economic performance in general and government in particular.
I then argue that the widespread decline in economic growth that
followed placed pressures on government to meet these obligations.
The result has been painful retrenchment exacerbated by difficulties
adjusting to global economic and technological changes. I also note
the declining belief and role of government as a regulator and opera-
tor of enterprises. Governments now face chronic problems. Some
they can do little about; others require politically painful measures
that only pay off far in the future. Instead of undertaking these
measures, avoidance, denial, and blame are common. When problems
aren't dealt with, it is no surprise that citizens experience considerable
disillusionment.

Economic performance therefore seems to be a prime suspect.
Polling data, however, suggest other factors may play a more important role. First, the timing is wrong. Although corresponding to the
beginning of a period of high inflation, the major rise in dissatisfaction

with government actually *predates* the period of slow productivity growth, increasing inequality, globalization, and technological change associated with the information revolution and corporate restructuring. While all these factors may have made restoring faith in government difficult, they do not appear to have been the initial source of the loss of faith. Second, in other parts of the world, similarly poor economic performance has been associated with continued trust in government, and, third, in the United States declining trust in government is pervasive. It has occurred to a similar degree and has moved synchronously among Americans regardless of income, ages, education levels, occupations, and geographic locations. This decline in trust apparently does not correlate with people's own economic experiences or with their expectations about the government's economic responsibilities; indeed, the decline is prevalent both among Americans who have fared relatively well in the economy and those who have fared relatively poorly. Thus, while economic factors may have been contributory, other factors must have been important. In particular, developments in the late 1960s and early 1970s—the Vietnam War, social changes, and Watergate—seemed to have convinced Americans that government (and other institutions) could not be trusted. In addition, during this period Americans felt that the government fell increasingly under the influence of special interests and became less responsive to individual citizens. Nevertheless, these conclusions are tentative, and there is considerable scope for additional research, both on the nature of economic performance and on the channels by which it affects confidence in government.

Performance

The first twenty-five years after World War II was a golden era that gave rise to heightened expectations about economic performance that subsequently proved unsustainable. As indicated in Table 4-1, per capita incomes in the United States grew more rapidly than in any previous quarter century, averaging 2.2 percent annually. Yet Europe and Japan grew even faster. Europe closed much of its gap in per capita incomes with the United States. Japan, starting from much lower

Table 4-1. U.S. Growth, 1870–1995

	GNP	GNP per Employee	GNP per Capital Output	Output per Work Hour in the Business Sector
1870–1913	4.3	1.9	2.2	
1913–29	3.1	1.5	1.7	
1929–50	2.9	1.7	1.8	
1950–60	3.2	2.1	1.4	
1960–73	4.3	2.2	3.0	3.4
1973–79	2.9	0.3	1.8	1.4
1979–89	2.7	1	1.8	1.2
1989–95	1.8	0.7	0.7	1

Sources: 1870–1960: Historical Statistics of the United States, colonial times to 1970; 1960–95: Economic Report of the President.

income levels, did likewise, completing the transition from developing to developed economy.

Expanding Government

As growth exceeded expectations, the welfare state expanded. Governments sought not only to provide basic benefits for the poor but broad support for housing, health, education, and retirement. In Europe, driven by the desire for a solidaristic "social wage," governments made most benefits available to all, whereas in the United States means testing was more common. Nevertheless, social expenditures on education, health, old-age pensions, and welfare grew rapidly on both continents—between 1960 and 1975, the share of such spending in gross domestic product typically increased by about ten percentage points.[1] Associated with the rise in government social transfers was an increase in taxes, particularly those imposed on employment.

Governments also assumed increasing obligations for economic outcomes beyond achieving full employment. In Europe, governments frequently tried to maintain employment in particular regions, firms, and even jobs. Traditional regulatory objectives such as safety on the job and other rules governing employment were expanded. In some countries, measures were taken to ensure worker participation in management decision-making and government oversight of plant closures and layoffs. In both Europe and Japan, the state also implemented industrial policies to promote industries of the future and to aid those in decline. When market forces seemed inadequate, states nationalized private firms, allocated credit, encouraged mergers, nurtured national champion firms, and, in Europe, operated state-owned industries. In the United States, policies were more laissez-faire, but the government nonetheless regulated numerous sectors and did intervene occasionally to bail out troubled firms and protect troubled industries.

Stagflation

In the early 1970s, however, growth slowed, and wage demands outpaced growth in productivity. In 1973, in a highly inflationary outburst, a synchronized global expansion and soaring commodity prices heralded a new era of stagflation. Growth declined throughout the developed world: the pace between 1973 and 1990 was typically about one-third slower than in the 1950s and 1960s (see Table 4-2). Growth was also more volatile, as bouts of inflation were followed by severe cyclical downturns. In the 1990s, inflation was kept in check, but growth was even slower than between 1973 and 1990.

These growth slowdowns have taken different forms. In the United States, employment has increased but average earnings have grown very slowly. In Europe, output per worker and real wages have risen steadily (although more slowly than in the 1950s and 1960s), but unemployment has increased significantly and labor force participation has fallen.[2] Japan fared considerably better in both sustaining real-wage growth and employment growth until the early 1990s. More recently, however, it experienced stagnation and growing overt and disguised unemployment.

It has been difficult, under these circumstances, for governments to honor the commitments assumed during more prosperous periods. Policies have cycled between measures to avoid change and measures to adjust to it. Initially, governments often tried to stabilize employment, maintain entitlements, and aid firms and workers in distress. Later, however, layoffs, cuts in aid, and fiscal retrenchment became inevitable. Similarly, regulatory efforts to prevent change and to protect domestic industries have been followed by deregulation, privatization, and trade and international financial liberalization.

Table 4-2. Average Annual Growth Rate for Ten Nations, 1870–1995

	1870–1900	1900–25	1925–50	1950–73	1973–90	1991–95
GDP/GNP						
United States	4.3	3.5	2.7	3.6	2.5	1.9
Canada	3.1	3.3	3.9	5.1	3.3	1.6
Japan	2.5	3.1	0.9	8.9	4.1	1.3
United Kingdom	2.1	0.9	1.8	3.0	1.9	1.2
France	1.6	1.2	1.1	5.1	2.5	1.1
Germany	2.7	1.7	1.8	5.7	2.1	2.2
Italy	0.9	2.2	1.4	5.4	2.9	1.2
Denmark	2.4	2.7	2.7	4.0	1.8	2.0
Netherlands	2.0	2.7	2.2	5.0	2.0	1.9
Sweden	2.5	2.9	3.1	3.8	1.9	0.2
Weighted Average*	3.0	2.7	2.0	5.2	2.8	1.6
GDP/GNP per Capita						
United States	2.0	1.7	1.6	2.2	1.5	0.8
Canada	1.8	1.0	2.3	3.0	2.2	0.5
Japan	1.6	1.9	-0.5	7.7	3.3	1.0
United Kingdom	1.1	0.5	1.3	2.6	1.7	0.8
France	1.5	1.1	1.0	4.1	2.0	0.8
Germany	1.7	1.2	2.8	4.8	2.0	1.6
Italy	0.2	1.4	0.7	4.7	2.6	1.5
Denmark	1.4	1.5	1.8	3.3	1.6	
Netherlands	0.8	1.2	0.9	3.8	1.4	
Sweden	1.8	2.2	2.5	3.2	1.6	
Weighted Average*	1.6	1.5	1.2	4.0	2.1	1.0

*Uses size of GNP in 1990 as a fixed weight.
Sources: 1870–1950: Maddison 1982, in Lipsey and Kravis 1987, 9; 1950–60: OECD National Accounts; 1960–90 IFS Yearbook 1990 (data tapes); 1991–95: OECD Economic Outlook and International Monetary Fund World Economic Outlook.

Growing Inequality

In the United States, incomes have not only grown slowly but have become less equal. This is evident in measures of household incomes, hourly wages, and wealth.[3] As Figure 4-1 shows, while households in the upper two quintiles enjoyed some income growth between 1979 and 1993—the top 5 percent enjoyed the greatest rise—the other quintiles experienced absolute declines, with the lowest quintile's incomes falling by the highest percentage. Wage data display similar patterns when grouped by education, occupation, or skills. As shown in Figure 4-2, for example, blue-collar workers, particularly those less skilled and less educated, fared especially poorly in the 1980s. As measured by the Employment Cost Index, real white-collar compensation increased 17 percent between 1981 and 1995, whereas blue-collar compensation was up just 4.8 percent.[4] Moreover, an additional increase in inequality has occurred among workers with similar edu-

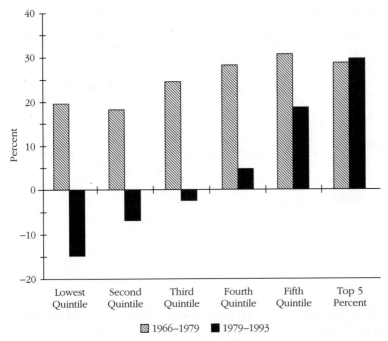

Figure 4-1. *Changes in average real family income by quintile. Real incomes have fallen or stagnated for most American families since 1979. Note that family income is deflated by the CPI-U-XI.*

Source: Department of Commerce.

cational, occupational, and industry backgrounds—so-called within-cell inequality.

Rising inequality is evident in other English-speaking developed economies—the United Kingdom, Canada, Australia, and New Zealand. In continental Europe, however, wage differentials were either broadly unchanged or increased only slightly. There is evidence of only small increases in the premiums on schooling and in the age-to-earnings profiles in some European countries.

Since 1973, European countries have experienced high levels of unemployment particularly concentrated on younger workers and the long-term unemployed. An important question is the degree to which institutional and regulatory factors in Europe have repressed wage adjustments, impaired work incentives, raised unemployment, and slowed labor-force growth. The comprehensive OECD Jobs Study, for

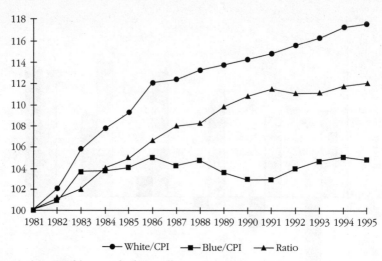

Figure 4-2. *U.S. blue- and white-collar compensation (1981 = 100)*

Source: Employment Cost Index.

example, concludes that all developed countries have experienced a shift in demand away from unskilled jobs. In countries in which relative wages have been flexible, trends in both relative employment and unemployment rates of the unskilled changed little during the 1980s. In countries with less wage flexibility, the effects have been felt in employment performance.

Painful Choices

Until the early 1990s, Americans used two mechanisms to limit the impact of slower productivity on consumption growth. The first was rapid labor-force growth. Instead of working smarter, Americans worked harder. Employment increased rapidly as the large numbers of women and postwar baby boomers joined the labor force. This put great pressure on working women, who often found themselves responsible as both breadwinners and homemakers. Nevertheless, it allowed the United States to stave off the impact of slower productivity growth on aggregate growth until the early 1990s: between the cyclical peaks of 1973 and 1989, U.S. GDP (in 1987 dollars) averaged an annual growth rate of 2.5 percent.

The second mechanism was to borrow. In the 1980s, U.S. consumption growth outpaced GDP (by 0.3 percent annually) because the country borrowed—from both the future (by investing less) and the rest of the world. Between 1980 and 1988, real consumption spending increased by 32 percent, and the share of gross private domestic investment in GDP fell from 17.3 percent to 13.2 percent. In 1992, the current account shifted from balance to deficit, and of course the federal budget deficit soared, peaking at 4 percent of GDP in 1986.

By the early 1990s, however, these options were no longer available. In the United States, the baby-boom generation had long been absorbed into the work force, and female participation rates leveled out. According to the Bureau of Labor Statistics, between 1995 and 2005, the labor force will grow at just over 1 percent annually—half the pace recorded in the late 1970s. (The labor force is expected to grow even more slowly thereafter, actually declining at 0.2 percent annually between 2010 and 2030.) Adding these labor-force projections to the 1 percent annual growth in productivity suggests that America's potential long-run GDP is growing at just over 2 percent.[5]

In the medium term, Europe and Japan may have more room than the United States to grow by reducing unemployment. According to estimates by the Organization for Economic Cooperation and Development (OECD), between 1997 and 2000 for example, growth rates of 3 percent and 3.8 percent annually could be achieved in Europe and Japan, respectively.[6] Once cyclical unemployment is eliminated, however, the OECD estimates potential growth at 2.8 percent and 3 percent for Europe and Japan, respectively. Unfortunately, structural unemployment in Europe remains high, at around 9.5 percent.[7]

In the 1990s, U.S. spending patterns have been aligned more closely to incomes. In particular, the structural federal budget deficit has been reduced, primarily through lowering expenditures on defense and discretionary government spending. In both Europe and Japan, however, persistent unemployment has led to a dramatic deterioration in fiscal positions. Budget deficits there must now be reduced in an environment of high unemployment. This task is becoming particularly difficult because the aging of populations throughout the developed world requires rising expenditures to meet existing pension and health care obligations.

Explanations

The sources of these problems are not well understood. Despite its economic importance, the productivity slowdown has not been given the research attention it deserves. With the wisdom of hindsight, at least, some of this slower growth might have been expected. In the 1950s and 1960s, the United States had enjoyed access to an unusually large residue of innovations that depression and war had prevented from being fully exploited. Europe and Japan enjoyed access to U.S. know-how and could benefit from relative backwardness. By the 1970s, both of these sources of rapid growth had been largely exhausted. But productivity growth has been even slower than an extrapolation of earlier historical trends would have predicted.

The slowdown in the United States is particularly evident in sectors outside of manufacturing—a perplexing development given the rapid increase in the use of computers, which might have been expected to be particularly beneficial in the services sector. It seems that the full potential of the computer is not being realized. Equally perplexing is the fact that major corporate restructuring and downsizing do not seem to have raised productivity outside of manufacturing.

Inequality. The sources of growing inequality in the United States and unemployment among the unskilled in Europe are also being hotly debated.[8] In both Europe and the United States, alarms have been sounded about the role of trade and international investment in shifting the demand for unskilled labor. In the United States, the debate over the North America Free Trade Agreement (NAFTA) in the early 1990s crystallized concerns over wage performance that are best captured by Ross Perot's allusion to the "giant sucking sound" of jobs as they move southward.

In Europe, the recessionary environment of the 1990s sparked similar fears of "delocalization"—that is, that firms are relocating to low-wage countries. In his best-selling book, Sir James Goldsmith also voiced concerns about trade and immigration in France, and the French Senate issued a special report blaming delocalization for much of France's ills.[9]

In Japan, the debate has become particularly heated in recent years; it is couched as a concern about the "hollowing out" of the economy. The Japanese have not seen an increase in inequality, but there are fears that Japanese industry is caught in a squeeze, as newly industrializing economies move into basic manufacturing industries that Japan once dominated, while Japan has not been sufficiently successful in entering high-technology industries of the future such as software, finance, and advanced microprocessors. The strengthening of the yen in the mid-1980s initiated these concerns as Japanese manufacturers began to invest outside of Japan in increasing numbers. After a period of respite in which a booming domestic economy laid some of these fears to rest, the association of slow growth and a strong yen have again brought them to the fore. As Japanese firms increasingly relocate abroad, fear is voiced about the ability of Japanese manufacturers to maintain their basic institutions such as lifetime employment and strong corporate groups.

Moreover, concerns have been voiced about international labor-market competition, not simply in terms of wages but also with regard to the regulatory environment. In Canada, free trade with the United States was seen by some as a threat to the Canada's welfare state. Some Japanese are worried about the continuous pressures from abroad to conform to international rather than domestic norms of behavior and the need for "a Japan that can say no." In Europe, an important aspect of creating a single market has been the "social dimension"—the effort to ensure that minimum labor standards prevail throughout the European Union. In France, a furor was raised when the Hoover corporation moved from Dijon to Scotland, purportedly because of both lower wage costs and lower labor standards. In the European debate about freer trade with Eastern Europe and Asia, concerns have been raised not simply about low wages but also about "social dumping"—that is, the downward competitive pressures that are allegedly placed on labor standards as a result of trade. In the United States, concerns about workers' rights have been reflected in U.S. international trade legislation. Indeed, both France and the United States have proposed that workers' rights be an important consideration in the post–Uruguay Round agenda.

These concerns are examples of more pervasive fears about globalization and its effects on national autonomy.[10] While the world remains organized politically into nation-states, the economy is becoming increasingly global. Over the postwar period, declining trade barriers and transportation costs and improvements in communications have expanded the role of international trade and investment in all economies. National economies are thus increasingly affected by external economic developments.[11] Multinational firms and international capital markets have a growing influence on domestic policies.

In addition, international governance has become more and more pervasive, extending to policy areas that were once thought of as exclusively matters of domestic concern—areas such as subsidies, product standards, intellectual property, and antitrust. While international agreements may bring gains in global efficiency, they also constrain domestic sovereignty. National governments are still held responsible for economic outcomes, but they are increasingly unable to act independently to meet these responsibilities.

Technological change is also seen as having contributed to growing inequality.[12] In particular, technology appears to have shifted toward requiring the more intensive use of skilled and educated workers. The spread of computers, information technology, and new forms of labor–management relations may also have been important. Perhaps even more than globalization, technology is a factor largely beyond the control of government. While the government may attempt to limit its application and cushion its impact, the interaction of technology and market forces usually forces structural adjustment.

Inequality, particularly that occurring within cells, could also result from other institutional changes—some reflecting technological imperatives, others the impact of deregulation and other sources of increased competition. Both large firms and unions are playing a reduced role in employment. As a result, fewer workers are having their pay determined by prevailing bargains and norms, while more are subject to the vagaries and idiosyncrasies of practices in smaller firms. In addition, even within larger firms, an increased role for performance-based pay, coupled with improved monitoring of individual efforts, could be important.

Policies.   Whatever their causes, it is not easy for governments to address the problems of slow growth, structural unemployment, and increasing inequality. To stimulate growth, greater investment is required, but the payoffs from increased investment on a feasible scale are unlikely to be large compared with the size of the slowdown. The effects would only be perceptible over the long run. In the short run, taking these steps requires additional reductions in public and private consumption, neither of which are attractive in a slow-growth economy.

Indeed, the measures required to deal with the productivity slowdown and raise national savings through budget reduction can be compared to the decision to give up smoking. First, the evidence on the health benefits has taken a long time to become clear: enough controversy existed so that people could find support for contradictory views. Second, in the short run, giving up smoking makes one feel worse, not better. Third, the benefits show up in the long run and are uncertain.

Undertaking structural reforms is equally difficult. First, there is uncertainty surrounding the sources of change and the appropriate solutions. Second, implementing changes is difficult. In Europe, for example, tackling structural unemployment is often seen as requiring increased labor-market flexibility. Recommended measures such as lowering subsidies, payroll taxes, minimum wages, and relaxing labor-market regulations and other rules all engender considerable ideological debate and face considerable political resistance. In Japan, similarly, reforms require deregulation, market opening, and reducing the power of government bureaucracy—again measures supported by powerful vested interests. Finally, the payoffs are uncertain, and because they are often clouded by cyclical changes, they are hard to detect in the short run.

Trying to reverse the current trends in trade or stifling technology could well damage living standards even further. Nor is it simple to reduce inequality directly through income redistribution. In the United States, the most significant redistribution of the income pie has actually been among workers rather than between capital and labor. Again, solving this problem honestly is particularly difficult, as it requires redistribution not from a relatively small class of capitalists but rather from the much more powerful intellectual elite. It is no wonder that there has been virtually no discussion of this possibility.

The chickens, therefore, appear to have now come home to roost. Given slow productivity growth, consumption in the United States is constrained by productivity performance to sluggish growth for the foreseeable future. Despite growing inequality, fiscal policies that redistribute income or other transfers to reduce the impact of structural change have limited scope. On the contrary, given high budget deficits and growing demands on government programs, the welfare state is being forced to shrink. If citizens hold their governments responsible for their well-being and look for government assistance during times of trouble, it is no surprise that they are increasingly disappointed.

Denial.   Given these painful choices, it is also no wonder that denial and the search for magical quick fixes plays an important part in the discourse. Some claim that the productivity slowdown reflects measurement error because productivity growth in services and other sectors is particularly hard to measure (indeed, significant problems lead to an overstatement of inflation in the U.S. consumer price index). Many of these measurement problems are not new, however. Before 1973, significant gains in productivity were recorded outside of manufacturing. If we claim that the slowdown reflects measurement error, we must argue that these problems have become greater since 1973. In his 1994 presidential address to the American Economic Association, Zvi Griliches argued that gross national product has in fact become more concentrated in sectors in which progress is more difficult to measure.[13] Similarly, Robert Gordon argues that some of the slowdown in service-sector productivity is attributable to measurement error.[14] Still, a precise and convincing account of the impact of measurement error has not been undertaken.

Others suggest that productivity is on the verge of improving. Indeed, until the early 1990s, this was standard U.S. government practice.[15] In the 1980s, supply-side economics and demographic changes—the aging of the work force—were looked on as potential saviors. In the 1990s, some believe that the services sector is undergoing a major structural transformation similar to that faced by manufacturing in the 1980s. They claim that computers will allow services industries to raise their productivity in response to deregulation and global competition. It will be a very pleasant surprise if they are right. Thus far, however, recent productivity growth lies well within the range generally expected for a business-cycle recovery. Moreover, the gains in productivity during the recovery between 1992 and 1996 have again been heavily concentrated in manufacturing.

Another line of argument blames people's expectations. Robert Samuelson has argued that Americans' dissatisfaction is a matter of perception rather than reality.[16] He suggests that by historical standards, economic performance over the past few decades has actually been strong. He argues that people have come to expect too much, partly because they have extrapolated the very unusual experience of the 1960s and assumed it could continue forever. A key question, therefore, is how recent experience compares with prewar performance.

As indicated in Table 4-1, the period since 1973 has actually been a uniquely poor one for U.S. productivity growth, and the period since 1990 has been similarly poor for the growth in per capita incomes. Productivity growth since 1973 is slow in comparison with the pace over the past 150 years and not just with the rapid growth achieved in the early postwar period. Measured between the cyclical peak of 1979 and 1995, for example, output per hour in the business sector grew a scant 0.8 percent annually. By contrast, had the 2 percent pace of the previous century been maintained, compensation would have increased by almost 50 percent. Between 1973 and 1989, America was able to maintain per capita income growth at a pace of just under 2 percent, which, while slower than in the 1960s, was quite in keeping with the historic performance. But this improvement was predicated on faster labor-force growth. With the decline in labor-force growth in the 1990s, output per capita has fallen in line with output per worker, growing by less than 1 percent annually. In sum, Samuelson is wrong. Americans who are using their history as a benchmark have every right to feel disappointed.

A final argument points to America's improved relative performance compared with other major industrial economies. The United States ranked first among developed countries, for example, in the Global Competitiveness Report, published by the World Economic Forum.[17] Indeed, in the 1990s, U.S. growth has been slightly more rapid than in developed countries as a whole. Manufacturing productivity in the United States has similarly been in the middle of the pack, and American firms have increased their technological lead in high-technology sectors such as software and semiconductors and have improved their performance in basic industries such as steel and automobiles. In addition, the United States has been more successful in sustaining employment growth. Perhaps Americans should not be dissatisfied with the performance of their country, which may well have adjusted to global shocks better than other countries. But this relative performance makes little difference to blue-collar Americans whose paychecks are barely growing.

Blame.   Instead of facing the fact that the slowdown reflects their own failures to improve productivity, Americans have also looked around for others to blame. Some finger the rich, pointing to soaring corporate profits and executive salaries. Others finger the poor, pointing to welfare spending and social programs. Some finger foreigners, pointing to trade and immigration. But the real source of slow growth is not that someone else has taken a much bigger slice of the pie. It's simply that the pie has not grown.

It is also increasingly common to see the finger pointed at government, which is often blamed for slowing growth both directly and indirectly. The direct channels involve distortions to incentives via high taxes, wasteful spending, and inefficient regulation. The indirect channels involve the impact of government policies on changing social norms, attitudes, and ethics. As Joel Slemrod points out, however, many problems make these effects difficult to measure. Incentive effects operate at the margin, and thus average tax rates may not accurately reflect the impact on incentives. And means-tested transfers have made matters even more complex. Similarly, tax shelters and other mechanisms for avoiding payment of taxes may lead to an overstatement of the impact of high statutory marginal rates. Effects operating through indirect channels are even more difficult to measure, because they operate over the very long run. Problems also arise because causation runs in both directions; high incomes lead to more government involvement, as citizens demand higher levels of public goods.[18]

In sum, slow growth and rising inequality present serious challenges to governments intent on maintaining their obligations. The extent of these problems is often challenged, their causes are uncertain, and the remedies they require are politically difficult. Indeed, government is frequently seen as part of the problem, rather than the solution. Under these circumstances, the economy could well explain why trust in government has eroded.

Needs and Preferences.   It is also quite possible that, even with unchanged economic performance, dissatisfaction could rise if needs become greater. For example, families may become less secure if they have to rely on a single breadwinner when previously there had been two. David Ellwood has emphasized that the United States has seen a remarkably steady rise in the percentage of families headed by a single parent. This increase does not seem related to economic conditions or public incentives but reflects independent demographic and social forces. This could therefore be an independent source of dissatisfaction: because the wages of the single breadwinner cannot be supplemented by another income, family insecurity increases.

Dissatisfaction could also rise with unchanged performance if needs become more disparate. The poor and the rich may want different things from government. It is also possible, therefore, as John Donahue has noted, that growing inequality in incomes could lead to dissatisfaction by making it more difficult to match policies with preferences. Greater inequality consequently makes pleasing the public more difficult, and because the United States has shifted toward increased inequality in the 1980s, this, too, could lead to increased dissatisfaction, even if policies and performance were unchanged.

Perceptions

Thus far I have made a plausible case for why both economic performance and demands for that performance could have shifted to raise dissatisfaction with government. But as I elaborated earlier, the links between economic performance and trust in government are not straightforward. Considerable research has been conducted on the links between economic performance and voting behavior, although most of the emphasis has been on people's votes for particular administrations, rather than their trust in government in general.[19] In addition, research has been undertaken on what people in different nations expect from government.[20] In the United States, these expectations, while different for different social groups, appear to have been remarkably constant over the past three decades.[21]

Consider, for example, the responses to the surveys on trust in the federal government reported by National Election Studies. In Table 4-3, replies to these surveys have been aggregated so that those indicating trust in the government "just about all of the time" score 100; "most of the time," 67; "some of the time," 33; and "none of the time," 0. This survey makes clear the precipitous decline of trust in government that occurred steadily between the mid-1960s and 1980.

In 1966, trust peaked with a score of 61 percent. By 1972 it had fallen to 38 percent; by 1974, to 29 percent; and by 1980, to 27 percent. The large 16-point decline between 1966 and 1968 occurred during a period of strong economic growth, which suggests an important role for the Vietnam War and the social upheavals and violence in 1968 rather than the economy. The precipitous 10-point decline between 1972 and 1974 does correspond with the OPEC oil shock and heightened inflation, but it is more importantly associated with Watergate. Significantly, trust in government continued to erode between 1976 and 1978 despite the recovery of the economy, and it then recovered between 1980 and 1982 despite the deepest postwar recession. Similarly, trust was eroded to an all time low between 1992 and 1994, again despite the recovery of the economy. This timing suggests that, first, the erosion of trust certainly predates the period of growing inequality (essentially a post-1980 development), the productivity slowdown (which became apparent in the late 1970s), the globalization of the economy, and the technological impact of computers and telecommunications. It also suggests that trust is not tightly correlated with a particular economic indicator such as inflation, unemployment, or growth. Certainly, at times, the economy's performance may have made it more difficult to regain confidence in government, but the initiating factors appear to derive from elsewhere.

Equally revealing are the tabulations in which the responses are broken down into social and other groups. As reported in Table 4-3, these are remarkably similar. Relatively small differences exist between males and females and among respondents of different incomes, occupations, ages, and geographic locations. (The one striking difference is for race, with blacks more trusting of the government than whites in the 1960s, and then less trusting thereafter.) It is noteworthy that the loss of trust in the late 1960s was so widely shared by Americans. Raymond Vernon has suggested that if the international economy is generating distrust in government, the evidence for distrust ought to be strongest among those groups who are generally hostile to free trade, immigration, and investment. We might expect, for example, greater distrust among unionized workers. But this does not appear to have been the case. Similarly, if poor wage growth is driving dissatisfaction, unskilled blue-collar workers might be expected to be particularly mistrustful. But again, this is not evident.

Table 4-3. Trust in Government Index: Selected Years, 1958–94

	1958	1964	1966	1968	1970	1972	1974	1976	1978	1980	1982	1984	1986	1988	1990	1992	1994
All	49	52	61	45	39	38	29	30	29	27	31	38	47	34	29	29	26
Male	51	52	60	43	39	38	30	31	30	27	32	37	46	35	29	28	26
Female	49	51	62	47	40	38	29	30	29	27	31	38	47	33	30	29	26
White	49	51	60	44	40	39	30	31	29	26	31	38	48	34	29	28	26
Black	50	57	69	54	33	38	24	27	32	34	33	34	40	31	28	30	29
Grade School/Some High School	49	51	59	43	36	36	26	29	31	28	32	37	42	32	31	33	29
High School Diploma	49	54	62	46	42	37	29	30	28	26	32	38	49	33	29	28	25
Some College, No Degree	50	50	62	45	42	40	33	31	29	25	28	37	45	34	27	27	25
College Degree	52	52	64	50	41	41	34	35	32	29	34	39	49	37	29	28	27
Family income 0–16 percentile	49	50	58	46	35	37	30	33	30	31	32	38	44	32	32	33	30
Family income 17–33 percentile	49	51	58	43	36	35	22	30	28	26	32	37	47	32	29	29	27
Family income 34–67 percentile	51	53	62	45	38	37	31	31	30	26	30	37	47	33	29	27	25
Family income 68–95 percentile	50	52	63	47	43	40	30	33	32	26	32	38	49	37	30	28	25
Family income 96–100 percentile	50	54	63	45	43	45	38	32	30	26	33	42	49	42	30	28	27
Professional	51	51		45	41	41	33	31	30	28	32	38	47	35	29	28	25
White-Collar	51	52		46	42	38	30	27	29	24	31	36	49	34	31	28	25
Blue-Collar	49	52		42	38	34	27	33	28	26	31	37	45	32	27	27	25
Unskilled	48	60		50	31	33	26	33	32	31	30	33	41	30	33	26	28
Farmers	48	52		41	29	34	30	32	28	18	31	39	40	31	28	37	26
Housewives	49	51		48	40	39	29	28	29	26	31	41	48	36	29	31	25
Union Household	48	54	61	45	40	35	29	31	29	26	32	34	47	33	28	25	26
NonUnion Household	50	51	61	45	39	39	30	30	31	27	31	39	47	34	29	29	26
South	48	50	55	43	36	37	28	30	31	27	32	37	47	33	29	31	29
North	50	52	63	46	41	38	30	31	29	26	31	38	46	34	29	27	25
Born 1959–74									35	34	39	40	45	38	33	30	27
Born 1943–58		51	68	49	43	39	32	30	30	25	39	40	45	38	33	30	25
Born 1927–42	51	54	65	48	41	37	28	30	28	27	30	38	48	32	28	28	25
Born 1911–26	50	51	61	43	39	37	27	30	29	26	31	35	48	33	25	25	29
Born 1895–1910	47	49	58	42	35	37	28	32	28	28	32	39	45	27	34	32	30

Source: The National Election Studies.

Moreover, the unanimity on this issue is atypical of many survey responses. There is, for example, an interesting contrast in the response to this question and another in which people are asked whether the government should guarantee every person a job and a good standard of living or if each person should do so on his or her own. The response to this question does not have the strong shift over time that is evident in the trust question, and it does indicate quite stark differences in opinion among groups. Women, blacks, and people with lower educations, lower incomes, and lower skills tend to believe that people should not be left on their own by the government. Similarly divergent views are apparent in the breakdowns in response to the question of whether government services should be cut. The divergences in these responses suggest that the declining trust in government is not related to people's views about the government's responsibilities or its role in the economy.

As shown in Figure 4-3, at the same time that trust in government declined, there are noteworthy increases in the percentage of respondents who believe that the government is wasteful, responsive to the needs of special interests, and remote from the interests of ordinary citizens. It is this sense of alienation, which is not necessarily linked to a single event or economic performance, that appears particularly important in the loss of trust. These data suggest that trust in government is a pervasive social phenomenon, that American citizens tend to share perceptions about this question even though the actual performance of the economy and their own economic circumstances may be quite different.

Conclusions

This chapter has briefly surveyed economic performance and perceptions. Economic performance could plausibly be the source of declining trust in government. On the one hand, based on government's previous performance, people have high expectations about what it can do. On the other hand, the problems faced by government are far more difficult to deal with. Governments have assumed obligations to boost growth, maintain full employment, ensure equity, and

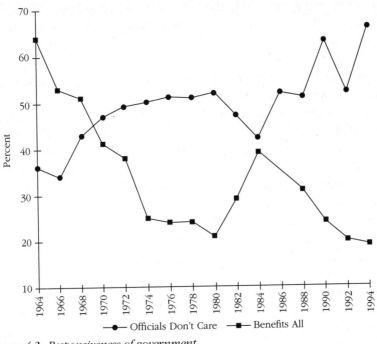

Figure 4-3. *Responsiveness of government*

Source: National Election Studies.

provide for the social welfare of their citizens. But these obligations have not been met in the past two decades. Income growth has slowed, inequality has increased in the United States, and unemployment has risen in Europe and Japan. On all three continents, people fear international competition and its impact on incomes and sovereignty.

How to respond to these problems remains hotly contested. The measures of performance have been questioned, and the reasons for these poor outcomes are disputed. Governments appear less able to determine the economic fortunes of their citizens. Economies are more open, structural changes appear larger, government fiscal policies are tightly constrained, and the policies that might credibly work require making tradeoffs between present and future generations and among politically powerful interest groups. Under these circumstances, it becomes attractive for leaders to try to shift blame, divert attention, and avoid taking these painful measures. The result is that, inevitably, the problems are not dealt with, and mistrust and disillusionment grows.

While this appears to be a plausible argument, it does not provide an adequate account of declining trust in government. While it may point to factors that have made restoring faith in government more difficult, it does not adequately account for the dramatic declines in trust that are evident in U.S. polling data. The timing and nature of these responses suggest that events such as the Vietnam War and Watergate, and a perception that the expansion of government actually alienated it from the needs of ordinary citizens, are far more important factors. Nevertheless, as this chapter makes clear, our understanding of the links between economic performance and trust leaves much to be desired. Whatever the uncertainties associated with actually measuring economic performance, they are small in the face of the uncertainties about the mechanisms by which that performance translates into a trust or lack of trust in government.

CHAPTER Five

Social and Cultural Causes of Dissatisfaction with U.S. Government

Jane Mansbridge

Introduction

Social and cultural changes can cause satisfaction with government to decline both indirectly, by affecting government performance (that is, making it harder for governmental institutions to act in ways that satisfy its citizens), and directly (holding performance constant), by affecting citizen attitudes, as a society becoming more cynical overall directs part of its anger at the government.

Most of the effect of social and cultural changes on the degree of satisfaction with government in the United States over the past thirty years has, I believe, worked indirectly, by reducing the caliber of government performance. Sociocultural changes have produced new problems, with consequent demands for governmental solutions. Sociocultural changes have also independently produced rising expectations for governmental action. Both of these trends have generated governmental "overload"—a situation in which citizens ask the government to solve problems it cannot solve, ask the government to do more things (and more incompatible things) than it can do, and ask the government to solve problems without being willing to sustain taxation adequate to finance the efforts that would produce a solution. As Richard Neustadt shows in Chapter 7, these greater demands on government operate within a system designed to go slow. High levels of citizen distrust make it go slower still.

Some of the effect of sociocultural changes on satisfaction with government works more directly, by producing dissatisfaction regardless of performance. An expected decline from an "unnatural" high of satisfaction with democratic governments after World War II, the rise of postmaterial values that include criticism of all authority, the increasing cynicism of the media for reasons intrinsic to that industry, and increases in the public perception of corruption that derive from relatively successful attempts to reduce corruption—all these factors must have had direct effects on decreasing satisfaction with government. Declines in optimism more generally also have had their effect. Most important, issues of race, ethnicity, and competing cultural values have split the citizenry in ways that one would expect to promote distrust of any entity that attempted to govern forcefully in the name of all the people.

Governments often have to make hard decisions. They must impose unpopular costs in order to produce popular benefits. If deference to elected and appointed authorities declines, citizens are less likely to assume that the individuals who make decisions are acting in the public interest. They are more likely to suspect the outcome. As deference declines, so does trust.

When a decline in deference is irreversible, the deficit in trust can be made up only by greater public participation in decisions. Not all participation, however, can meet this need. That participation must take place in a structure that forces citizens themselves to face the hard decisions. In a highly decentralized unit, such as a town meeting or a family, citizens and family members know that they cannot have what they are not willing to pay for. They know, too, that they cannot have other incompatible goods. This knowledge encourages them to think through more carefully the implications of their choices and to ask themselves what they most want. If citizens are no longer willing to trust governmental authorities to investigate potential outcomes and make these hard choices for them, new forms of participation must be designed to allow citizens to make the choices well and for themselves.

Performance and Overload

Rising Problems

The words "governmental overload" suggest a fixed governmental capacity, which in some conditions becomes overloaded. But "overload" is a relative term. Some governments do far more than others in, say, reducing unemployment or in providing full health insurance. Each government becomes "overloaded" only in relation to what its citizens expect and will pay for. In considering performance, therefore, rising problems and rising expectations must be first treated somewhat separately, then linked.

It seems likely that several of the greatest problems of contemporary democratic governments have social and cultural changes among their causes. In the United States, crime and children in poverty exemplify such problems. Each has causes that are both hard to puzzle out and undoubtedly linked in some way to social and cultural changes.

Crime has been hard to measure and compare over time until the advent of victimization studies. Earlier measures—namely, the numbers of crimes recorded by the police—depended too heavily on variations in enforcement efforts. But because homicide has always called forth strong enforcement efforts, homicide rates can serve as a rough proxy for violent crime, the kind of crime that frightens citizens most.

Figure 5-1 indicates that homicide rates rose dramatically in the United States between 1960 and 1975,[1] exactly the period in which distrust in the federal government rose, almost equally dramatically.[2] It is of course conceivable that, if any causal connection exists between the two events at all, rising distrust in government caused the rise in crime, as witnesses of criminal behavior became less likely to report criminals to the police. It is somewhat more likely, however, that rising crime caused rising dissatisfaction with and therefore distrust of government. The most likely relation is that a cause external to both trends—for instance, a growing disrespect for social norms and traditional authority—was responsible for both the rise in homicides and the distrust in government during the period in question. Cross-national studies could illuminate this relationship.

Why did homicides in the United States rise in this period? No one

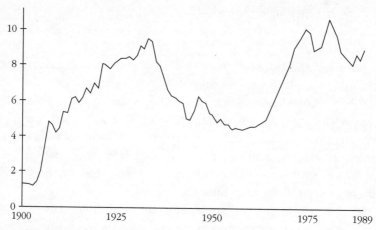

Figure 5-1. Homicide rate trends, 1900–88 (rate per 100,000 population)
Source: Vital Statistics of the United States, National Center for Health Statistics.

knows, but people speculate about declining social cohesion, the permissiveness of the 1960s, the burgeoning number of young males, violence in the movies and television, the training in violence and the brutalization of the Vietnam War, and the virtual end of the death penalty. These causes are almost entirely social and cultural. Their effect was to create a problem that citizens turned to government to solve.

The period from 1965 to 1990 also saw an increase in the number of children whose families could not keep them out of poverty without government help. This problem seems directly linked to social changes in marriage patterns. The ratio of marriages to divorces in the United States has declined from 4.3 to 1 in 1950 to 2 to 1 in 1990. The proportion of married to unmarried adults declined from 72 percent in 1970 to 61 percent in 1990. More children, therefore, found themselves living in families with only one parent and uncertain financial support. Table 5-1 shows that the percentage of children living with two parents declined from 85 percent in 1970 to 69 percent in 1994. Most of the children living with one parent were living with their mother, whose earning power was usually lower (sometimes far lower) than that of their father and whose child-care responsibilities often prevented her from taking full-time work in the paid sector.

As with crime, the exact causes of these changes in the family are

Table 5-1. Living Arrangements of U.S. Children 1970 and 1994
             (Numbers in Thousands)

Living Arrangements	1970	1994
Children under 18 years	69,162	69,508
Percent living with		
Two parents	85	69
One parent	12	27
Mother only	11	24
Father only	1	3
Neither parent	3	4

Source: "Marital Status and Living Arrangements, March 1994," *U.S. Bureau of the Census Current Population Reports,* Series P20-483, U.S. (Washington, D.C.: Government Printing Office, 1996), ix, table D.

hard to trace. Barbara Ehrenreich suggests that around 1950, the values of American males began to change, with the rise of *Playboy* magazine and its philosophy, the *On the Road* model of poets and writers of the beat generation, and even the pop medical science of Type A (overworking) and Type B (relaxed) differential risks of heart attack.[3] These trends produced among men a gradual revolt against the postwar model of hardworking dedication to family, and among women a slower but inevitable reaction of self-protection by joining the paid labor force.

The longer run saw a gradual rise in female entry into the paid labor force beginning in 1930 and continuing steadily upward till the present. This change seems to have been facilitated, if not caused, by two technological patterns. First, opportunities increased for workers in the service sector, where upper-body strength was not a prerequisite for reasonable pay. Second, technological innovation made it unnecessary for a full-time male worker to be supported by the full-time unpaid work of a female.[4] Household and service innovations, including not only time-saving appliances but also cheaper commercial laundries and food outlets, reduced the necessity for work in the home. At the same time, greater gender equality in education and the increasing need for educated workers in the paid work force made it possible for women to begin to earn a living wage. Female work force entry in turn made exit a conceivable, though not perfect, option from abusive, insupportable, and even just disagreeable marriages.

As divorce and births out of wedlock increased across the board, the number of divorced and unmarried women from low-income and

Black families increased at the greatest rate. When the options of divorce or nonmarriage became more financially and socially available, the strains of marriage on a low-income family seemed most likely to tear these families apart. As a result, fewer children from low-income families had the psychological and financial support of two parents, thus reducing their own economic chances still further.

Some attribute the decline of the nuclear family to an increase in selfishness, egoism, or individualism among both fathers and mothers. An increase in egoism would lower parents' efforts to marry or stay together for the sake of the children. We have very poor data on personal or public altruism. Behavioral measures, such as charitable giving or the giving of blood, seem to vary greatly according to tax policy or the efforts of blood-donation organizations. Changes on those measures cannot therefore be used to measure larger changes in responsibility for others.[5] Indeed, we have no survey data to suggest that trends in altruistic sentiments have any demonstrable relationship to the long-term upward trend in divorce and nonmarriage.

The speculation that individualism and capitalism in combination and over the course of generations "sweep away all values beyond self-gratification, and all social ties except those that yield each party immediate benefit"[6] requires further articulation to suggest why individualism and capitalism should produce these effects on the family beginning in the 1950s and not earlier. The specific mechanisms may be globalization and the logic of free trade, which erode "the capacity of any government to soften the hard edges of capitalism—and particularly its tendency toward extreme, demoralizing inequality."[7] It is true that analyses that blame the decline of the family on, say, welfare policies specific to the United States or Federal Reserve policies designed to keep unemployment above target levels ignore the more general problem of family breakdown throughout the Western world. But it is also hard to find specific changes in globalism and free trade that map well against the time trends describing the decline of the nuclear family.

In the United States, the theory that government policies themselves caused the decline of the family seems only at first glance to fit the time trends better. First, no-fault divorce law swept the states in the 1970s largely as a result of professional legal associations working behind the scenes on reform committees in each state. Their efforts, directed at cleaning up what many of them considered a disgrace to the legal profession, were resolutely kept out of the political arena.[8] This state-based institutional change facilitated—but was itself caused by—the larger social and cultural change of increased divorces. Second, federal and state support for single mothers became more generous between 1964 and 1974. Yet these policies affected only a small percentage of the population. They also grew steadily less generous after 1980 without reversing the trend that began in the 1960s.

The most probable single cause of the growing number of children living with one-parent families is that societal norms regarding premarital sex, illegitimacy, and divorce have changed fairly dramatically over time, for a mix of social and cultural reasons. The percentage of the U.S. population believing that premarital sex is "always wrong" or "almost always wrong" declined from 47 percent in 1972 to 37 percent in 1982; it declined more slowly thereafter, to 35 percent in 1995. The growing ease of contraception, beginning with the availability of birth-control pills, lowered the physical sanctions for out-of-wedlock sexual relations, and undoubtedly had an effect on gradually lowering the social sanctions as well. Young people's demands for "sexual liberation" along with other forms of liberation marked what critics would later condemn as the excessive permissiveness of the 1960s. Across classes, a growing tolerance of premarital intercourse—and later, of children born out of wedlock—followed fairly directly from the new rejection of traditional norms.

Lest the past appear too golden an age, Table 5-2 reveals that in the United States the percentage of children living with their natural mother and father at age sixteen was even higher between 1961 and 1970 than it had been forty years earlier. Increases in divorce had not quite made up for decreases in mortality. The big changes came in the period from 1970 to 1990.

As another caveat to the golden age theory, Table 5-3 indicates that from 1921 to 1990 the number of a child's siblings has steadily declined. High numbers of siblings are associated with low scores on standardized tests, low grades in school, low participation in higher education, and low income after graduation.[9] The causes of this rela-

Table 5-2. Living Arrangements of U.S. Sixteen-Year-Olds by Decade: General Social Survey

	Year Respondent Was 16		
Living Arrangements	1921–30	1961–70	1981–90
Households Included			
Natural mother and father	74.5	77.8	67.6
Mother and stepfather	2.9	4.6	7.0
Mother only	8.6	10.3	15.2
Father and stepmother	3.0	1.3	2.9
Father only	3.7	1.6	2.8
Other relatives only	5.1	1.2	1.4
Total	100.0	100.0	100.0
Overall Percentage Who Lived With			
Natural mother	86.0	92.7	89.8
Natural father	81.2	80.7	73.3
Neither natural parent[1]	7.4	4.3	4.4
Number of cases[2]	2693	6583	1217

[1] Includes residents of institutions.

[2] Unweighted N. When computing percentages, respondents are weighted by the number of adults in their household so as to compensate for the fact that the General Social Survey includes only one respondent per household.

Source: General Social Survey, Cumulative File, 1972–93. Tabulations by David Rhodes. Estimates are based on retrospective reports by random samples of English-speaking respondents age eighteen and over. The estimates are not precisely representative of Americans who are sixteen-year-olds in the relevant decade because they include English-speaking immigrants who were not living in the United States when they were sixteen and because they omit individuals who have died. The bias introduced by differential mortality is likely to be largest for those who turned sixteen between 1921 and 1930, who are typically seventy-four when interviewed.

tionship are complex, but they may be affected both by income per household member and the amount of time the parents can spend with each child.

Nevertheless, from the perspective of children from the lowest income brackets, the financial and, to some degree, the psychological results of trends in the United States toward divorce and nonmarriage from 1950 to the present have been a disaster. For a complex mix of social and cultural reasons, mothers and fathers who are themselves poor are now less likely to be living together and so less able, other things equal, to support their children in a way that will help those children escape from poverty as they grow older.[10] In England, France, and Sweden, rates of out-of-wedlock births are now as high as or higher than in the United States, but higher governmental safety nets in the European countries have dramatically reduced the problem of child poverty.

Like crime, the increasing problem of children in poverty had so-

Table 5-3. Number of Siblings Ever Born by Decade They Reached Sixteen: General Social Survey

Number of Siblings	Decade in Which Respondent Reached 16			
	1921–30	1941–50	1961–70	1981–90
One or more	95.4	92.8	95.2	95.7
Two or more	85.4	77.4	78.9	73.5
Four or more	62.0	48.1	41.5	31.1
Six or more	42.0	29.2	21.0	14.7
Median[1]	5.8	3.9	3.5	2.9
Number of cases[2]	2694	3865	6588	1218

[1] A median of 5.8 indicates that the smaller half of the distribution included all respondents reporting fewer than five siblings and 80 percent of those reporting exactly five siblings.
[2] Unweighted N. When computing percentages, respondents were weighted by the number of adults in their household so as to compensate for the fact that the General Social Survey interviews only one respondent per household.
Source: General Social Survey, Cumulative File, 1972–93. See table 5.3.

ciocultural causes but was seen to require governmental action. Neither trend responded to governmental efforts to affect the causes, whether under Republican administrations or Democratic ones. Both problems led to asking more of government than it could do, given a national political commitment to a limited welfare state. Both problems also produced deep social cleavages regarding the right response to these problems. No radical solution—such as abolishing divorce or providing generous guaranteed child support—would be politically possible under these circumstances. Any politically realistic governmental attempt to address the problems was therefore unlikely to affect their underlying causes. And any governmental attempt to address either their causes or their effects was bound to alienate large numbers of citizens, whose diagnosis of the problem produced the opposite solution.

Rising Expectations

After the Great Depression, expectations of what government should do gradually changed in all industrialized nations. In the United States, people realized, often for the first time, that their difficulties getting jobs were structural and not their own fault. Moreover, it slowly turned out that government could do something about those difficulties. Keynesian monetary policy made national governments far more the protectors of their nations' economies than they had been even in the mercantile era and the era of the great transcontinental railroads. As a result, the citizenry at present expects its government to produce a continually growing economy without recessions—a feat no economist knows fully how to achieve. The American people's satisfaction with government, as reported on surveys, is fairly closely related to how well they think the national economy is going. This relation is far stronger than with how well individuals think their own economic lives are faring.[11]

Increased expectations regarding health care are straining the financial capacity of all of the older democracies.[12] The increasing costs of providing for health and the growing aging population dramatically restrict governmental opportunities for any innovation that has a monetary price tag.[13] People in every industrial country seem to experience rising expectations and dissatisfaction regarding health care regardless of whether a country is spending 8 percent of gross domestic product on health care (as in much of Europe) or 13 percent (as in the United States), and whether 100 percent of the country is insured (as in much of Europe) or much less (as in the United States). Satisfaction thus seems to derive not directly from performance but from the ratio of performance to expectations. And expectations are rising.

Ronald Inglehart in Chapter 9 hypothesizes that these rising expectations derive directly from economic development. As concerns for existential security were gradually met throughout postwar Europe and the United States, the citizens of those countries began to ask more of their lives than material comfort and more of their governments than material security. As people became more and more sure that they and their children would not starve to death or even go hungry for want of sustenance, they demanded more of their physical and social surroundings. Once citizens became assured that they would have either jobs or unemployment insurance, for example, they became increasingly concerned about the environment.

Robert Samuelson attributes rising expectations in the United States not to the end of the cold war but to the extraordinary period of prosperity that Americans experienced after World War II.[14] The postwar decades, he writes, created an inflated sense of what Americans could expect. The benefits of those decades were in no way the norm in American history. Yet for one long generation, prosperity and benefits reached astronomical heights, creating a false belief that things would only continue to improve. A "politics of overpromise" accentuated these unrealistic expectations, as federal and state governments became committed to ensuring equality, ending racism and sexism, and protecting a vastly expanded set of rights.

Many communitarian scholars, among them Mary Ann Glendon and Michael Sandel, see in the United States a growing concern for personal and individual liberty at the expense of concern for community, and a growing concern for rights in contrast to responsibilities.[15] As individuals focus on their own right to be left alone, they slough off the responsibilities they owe other members of their community, thus requiring government to take up the slack. The middle and professional classes in the United States may even be experiencing a declining need for community in the traditional geographic sense, as these groups form non–place-linked professional and cultural ties across different geographical areas in large cities and across the nation, and as pensions and the national government increasingly provide security in old age. A widespread decreased responsibility for family and community, if this could be documented, would create both new problems (for example, of declining child support) and new expectations of government.

A related version of the argument from lowered individual and family responsibility traces the cause of that lowered responsibility to government provisions for Social Security, health, unemployment, and aid to dependent children. In this hypothesis, the government policies themselves have created dependence on government, and that dependence has produced a decline in personal responsibility, which in turn reinforces the dependence on government, with growing expectations of governmental performance. This hypothesis is weakened by the seemingly greater responsibility in many areas among European families, who have had greater government protection in these areas than families in the United States. The thesis might be saved if one assumed different cultures in the United States and Europe and argued for a particularly negative effect of such government programs in the culture of the United States.[16]

Along the same lines, a growing "culture of rights" in the United States and, to a lesser degree, in Europe could also be directly, rather than indirectly, responsible for rising expectations of government. As each experienced good hardens into a right or an entitlement, citizens' expectations are ratcheted up in ways that make a return to lower norms difficult. The rights of the elderly to an old age free of poverty (and among the middle class replete with comfort), for example, are now nearly sacrosanct in both the United States and Europe. The right to adequate health care plays the same role in Europe and among those employed in jobs with full health benefits in the United States, with the meaning of "adequate" growing exponentially with new discoveries in medicine.

New rights also build on old, as women, say, claim the same level of scrutiny for claims of discrimination by gender as the U.S. Constitution provides for claims of discrimination by race. Just as the African National Congress of South Africa found itself committed by its ideology to proclaiming equal rights for women once it had proclaimed equal rights for Blacks, so, too, throughout the world the effect of seeing justice done in one area creates demands that justice be done in others.

Fred Schauer makes the point that when a new right is established, some people often have to "pay" in some way for others to enjoy that right. Typically the number of people paying the price is greater than the number of people enjoying the benefit. Recognizing a right thus often decreases aggregate utility, even when it is the right thing to do on nonutilitarian grounds. As a consequence, "people having a decreasing level of satisfaction with their level of utility may not be the surprising and unfortunate failing of a government or a society that is doing the wrong thing, but may instead be the unsurprising and inevitable consequence of a society that engages in the morally worthy enterprise of paying in the currency of its own aggregate welfare (and, therefore, satisfaction) for the rights of individuals who are often in the minority."[17] The current debate about rights often ignores or trivializes the cost of rights, assuming that the rights violator is detracting from the general welfare.

Another theory, sometimes connected with the rights debate and sometimes not, postulates a rising tide of individualism throughout the United States and Europe, promoted by the success of capitalism in the post-Communist era. If individualism is rising, that tide could well lead individual citizens no longer to moderate their demands on the government for the sake of the good of others. It could, in theory, also lead individuals to demand less of their governments, but this turn has not been as visible.

Because we have little evidence at this point on the social and cultural causes of rising expectations, it is not easy to determine what weight to give each of these various hypotheses in explaining the phenomenon. It seems fairly clear, however, that public expectations from government have risen, for social and cultural as well as for more structural economic and political reasons, and that these rising expectations have made it harder for governments to perform to their citizens' satisfaction.

Declining Nongovernmental Resources

Rising problems—for instance, of crime and child poverty—have often been met with declining resources outside government. In what Elinor Ostrom calls "co-production," for example, communities and families work with governmental institutions to produce desired outcomes. In controlling crime, community members report suspicious individuals to the police and show up as witnesses when required in court.[18] In helping children move out of poverty, mothers and fathers insist that the children attend school regularly, consult with teachers, and monitor their children's homework. When distrust of the police pervades a community, or when public spirit has been eroded by poverty and governmental neglect, communities fail to do their part in the co-production of crime control. When parents' resources are strained by a reduction in the number of adults who can bring in money and monitor the children's behavior, families fail to do their part in the co-production of education. Losses in community and family cohesion thus directly lower the resources of entities outside the government to handle social problems.[19]

Robert Putnam contends that losses in voluntary association membership in the United States further compound the problem.[20] Large numbers of organizations with local bases but state and national networks designed in the progressive era and highly active thereafter, have declined seriously in membership from about 1965 to the present.[21] The Elks, the Rotary Club, the League of Women Voters, the Parent-Teacher Association, and the Red Cross all were founded sometime between 1868 and 1920 and have recently gone into stunning declines. So, too, have church groups, labor unions, sports clubs, literary discussion groups, and a host of other associations. After examining several alternative hypotheses—including the entry of women into the paid labor force, greater geographical mobility and suburbanization, increased pressures of time and money, changes in marriage and family structures, the rise of the welfare state, and generational effects—Putnam suggests that although each of these may have contributed something to this phenomenon, the rising number of hours the American population has spent watching television probably figures as a major cause of voluntary association decline.

If voluntary associations are decreasing, and governments can therefore delegate fewer societal problems to those associations, government overload is bound to increase. If fewer citizens have the experience of participation in voluntary associations, they may also have less experience of learning to moderate their demands for the common good.

The steady entry of more and more women into the paid labor force from the 1930s to the present, combined with their increasing entry into full-time rather than part-time work, must have had some effect on the nongovernmental resources available for solving social problems. It is not easy, however, to pinpoint these effects. As Putnam points out, employed women are more likely to join voluntary associations than are homemakers.[22] Yet the intensity and breadth of involvement of elite women in community associations must have fallen, thus probably reducing, if not eliminating their own participation, perhaps reducing the modeling effect they may have had on their husbands, and in the reduction of their time, diminishing the capacity of organizations like the PTA to provide the basis for cross-class alliances and interactions.[23]

Yet Putnam's data on associational decline have been challenged from several directions. Everett Ladd has produced several surveys that show a large increase in social service activities over the past twenty years, an increase in per capita charitable giving, and no decrease either in church attendance or in the number of volunteers as a percentage of the population. Ladd argues that PTA membership decline reflects no more than changes in the size of the school-age population, and that parental involvement is "very high and if anything increasing."[24] Surveys cited by Sidney Verba, Kay Schlozman, and Henry Brady show slight increases between 1967 and 1987 in the percentage of people reporting working "with others on a local problem," active "membership in a community problem-solving organization," and having formed a "group to help solve local problems." They also show a higher percentage of citizens contacting local, state, and national officials on issue-based, rather than personal, problems.[25]

Nevertheless, everyone agrees on the decline in voting turnout in the United States from 1960 to the present. Although that decline has not reached the historical low of 49 percent in 1920 and 1924, it is significant.[26] Theda Skocpol blames the decline in turnout on the replacement of locally rooted political parties by television advertising, polling, political consultants, nationally based lobbying groups, computerized modes of data analysis, and direct-mail targeting.[27] Steven Rosenstone and John Mark Hansen blame it on both weakened social involvement and the declining age of the electorate, but primarily on declines in mobilization.[28] Parties are forgoing personal contact with voters, and the 65 percent decline in unionization since 1954 has critically reduced the resources for mobilizing lower-middle-income and working-class voters.[29] The question is whether this decline is causally related to the decline in trust in government. As for Putnam's television hypothesis, it does seem that the more time citizens watch television, the less likely they are to engage in every type of political participation, including voting. (They also know less about politics, feel less able to affect government, and are less interested in politics.) Citizens who watch the network *news* are more likely to participate politically, probably because their interest in politics leads them to both watch and participate. The causal direction of these connections is not clear.[30]

Inglehart in Chapter 9 points out that "elite-directed" participation—such as voting in elections and party loyalty—is falling in most European countries, but "autonomous and active" forms of political participation—such as discussing politics and signing a petition—are increasing. Inglehart's European findings are consistent with Verba, Schlozman, and Brady's data on increased contacting in the United States. These active forms of political participation could produce more nongovernmental resources for solving problems, but if they are directed primarily at increasing demands on government, they may contribute indirectly to distrust.

By increasing international competition, globalization may also have decreased the private sector's resources for solving social problems. Although international trade accounts for only 25 percent of the U.S. gross national product, the effects of globalization may have been much greater through anticipated reactions. If large firms no longer perceive themselves as having a safe, mildly oligopolistic market position, they will be less likely to engage in the production of public goods, such as job training and community service. Nor will they be willing to engage in experiments such as on-site child care that could help solve some problems caused by the decline of the single-bread-winner family. Child-care and other "family-friendly" programs cost money. If the expenditures cannot be reimbursed through sufficiently lowered absenteeism and turnover, businesses will have no monetary reason to engage in them. Exhorting businesses to practice "enlightened self-interest" or "corporate responsibility" will be futile if those businesses have no way of preventing competitors from free-riding on their provision of public goods. If some firms provide job training, for example, they can be undersold by competitors who save by not providing such training, lure away the trained labor from the socially conscious firms, and charge less for a comparable product. Slightly protected markets facilitate corporate responsibility. Highly competitive markets erode it. If extreme competition becomes widespread, it will produce a corporate culture indifferent to social problems.

Perceptions

Social and cultural changes leading to government overload provide, as we have seen, indirect explanations for declines in government performance in all or most of the advanced industrial democracies. Other social and cultural changes have undoubtedly led, directly and independently, to increased negative perceptions of government, holding government performance constant. These changes include a decline from the postwar moment of self-congratulation and expanding economy, the recent end of the cold war (creating among elites "an ever more foggy sense of the national interest"[31] and greater willingness to engage in paralyzing partisanship once they were deprived of an external enemy who would make governmental paralysis look like treason), a widespread decrease in deference to authority with a concomitant upswing in cynicism, a decrease in interpersonal trust, a decrease in optimism, increasing negative coverage of governments in the media, greater publicity regarding corruption, and the major social fissures that began in the 1960s. These factors all seem to have contributed to negative perceptions of government in ways that would probably have produced declines in trust in government even if the ratio of government performance to expectations had not itself become less favorable.

Ronald Inglehart argues in Chapter 9 that economic development promotes "existential security." We have seen how this might have increased other demands on government. Inglehart contends that it also reduces the tendency for mass publics to defer to authority, creating increased skepticism toward authority, criticism of political leaders, and citizen action aimed at discrediting one or more branches of government. Gary Orren in Chapter 3 documents declines in the trust that citizens of some of the older democracies feel for one another. Eric Uslaner shows that in the United States most of this decline in interpersonal trust can be explained by declines in optimism.[32] Tom Patterson documents the increasing negative coverage of governments and elections by the media in both the United States and Europe.[33] Some trends in reporting, such as the greater coverage of sex scandals, have greatly undermined the "dignified" aspect of government. At the same time, the information revolution, which allows citizens of every country to demand the best of what others offer without the concomitant costs, may well have produced greater perceptions of government failure.

In Great Britain, the "Americanization" (or politicization) of the civil service has led to a shift in institutional norms from one of public service to one of serving the policy and ideological demands of the party in power. This social and cultural change undoubtedly contributes in part to public distrust of government.

In the United States, the growth of entitlement programs that are not conceived as a return for services to the commonweal, that did not arise from a politics bridging class, and that do not work in partnership with voluntary associations may well have produced a mixture of disillusionment and anger with the federal government.[34]

Also in the United States, a growing public perception that "quite a few of the people running government are a little crooked" (Figure

3-2 in Chapter 3) coexists with a perception among responsible Washington insiders from both political parties that the actual levels of direct corruption, in the sense of bribe-taking, have considerably diminished, or at worst remained constant, over this period.[35] Incoming administrations and congresses have slowly raised ethical standards and instituted mechanisms for policing those raised standards. As a consequence, more violations are publicized. A content analysis of the media would probably reveal more coverage of scandal in Washington in the 1990s than in the 1950s and 1960s. But this is probably the result of more demanding social and cultural norms, not more nefarious behavior.

The most important direct sociocultural causes of distrust in the United States, however, probably result from the major social and cultural rifts the nation has experienced since 1960. Joseph Kalt argues that successful governments have a good match between their institutions and the shared norms of the citizenry regarding the structure, scope, location, and source of government.[36] It follows that if a population begins to develop heterogeneous and conflicting norms about what their governing institutions can and should do, those institutions will experience less solid support.

As the welfare state has grown to try to meet the rising expectations of the postwar generation, and as Keynesian economics has ceased to command the deference of both right and left in Europe, deep rifts have appeared among the citizens and ruling elites of the United States and Great Britain regarding the proper role of government in the economy and social welfare provision. In Great Britain and to a lesser degree elsewhere, the postwar consensus on the welfare state has fallen apart, producing increased uncertainty over goals and more bitter partisanship.[37]

The "culture wars" have probably riven society most dramatically in the United States. Ethnicity, race, postcolonial status, gender, sexual preference, and attitudes toward the family, abortion, drugs, immigration, and war have all split European and U.S. populations on issues that are less susceptible to political compromise than earlier issues, which had more monetary bottom lines. Declines in shared norms on these social issues have produced either governmental deadlock or policies that angered a major fraction of the population.

In the United States, race has probably played an important role in creating or exacerbating distrust in government. African Americans, who had little reason to trust a White-controlled government in the first place, have not had their distrust assuaged by government actions in the civil rights era and thereafter. Middle-class African Americans, who arguably gained the most from these policies, are among the most alienated.[38] Many Whites, on the other hand, have felt that policies such as affirmative action have gone too far. President Nixon's "southern strategy," designed to tap southern conservatism and anger over federal actions on behalf of African Americans, succeeded in both reducing the strength of the Democratic party and increasing Black–White tensions in the country. In the cities, the effects of school busing turned many White working-class citizens against the federal government. Federal laws against discrimination in employment convinced some White citizens that their jobs were being taken away to help Blacks.

At the same time, many in the "silent majority" saw liberal governments in Washington backing proposals like the Equal Rights Amendment for women, which they believed furthered the social disintegration that had begun in the permissive era of the 1960s. The increasing social acceptance and visibility of gay men and lesbians, continuing difficulties in controlling adolescents' use of drugs, and the growing acceptance of premarital sex and illegitimacy all fostered a sense among conservatives that the country was spiraling out of control.

The surge in trust in government during the administration of President Reagan probably resulted in part from his implied reassurance that these movements would be slowed or brought to an end. It also probably resulted in part from his continued stress on shared values within the nation. Finally, it may have resulted in part from a public perception of reduced "bickering" in Congress, for as the Democrats were about to try to block a series of Reagan initiatives, the attempted assassination of the president made those moves untenable. Reagan himself reduced the perception of bickering by rarely vetoing legislation explicitly, preferring a "pocket veto."

If these social rifts are at the base of much of the distrust of government, it is not likely that trust will replace distrust in the near future. Immigration, multiculturalism, and the continuing politics of race are likely to continue to divide the nation in the near future.

Hard Decisions

With the growth of entitlements, including the burgeoning costs of health care and old-age pensions, democratic governments of the future will have fewer and fewer resources to meet the greater and greater expectations of their citizens. The days of hard decisions are upon us.

When there is no "win-win" solution, and someone's ox must be gored, minimal trust in those who must make the decision results in the losers refusing to believe that the decision was fair. That refusal in turn produces both a politics suffused with bitterness and, in time, greatly reduced compliance with the law.[39] A society with characteristically low compliance with the law cannot succeed in competition with more spontaneously cooperative societies, because it will have to spend more of its collective resources on monitoring and sanctions.

To reverse the trend of distrust in U.S. government that we witness, we must (1) understand better the sources of this growing disaffection from government in so many of the older democracies, (2) establish reliable measures of government performance and believable measures of government corruption, and (3) create institutions that encourage citizens to look at problems from more than one perspective and that engage them in the weighing that hard decisions require.

This chapter will have succeeded if it has dispelled any lingering certitude about this problem. There is considerable work still to do, using cross-national comparisons and investigating the few variations among subgroups and changes in the trend in the early 1980s and in 1996. It has, however, sought to organize the issues and clarify the problems. It has suggested, as a hypothesis, that most of the explanation for declining levels of trust in U.S. government derives indirectly from increased government "overload," caused in part by new sociocultural problems, rising expectations, and declining willingness to pay for partial solutions to these problems. Another part of the explanation surely derives directly from a combination of social and cultural causes: a decline from a post–World War II high, mounting cynicism about authority, increasing negativism in the media, and growing normative divisions within the country. When a leading figure such as President Reagan can momentarily rekindle the postwar high, dampen the cynicism about authority, master the media, and soothe or paper over the country's divisions, trust in government will increase, but only to diminish again after that momentary effect.

A decline in voluntary association membership ("social capital") is probably not a major cause of declining trust in government, because so many measures do not indicate declines in voluntary association. Nor is it likely that declines in the nuclear family have affected distrust, except to some degree indirectly, by creating one more unsolvable problem for government to grapple with, and one more issue over which the public can deeply disagree.

Although we cannot yet be certain of the causes of the decline in trust, we should be concerned about that decline. Liberals and conservatives alike should worry that declining trust will undermine both patriotism and government efforts to help the most vulnerable. Declining trust will erode the citizenry's willingness both to pay taxes and to fight for the nation's security. Expanding demands on democratic governments and declining trust in those governments will inevitably place on governmental systems pressures that were unforeseen by the framers of any existing constitution. When a major economic crisis next emerges, as history suggests it will, the governments of the major democracies will be far better off if they have found ways to become sufficiently resilient, competent, and just to respond in ways that the public will trust. They will also be better off if they have found ways to engage their citizens in the hard governmental choices that ideally citizens as well as their representatives should make for themselves.

CHAPTER Six

The Polarization
of American Parties and
Mistrust of Government

David C. King

By most appearances in the early 1990s, the United States seemed in the midst of a conservative shift. On the national stage, liberalism was an opprobrium, the dreaded "L" word. Bill Clinton prevailed in the 1992 presidential campaign while running to the middle and claiming to have abandoned "old-style liberal solutions." When his first two years in office betrayed that promise, the president's popularity plummeted. Republicans seized both houses of Congress in the 1994 elections—for the first time in forty years—and made great gains in governors' offices and state legislatures as well. These victories were widely interpreted as further repudiations of traditional liberal policies. With Republicans picking up more congressional seats than any election since 1942, a modern record number of Democratic legislators announced they would not run again. Republicans say they heard the country giving them a conservative mandate. Yet in the mid-1990s, the most conservative plans were repeatedly dashed as a fickle public turned against Republican party leaders. By the summer of 1996, House Speaker Newt Gingrich's political fortunes could hardly have been worse, and President Clinton's reelection was assured.

One lesson that Democratic and Republican party leaders claim to have learned in the mid-1990s is that there are great political rewards for being "centrists." While extremists may be praised within wings of their own parties, they do less well in general elections and find it more difficult to build bipartisan coalitions in Congress and the White House. Following acrimony in the 104th Congress (1995–97), President Clinton predictably called for a new era of bipartisanship. "Today," said the president in December 1996, "the clamor of political conflict has subsided. A new landscape is taking shape. The answer is clear: the center can hold, the center has held and the American people are demanding that it continue to do so."[1] Republican leaders on Capitol Hill quickly agreed. Anthony Downs, the progenitor of median voter theories in economics and political science, could not have scripted a finer exchange.[2]

In theory, at least, a move to the center—the "sensible center," to use Richard Darman's phrase—makes perfect sense.[3] That is where the votes are, and that is where compromises are forged. In practice, however, both political parties have been growing more extreme over the past three decades, and it is unlikely that postelection promises of bipartisanship will quickly reverse historic trends. Furthermore, the public's mistrust of government is unlikely to be reversed unless and until politicians and their parties stage a concerted return to the sensible center. The politics of polarization *is* the politics of mistrust.

This chapter's thesis is that the American electorate has been relatively stable in its policy and ideological preferences, while the political parties have become more extreme. Americans have not been shifting their basic preferences wildly. Rather, political elites have grown more ideologically distant—widening the gap between citizens and government. That growing gap, which I document in this chapter, has been filled in with mistrust and with a newfound habit of splitting tickets between the increasingly polarized parties.

My argument is built around a series of questions. First, however, I will assert—and later demonstrate—that both parties have grown more extreme since the early 1960s and the breakdown of the New Deal Democratic coalition. Before exploring that evidence in detail, I ask and answer two questions: Have Americans become appreciably more liberal or conservative? Have Americans appreciably changed their partisan allegiances? The answers will prove instructive in deciphering an important cause of growing mistrust toward government:

namely, that the parties have been polarizing, making the preferences of parties and political elites more distant from the concerns of most Americans.

Trends in Political Ideology since the 1960s

A person's political ideology is a shorthand way of categorizing what one knows about politics, and it is used for speedily assessing new political observations. People with highly refined ideological antennae have an especially well-structured way of thinking about politics, and these ideologues judge political propositions based on how liberal or conservative they seem. Although most Americans are not highly ideological, most have preferences one way or the other. As noted, by the early 1990s, the United States seemed in the midst of a conservative shift, only to reject the most conservative proposals in Congress by the mid-1990s.

Evidence from public opinion polls consistently shows that the country's basic balance between liberals and conservatives changes only gradually, not all at once. The National Election Studies, conducted every two years by the University of Michigan's Institute for Social Research, is our best snapshot of political attitudes.[4] The 1970s began with a politically moderate president in Richard Nixon. President Jimmy Carter was considered more centrist than most nationally known Democrats, and he gave way to a Barry Goldwater conservative in President Ronald Reagan. Given these hints about the national mood, one would expect that Americans' underlying ideologies were shifting to the right. Evidence on this is shown in Table 6-1, which tracks voters' self-placements along the left–right dimension.

At least in terms of what Americans call themselves, the nation became gradually more conservative throughout the 1970s and 1980s, but without any wild swings one way or the other. "Extreme" conservatives and "extreme" liberals have fluctuated between 1 percent and 3 percent of the population over the last quarter-century. The combined percentage of self-identified conservatives and extreme conservatives stood at 11 in 1972 and 16 in 1992. Self-identified conservatives peaked in 1994, which may indeed indicate a lasting change, but it is too early to say. Notice, however, that in virtually every year the modal

Table 6-1. Liberal-Conservative Self-Identification, 1972–94

Percent	1972	1974	1976	1978	1980	1982	1984	1986	1988	1990	1992	1994
Extremely Liberal	1	2	1	2	2	1	2	1	2	1	2	1
Liberal	7	11	7	8	6	6	7	6	6	7	8	6
Slightly Liberal	10	8	8	10	9	8	9	11	9	8	10	7
Middle of the Road	27	26	25	27	20	22	23	28	22	24	23	27
Slightly Conservative	15	12	12	14	13	13	14	15	15	14	15	15
Conservative	10	12	11	11	13	12	13	13	14	10	13	18
Extremely Conservative	1	2	2	2	2	2	2	2	3	2	3	3
Don't Know"/"Haven't Thought about This"	28	27	33	27	36	36	30	25	30	33	27	22

Source: American National Election Studies, 1972–94.

response was "don't know" or "haven't thought much about this." A plurality of Americans cannot identify themselves along an ideological spectrum, and we should suspect that these voters may grow more restive if and when the political parties portray their positions in highly ideological terms.[5]

The American trend toward a slightly more conservative electorate is similar to what one finds in Western Europe over the same period.[6] Political scientists, however, would warn us against reading too much into Table 6-1. While three-quarters of Americans can place themselves along the ideological spectrum, an overwhelming majority of voters are not true ideologues in that their political ideologies do not highly constrain or structure the ways they behave.[7] On the high end of estimates by political scientists, no more than one-fourth of Americans show consistent signs of ideological thinking. Furthermore, half of the jump in self-identified 1994 conservatives came from the "don't know"/"haven't thought much about this" category. For many Americans, calling themselves liberals or conservatives is a momentary fashion statement without much depth. Today the "L" word and leisure suits are equally out of style.

Instead of depending on self-identification, we might find additional evidence of preference changes by looking at public opinion on policies that can be termed generally liberal or conservative. We briefly explore six such issues:[8] (1) support for the proposition that there should be a government-guaranteed standard of living;

(2) feelings that the federal government is too powerful; (3) support for cutting government spending; (4) opposition to government-directed health insurance programs; (5) opposition to abortion; and (6) opposition to federally mandated affirmative action programs.

An increasingly conservative nation is likely to be ever more supportive of laissez-faire economic policies. The National Election Studies respondents have been asked the following question since 1972: "Some people feel that the government in Washington should see to it that every person has a job and a good standard of living. Others think the government should just let each person get ahead on his/their own. Where would you place yourself on this scale, or haven't you thought much about this?"[9] In 1972, 40 percent of the respondents gave conservative responses, saying that folks should get ahead on their own without any government guarantees. The percentage varied slightly over the next two decades before peaking at 44 percent in 1994, up just four points in twenty-two years. Despite extensive debate over the nature and scope of welfare policies, the country's fundamental orientation on the role of government in guaranteeing a standard of living has hardly changed at all. Of course there is bound to be fuzziness in how people have interpreted this NES question over the years, but the lack of erosion is noteworthy. (See Figure 6-1 for a summary of the survey results.)[10]

Likewise, the percentage of Americans who say that the "government is getting too powerful" has changed very little since the mid-1960s, when Great Society programs were conceived.[11] In 1966, 39 percent of Americans thought the federal government too powerful, and after fluctuating modestly throughout the 1970s, the number was 40 percent in 1994.[12] Forty percent may seem high, but it is not the modal response in most years. Rather, a plurality of Americans profess no opinion on the subject, which is hardly what one expects if there is a widespread revolt brewing against basic governmental powers. Not surprisingly, in every year since 1968, more Americans have considered the federal government too strong than considered it too weak, but I interpret this as a robust sign of a Lockean nation.

Even if Americans have not changed their ideas about the appropriate scope of government, we might expect taxpayers to want to see government services and spending cut. Since 1982, the NES has asked whether the government should provide fewer services, even

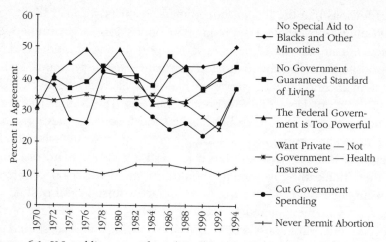

Figure 6-1. *U.S. public support for politically conservative propositions*

Source: American National Election Studies, 1970–94. See text endnote for variable numbers and question wording.

in areas such as health and education, in order to reduce spending. The responses have been virtually identical every two years since, with about 20 percent strongly favoring cuts, 15 percent strongly opposing cuts, and the rest somewhere in between. Americans simultaneously demand lower taxes and higher spending, which leaves government officials having to balance the people's desires for public goods and for private consumption.[13] Spending cuts sound good as long as one's own cherished programs are preserved, and this has contributed to stable support for government spending throughout the last twenty-five years.

Perhaps these first three questions were too general—too philosophical—to capture a conservative shift in public opinion. The early Clinton administration focused on national health insurance, so we will as well. Since 1970, the NES has asked about the desirability of a national health plan.[14] Here, too, public opinion appears to have been stable, with about 33 percent of Americans consistently preferring private to government insurance plans. The number reached 37 percent in 1994, just as President Clinton's health proposal was being debated. So while there have been some fluctuations in opinion about national health insurance over the past twenty-five years, there has been no general conservative trend here either. At least that is what the poll results seem to show, but it is likely that these numbers understate conservative trends. When people were asked about national health care in early 1970s, they likely had a big government solution in mind, possibly patterned on the British model. By the early 1990s, the whole debate had shifted to the right, and national health insurance was more likely to mean "managed competition" among "health maintenance organizations," two concepts not widely discussed twenty years earlier. This is a classic problem with public opinion data, because underlying frames of reference may change over time.

Abortion, however, is an altogether different type of issue. An abortion in the mid-1990s is fundamentally the same procedure that it was in the mid-1970s. The politics of abortion, however, has changed dramatically. Partisan cleavages on abortion cut across various factions of both parties in the mid-1970s, but today the cleavages reinforce party lines. The NES has asked about abortion since 1972. Consistently, a little more than 10 percent of Americans have held that "abortion should never be permitted."[15] Among the public, that figure has barely budged, even as both political parties have become more extreme in their platforms and their rhetoric. At least with respect to this highly visible measure of moral conservatism, the country's basic preferences have changed very little.

In one area, government aid to blacks and minorities, the country has indeed become more conservative since the mid-1980s. Half of the NES respondents now agree that "the government should not make any special effort to help blacks because they should help themselves." That percentage is up from one-third of the population in 1984.[16] In the current environment, anti–affirmative action proposals such as California's Proposition 209 of 1996 have wide support, whereas only a decade ago such proposals would have been scarcely imaginable.

In summary, the evidence from various conceptions of political ideology shows a gradual, slight, and recent trend toward conservatism. If we look at how Americans describe themselves, we can say that the country has been growing more conservative, with the greatest change coming between 1992 and 1994. We saw no evidence of rapid swings in the self-identification of voters between the political extremes, and it could be that these labels are—for many people—just fashion statements with little real meaning. Moreover, when we examined public opinion on six conservative issues, we found no marked trend, except for a recent appetite for cutting spending and rolling back affirmative action programs. Americans are becoming more conservative, gradually, but on core issues—such as the role and powers of the federal government—they are about as conservative today as they were twenty-five years ago.

Changes in Party Allegiances since the 1960s

The United States is more Republican today than it has been at any other time in my (and, if you were born after 1930, your) lifetime. This is unquestionably true when we look at the percentage of all elected offices (local, state, and federal) held by Republicans. And while Democrats are still a majority among party loyalists in the electorate, Republicans have made substantial gains since the mid-1980s. Witness Table 6-2. From 1952 through 1982, the Democratic party advantage was about 22 percent. Since then, the average has been closer to 10 percent. Moreover, the Republican party's gains have been noticeable among younger voters, particularly suburban whites socialized during the Reagan years. This may have a lasting impact on the balance of loyalties between the parties, because party preferences are established early and change slowly.[17]

Notice three things about the trends in partisan identification. First, Republican gains came at the expense of Democratic losses, not simply from any sizable decrease in the percentage of independents.[18] Second, the percentage of independents has been fairly stable for thirty years. It is true that Americans proclaim weaker partisan loyalties today than they did in the early 1960s, but most still say they favor one party over the other. Third, Republican gains were most noticeable in the early 1980s, when Ronald Reagan was the party's figurehead and father figure.

Depending on whom one listens to, the parties are either in grave danger or surprisingly healthy. The answer largely depends on which definition of "party" one uses, and political scientists, following V. O. Key Jr., distinguish among three senses of the word: partisan attachments in the *electorate,* parties as political *organizations,* and parties

Table 6-2. Party Identification, 1952–1994

Percent	1952	1954	1956	1958	1960	1962	1964	1966	1968	1970	1972	1974	1976	1978	1980	1982	1984	1986	1988	1990	1992	1994
Democrat (Including Leaners)	57	56	50	56	52	54	61	55	55	54	52	52	52	54	52	55	48	51	47	52	50	47
Independent	6	7	9	7	10	8	8	12	11	13	13	15	15	14	13	11	11	12	11	10	12	10
Republican (Including Leaners)	34	33	37	33	36	35	30	32	33	32	34	31	33	30	33	32	39	36	41	36	38	42
%Democrats Minus % Republicans	23	23	13	23	16	19	31	23	22	22	18	21	19	24	19	23	9	15	6	16	12	5

Source: American National Election Studies, 1952–94. Percentages do not sum to 100 because "apolitical" and "don't know" responses are excluded.

in *government*.[19] The prevailing wisdom is that parties are in some trouble among the electorate, especially so with the rise in split-ticket voting and a gradual decline in the number of self-identified "strong partisans." Meanwhile, parties as organizations are doing well both on the national level (with infusions of special-interest money) and on the state and local levels (with Republican clubs gaining a foothold in the once solidly Democratic South). As for parties in government, the evidence is mixed. Party influence and discipline are not particularly strong in executive branch bureaucracies, and parties are generally absent from the judicial branch. In American legislatures, however, partisanship is alive, well, and getting stronger.[20] Parties in the government may play an important role in solving our puzzle of voter volatility, but we should save that discussion of legislative partisanship until after we review what has happened to party loyalists among voters.

Partisanship is usually measured on a seven-point scale, with strong partisans at the extremes and pure independents in the middle category. Independent-leaning partisans are "almost" independent, or at least they claim they are, but they tend to align fairly closely with one of the parties. On average from 1952 to 1960, 36 percent of Americans described themselves as strong partisans. This figure declined six points, to 30 percent, for the 1984–92 average. Over the same period, the percentage of independent-leaning partisans jumped from 15 to 25, and the number of pure independents rose four points. Over the same two periods, loyalty to party labels among partisans in the voting booth declined roughly two points in presidential elections, six points in Senate elections, and nine points in House elections. Split-party outcomes in presidential and congressional elections rose from 25 percent of the congressional districts to 34 percent, and straight-ticket voting decreased about fifteen points.[21]

Although partisanship in the electorate is weakening, there remains a cadre of strong partisans, numbering near 30 percent. The preferences and motivations of strong partisans deserve special attention because *almost all of our politicians are drawn from their ranks.* The day-in and day-out drudgery of maintaining political organizations is performed almost exclusively by strong partisans. These people are also much more likely than the rest of us to belong to political interest groups, work to get a candidate elected, go to public meetings, give money to a candidate, write letters to public officials, and follow politics in the media.[22] Cross-national studies consistently find the strength of a person's partisan attachments to be the best predictor of political participation, and a recent analysis of partisanship in state governments found the same thing. Strong partisans are the "worker bees" of political parties.[23] If we want a good sense for what the parties are doing and what issues the parties are likely to pursue, we should look to the activists for clues.

Party activists are, on average, more extreme in their ideological and policy views than most voters, and for good reason. Potential activists have to become activated, and this is more likely to happen when the "other" party's positions seems especially onerous. From the perspective of a potential activist, the more extreme your own political views are, the more distasteful the opposition's alternatives appear. As choices between the parties become more compelling, it is easier for potential activists to overcome inertia. There is good empirical evidence of this effect throughout the United States and in Western Europe.[24] For example, James McCann has compared the policy and ideology preferences of four groups of American voters: mass-level partisans, partisans who attended a political caucus, caucuses attendees who also were campaign activists, and state-level party delegates. The percentages of Democrats who called themselves liberals in these four categories were 38, 50, 62, and 68, respectively. Activist Democrats are far more liberal than run-of-the-mill Democrats. Likewise, the conservatism percentages for the four categories of Republicans were 65, 80, 87, and 91, respectively.[25]

Party activists are not merely more extreme than average Americans; they are significantly less likely to compromise (they might say "betray") core beliefs. They are ideological purists, making them less likely to shift policy positions to attract the median voter. This has been documented by political scientists at every national party convention since 1956. To the extent that parties are dominated by these purists, it makes working with political opponents especially difficult.[26]

Parties as organizations are the creations of strategic political actors. I will argue later that the parties are becoming more extreme, that they are increasingly distant in their policies from what the average voter would like. If so, the change is almost certainly being driven by the preferences and activities of strong partisans. Since the mid-1970s, some of the strongest partisans have been showing up in Congress. Bills that read more like ideological litmus tests have been increasingly common—both among Democratic leadership through-out the 1970s and 1980s and now under Republican leadership in the mid-1990s.

That the parties have been getting stronger in Congress deserves close attention. Throughout the 1960s and 1970s, political scientists were commenting on the decline of partisanship in legislatures, espe-cially in the House of Representatives.[27] The House speaker's powers ebbed, and individual politicians gained more autonomy as their staff budgets increased and the committee system decentralized. Party voting on the House floor, and presumably in committees as well, dropped steadily throughout the mid-century among persistent calls for "responsible parties" to stem the tide of parochial interests and individualism. That analysis was essentially correct in its time, but the parties were never dead, and as House and Senate leaders began reasserting their powers in the mid-1970s, the parties reemerged.[28] A clear example of this is shown in Figure 6-2, which tracks the rise in "party unity" voting in Congress. A Republican legislator is now more likely to vote in agreement with a majority of the Republican Congress than at any time in the last five decades. Likewise, Democratic legis-lators are setting modern records for party unity. The trend toward stronger congressional parties as shown in Figure 6-2 is almost a mirror image of the decline in party loyalties that we found in the electorate.[29]

While party unity has been increasing in Congress, the percentage of centrist members has been decreasing in both parties. Sarah Binder, a Congress scholar at the Brookings Institution, has charted the recent disappearance of centrists. She defines "centrists" as those members whose ideology positions are closer to the midpoint between the two parties than to the median member of their own party. As we see in Figure 6-3, which is adapted from Binder's work, the percentage of centrists declined from about 25 percent of all members in 1980 to 10 percent in 1996. The evidence on congressional partisanship suggests two things: that each party is more internally cohesive when voting on the floor, and that there are fewer bipartisan coalitions today than

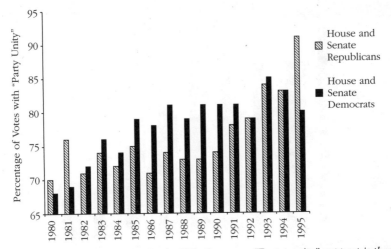

Figure 6-2. *Rising party unity in the U.S. Congress. "Party unity" support is the percentage of votes on which members voted "yea" or "nay" in agreement with a majority of their party.*

Source: Congressional Quarterly Weekly Report, January 27, 1996, 245.

just fifteen years ago. Rules and procedures are increasingly used to benefit the majority party at the expense of the minority.

George Wallace used to say that there isn't "a dime's worth of difference" between the two parties, but this is the case no longer. Today, perhaps, there may be fifteen cents worth of a difference—and the gap is growing. How did these developments in party allegiances happen, and how do these trends help us to think about the public's disaffection for government?

An important part of the answer is the demise of the New Deal coalition, which struck a grand bargain in the Democratic party between socially conservative southern whites and northern liberals. Over the first half of the century, Republicans had no significant presence in the old confederacy, and southern politicians gained national strength by joining in a partisan coalition with northern liberals.[30] Their alliance kept race off the agenda for several decades until it burst on the national scene in the early 1960s. Only then did party differences on race come into a sharp focus.[31] In addition to the white southerners and northeastern liberals, the New Deal coalition included midwestern anti-Communists, ethnic Catholics, and radical

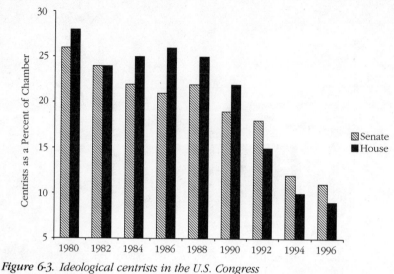

Figure 6-3. *Ideological centrists in the U.S. Congress*

Centrists are defined as members whose ideological positions (using D-Nominate and W-Nominate scores) place them closer to the ideological midpoint between the two parties than to the median member of their own party.

Source: Binder 1996.

social democrats in the Great Plains states and in the urban Northeast.[32] It was a strange-bedfellows coalition, but despite the factions, it persisted for more than thirty years. Putting the issue of race aside— and this is not an easy thing to do—umbrella coalitions are more likely to spawn centrist policies because extreme factions within the parties have to work out their differences before supporting national legislation.

The New Deal coalition is dead. For evidence we turn to Harold Stanley and Richard Neimi's compelling analysis.[33] Using NES data from 1952 to 1992 to explore the demographic characteristics of Democrats, they show a steady erosion of the New Deal coalition beginning in the early 1960s. A portion of their results is summarized in Figure 6-4. The figure reflects coefficient estimates from logistic equations predicting partisanship as a function of demographic variables. As such, each coefficient estimate controls for the effects of the other independent variables. We are left with relatively pure indicators of the impact on one's partisanship of being black, a native southern white, working-class, wealthy, and so on. The results are telling.

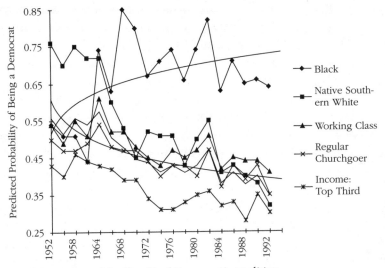

Figure 6-4. Erosion of the New Deal Democratic coalition

Entries are the means of the predicted probabilities of Democratic identification for all group members in each year, based on logistic equations, and controlling for other demographic indicators in the Stanley and Neimi model.

Source: Computed from Stanley and Neimi 1995, Table 9.1, based on the 1952–92 American National Election Studies.

In the early 1950s, native southern whites were overwhelmingly identified with the Democratic party. They were the Democrats also most likely to support conservative public policies. Contemporary with the civil rights movement (and long before Ronald Reagan's successful southern strategy), many southern whites abandoned the Democratic party. That most critical element of the "grand bargain" over race disappeared. Not even two native southern whites, Bill Clinton and Al Gore, could reverse the trend in 1992.

While the Democratic party was becoming less southern, it was also growing more secular. The mean probability of a regular church-goer self-identifying as a Democrat was about 0.50 until the late 1960s. By 1994 the probability dropped to 0.35 (again, controlling for all other voter attributes in the model). That is a 30 percent decline in the probability of regular churchgoers calling themselves Democrats. Many of today's Christian Coalition members would have been in the Democratic party thirty years ago. They would have been consulted on such issues as abortion, school prayer, and welfare reform. By the

1990s, a large portion of the Democratic party's activist base wanted nothing to do with the Christian right, and opportunities for productive policy coalitions were being lost.

The economic base of the New Deal coalition has also been transformed. In the late 1950s, Americans with family incomes in the top one-third had a 0.45 probability of being Democrats. That support eroded in the late 1960s and is about 0.30 today, for a 33 percent drop. At the same time that some relatively wealthy Americans were leaving the New Deal coalition, so was an important slice of the working class.

The old Democratic party was a big tent. Although the new Democratic party is a place that traditional liberals may find more comfortable, the tent is not so big anymore. Of course, it was not race alone that eroded the old coalition. As E. J. Dionne contends in *Why Americans Hate Politics,* the old political order "could not withstand the storms over the Vietnam War, race, feminism, and the counterculture. American politics has never fully recovered from the implosion of the Vital Center."[34] The Democratic party still has considerable ideological diversity, and William Mayer has recently shown that the party's faithful consistently reflect a broader ideological and policy range than Republicans.[35] That range, however, may well have diminished over the last three decades.

Meanwhile, the Republican party has been transformed by an infusion of southern whites and upper-class reinforcements. Adding to the party ranks were regular churchgoers and a smattering of the working classes, who are more likely than "Rockefeller Republicans" to push a conservative social agenda. Also in the 1960s, a cohort of young Republicans, many of them active in the 1964 Goldwater presidential campaign, became a strong force in the party.[36] The Republican party's base has headed south, and the party's proposals have become more conservative as a result. A generation ago, all of the Republican party leaders in Congress came from the North. Today the leadership is dominated by the likes of Trent Lott (Mississippi), Newt Gingrich (Georgia), and Dick Armey (Texas).[37]

With the demise of the New Deal coalition, the electoral bases of the two parties changed in ways that have made the parties both more ideologically cohesive and more ideologically extreme. That the parties are polarizing has been a recurring theme in recent journalistic critiques of modern elections. Political scientists, however, may instinctively suspect that polarization is an irrational strategy for the elites who are running the parties. The party locating its policy positions closest to the preferences of the median voter is supposed to get the most votes, or so we have been taught.[38] With that model in mind, it makes little sense to allow one's own party to become extreme, but that is precisely what has been happening since the decline of the New Deal coalition.

As evidence, we return to the National Election Studies and a measure of political ideology. Beginning in 1964, the NES staff has asked respondents to rate liberals and conservatives on a "feeling thermometer," ranging from 1 (very cold feelings for the group) to 97 (very warm feelings). An individual's ideology can be measured by the difference between the feeling thermometer ratings for the two groups.[39] In the analysis that follows, low scores indicate strong preferences for liberals. Preferences for conservatives get high scores.

At least among average Americans, conservatism has been very stable, with no statistically significant trend in either direction.[40] Americans are slightly more conservative (with an average thermometer score of 53) than they are liberal. Just as we saw earlier with respect to public support for politically conservative propositions (Figure 6-1), there has been no marked conservative trend over the past couple decades. The same cannot be said, however, for strong Republicans, as shown in Figure 6-5.[41] Strong Republicans have become more conservative, and this is significant in that Republican party activists are drawn almost entirely from their ranks. Likewise, strong Democrats have become more liberal, although the ideological shift has not been as steep.

The pattern in Figure 6-5—showing that the parties have been polarizing—is repeated when we examine the preferences of campaign activists. Accordingly, the data at hand are likely biased toward *understating* the amount of polarization.[42] From the average American's perspective, the two parties have indeed been growing more distant, as shown in Figure 6-6, which is strictly derived from the data in Figure 6-5. If we use the linear trend line as a guide, the gap was around fifteen thermometer points in the early 1960s and is more than twenty-two points today—a 47 percent increase in thirty years.

The basic evidence for polarization of the two parties seems unmistakable in Figures 6-5 and 6-6. Polarization is unlikely to con-

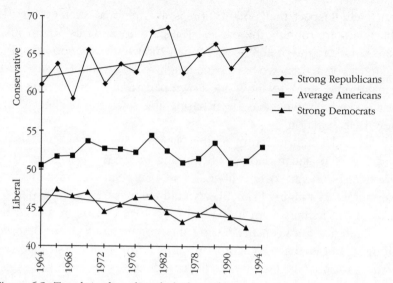

Figure 6-5. *Trends in the political ideology of strong partisans*

The questions were not asked in 1978. The 1994 data point is estimated from information available on the NES World Wide Web site but cannot yet be broken down by parties.

Source: American National Election Studies, 1952–92 Cumulative File, Variable No. 801.

tinue forever, however, because the basic Downsian logic of spatial policy locations cannot be ignored. For politicians, nothing focuses the mind as effectively as an electoral defeat like the one congressional Democrats suffered in 1994. President Clinton's 1996 "triangulation" strategy was Downsian in almost every respect. He staked out policy issues near the median voter in such areas as welfare reform and gay marriages, much to the consternation of Democratic party activists.[43] Of course, if a triangulation strategy made so much sense in 1995 and 1996, it presumably should have been attractive in 1993 and 1994 as well. But at that time the Democratic party seemed seized by its own extremes.

It is worth repeating the evidence presented here, because much of it may help us to understand how the parties have been complicit in the public's mistrust of government.

- *Polarization* Citizens who most closely identify with political parties have grown, on average, more ideologically extreme over the last three decades.

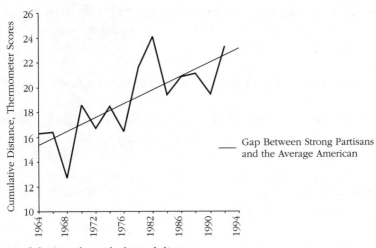

***Figure 6-6.** Growth in ideological distance*

Source: American National Election Studies, 1952–92 Cumulative File. Variable No. 801 (question not asked in 1978).

- *Alienation* Meanwhile, the average American has become only slightly more conservative, creating a growing gap between the preferences of political elites and average citizens.
- *Frustration with Partisanship in Congress* Within Congress, the parties have become both more extreme and more cohesive, while average Americans are likely to be slightly less partisan then they were in the 1960s.

Inflexible partisanship is corrosive within electorates and legislatures. Of course parties play a crucial role in democracies as political intermediaries, and we want them to be responsible by announcing proposals and then delivering on them. The art of politics, however, is the art of compromise, and strange-bedfellows coalitions tend to make better laws (easier to implement, more widely supported, and more likely to stand constitutional tests) than strict and homogeneous party coalitions. This is especially important in policy areas with highly heterogeneous constituents and interests. Partisanship is too often a barrier to strange-bedfellows coalitions, and bipartisan alliances have dwindled in Congress since the mid-1970s.[44] With our legislatures increasingly dominated by loyalists drawn from extreme elements in their own parties, legislators are inclined to inveigh against rivals. Is it any wonder why survey respondents accord politicians less respect when politicians are showing less respect among themselves?

How Mistrust Flows from Polarization of the Parties

Quite naturally, citizens are more trusting of politicians who share their concerns, and citizens are more accepting of political institutions that advance citizen interests. Indeed, the singular accomplishment of a democracy is that public officials have strong incentives to be beholden to their constituents' wishes. Imagine yourself in the position of the average American who, over the past three decades, has witnessed the political parties staking out positions ever more distant from where you want your representatives to be. Frustration and alienation would grow. It is not simply a question of which politicians are *closer* to you as much as *how far away they are* from your basic concerns.[45]

Is there any evidence that the distance one is from the parties has an impact on how much one trusts the government? From the data presented thus far, perhaps. The widening gap between the parties shown in Figure 6-6 covers the same period during which mistrust grew. Compare the slope in Figure 6-6 with the trust in government data presented in Gary Orren's Chapter 3. The trend lines seem related; they pass the eyeball test. But eyeball tests are rarely convincing.

A second test of the relationship between polarization and mistrust is to see whether people who say they mistrust government are, on average, more distant from the parties. Accordingly, I explored survey responses to the National Elections Studies for every two years since 1964, when the ideology thermometer ratings were first taken. An ideology score for each party and each year was generated, as reflected in Figure 6-5. For example, strong Republicans in 1970 scored, on average, about 65 on the (1 to 97) ideology rating. Strong Democrats scored close to 47, and the national average was 54. If an individual's ideological distance from the parties is related to mistrust, then citizens at the national mean should be more distrustful than citizens "closer" to one of the parties. By implication, as the parties move farther away from the average citizen, mistrust should rise.

That is precisely what the survey evidence shows. Using data from 11,756 respondents whose ideological preferences fell somewhere between the two party extremes, citizens who say that they trust the federal government to do the right thing "never" and "only some of the time" were statistically more likely to be farther away from the parties. The closest party cadre was 4.56 thermometer points away for citizens trusting government and 4.98 thermometer points for mistrustful citizens. At least in this bivariate way, mistrust seems to flow from polarization.

The basic argument of this book is that mistrust in government is a multicausal phenomenon, while much of the argument in this chapter has necessarily been unicausal. It is not my task to evaluate all of the competing hypotheses in one place, but an appropriate test of the polarization hypotheses should be multivariate. That analysis is presented in Table 6-3, which shows probit estimates for a model of distrust.[46] The results in Table 6-3 reflect the independent contributions that each of the variables makes to explaining mistrust. For our purposes, the actual sizes of the coefficient estimates is less important than whether we find statistically discernible results. Several of the results are illuminating beyond the issues raised in this chapter.

Recalling Robert Lawrence's provocative findings about the role of the economy in public evaluations of government (Chapter 4), it is clear that being unemployed is related to mistrust. We should, of course, be careful about generalizing from the probit estimates because the model does not test for national economic trends. Still, it seems that personal economic crises make citizens more willing to blame Washington for their problems and less willing to extend politicians their trust. Furthermore, white Americans are less trusting of government than are minorities. This may be a reaction among minorities to the civil rights movement, when the government shifted from prosecutor to protector of minority interests. Mistrust of government also falls with education but rises with age.

Trust in government is related to partisanship in two ways. First, as expected, trust is highest among strong partisans. The more professed affinity one has for a party, the more likely one is to trust the government—even when the government is run by the *other* party. Strong Democrats, for example, were more likely than weak Democrats to trust the government during the height of the Reagan admini-

Table 6-3. Probit Estimates for Model Predicting Mistrust of Federal Government

Independent Variable	Coefficient (standard error)	$P>|z|$
Distance to Closest Strong Partisans	0.014 (0.001)	0.000
Partisan Strength (1 = Low to 4 = High)	−0.089 (0.011)	0.000
Year of Survey	0.034 (0.001)	0.000
Age of Respondent (Years)	0.003 (0.001)	0.000
Gender of Respondent (1 = Male)	−0.030 (0.020)	0.139
Race of Respondent (1 = White)	−0.302 (0.035)	0.000
Respondent from the South? (1 = Yes)	−0.052 (0.022)	0.016
Respondent's Income (First to Fifth Percentile)	−0.015 (0.010)	0.122
Respondent's Education (1 = Low to 8 = High)	−0.027 (0.007)	0.000
Is Respondent Unemployed? (1 = Yes)	0.174 (0.042)	0.000

Number of Observations = 17,090
Pseudo R^2 = 0.0548

stration. This may be partly due to the sense among strong partisans that their *own* party is ready to "fight the good fight."

Second, to test the central proposition of this chapter, for every NES survey respondent I calculated the ideological distance to the closest group of strong partisans. The prediction is that the smaller the distance, the greater the trust. As the parties have polarized, more and more Americans have seen the parties drift away from their centrist preferences. The results in Table 6-3 are unambiguous on this point. The more distant the parties are from respondents, the more likely respondents are to say that they mistrust government, even after accounting for the effects of unemployment, education, age, year, partisan strength, and so on.

In elections with politicians making policy stands relatively close to average (or median) Americans, the vote choice is fairly well understood. Most of us begin with a bias in favor of the candidates matching our partisan identification, but this is tempered by issue positions, character, and retrospective evaluations of how the incumbents have been performing.[47] When evaluating issue positions, voters presumably seek to minimize the differences between their preferences and what a candidate is (strategically) offering. This logic works well when the parties are relatively close to the median voter, but we do not yet have a good sense for what happens to the vote calculus when the parties are extreme. One option is always to vote for the closest candidate, no matter how far away that might be. However, depending on what one's preferences are for the status quo, this might prove disastrous. Instead, it may make sense for voters to play a mixed strategy, splitting their votes between the parties to balance the extremes. Indeed, Morris Fiorina makes this argument, noting that along with transformations in the coalitions supporting the parties, "activists tried to impose programmatic government; voters responded with divided government."[48]

The style of analysis presented in Table 6-3—demonstrating that polarization is related to mistrust—was applied as well to split-ticket voting. The results there also indicate that the farther away one is from both parties, the more likely a voter is to vote for candidates from more than one party.[49] Political scientists are nowhere near a consensus on the causes of split-ticket voting, and Professor Fiorina's balancing hypothesis has met with considerable resistance.[50] In exploring the causes of mistrust, however, both mistrust and declining fidelity to parties appear driven by thirty years of polarization.

Conclusion

The spring of President Clinton's second term was replete with promises of moderation and bipartisanship. Indeed, the president's reelection owed much to his willingness to act more like a centrist and less like the liberal whom voters came to know in 1993 and 1994. While the Downsian logic of moderation seems compelling, both parties, however, continue to be most influenced by their extremes. There is nothing new in this, and we have seen that both parties have become more extreme over the past three decades—not just the last three years. It is unlikely that a couple of months of moderation by the president will return the parties to the broader-based coalitions that grew out of the New Deal.

Fundamental political orientations change gradually. We have seen that the country has indeed grown more conservative since the mid-1960s, but the changes have been modest. Americans have been remarkably consistent with respect to opinions on abortion, national health insurance, the powers of the federal government, and social safety-net issues. It now seems clear that the Republicans in 1995 and 1996 claimed a conservative mandate that most Americans were unready to give. Democrats, however, committed similar sins in the 1970s and 1980s—all of which culminated in President Clinton's national health care proposals in 1993.

Mistrust of government was on the rise long before President Clinton and Speaker Gingrich began their personal and political battles of the 1990s. Indeed, both men—as leaders of their respective political parties—are creatures of the polarizing trends documented in this chapter. Both men are born of political primaries that amplify the demands of the extreme wings. Both men rely on campaign resources drawn disproportionately from activists and strong partisans. And both men have to try holding together voting coalitions within the Congress, although their legislators are also subject to polarizing forces back home.

The demise of the New Deal coalition, the rise of the Republican party in the South, the declining fidelity to party labels, and the rising partisanship among political elites in Congress all point to a growing gap between the interests of political elites and the preferences of average Americans. That growing gap is being filled not by third parties—because our electoral system is profoundly hostile to third parties. The growing gap between elites and the rest of us is being filled with cynicism, mistrust, and frustration that our leaders do not care about "our" problems. One way out of this downward spiral may be for candidates, chastened by the prospect of electoral defeat, to adopt more centrist policies. This is especially difficult, however, when the parties are dominated by activists who are too often willing to sacrifice votes for the sake of ideological purity. Faced with such stark choices, voters may find mistrust to be a perfectly reasonable response.

Seven

The Politics of Mistrust

Richard E. Neustadt

The classic 1911 edition of the *Encyclopaedia Britannica* includes a lengthy article on the history of the United States. It was written by another Harvard professor, the distinguished historian Frederick Jackson Turner. Let me quote its last paragraph:

> At the close of the first decade of the 20th century the United States was actively engaged in settling its social economic questions, with a tendency toward radicalism in its dealings with the great industrial forces of the nation. The "sweat shops" and slums of its great cities were filled with new material for American society to assimilate. . . . Already the food supply showed signs of not keeping pace with the growth of population, while the supply of gold flowed in with undiminished volume. High prices became a factor in the political situation. Between 1890 and 1900, in the continental United States, farms were added in area equal to France and Italy combined. Even the addition of improved farm land in that decade surpassed the whole area of France or of the German Empire in Europe. But intensive cultivation and agricultural returns hardly kept pace with the growth of population or the extension of farms.[1]

In those days, the U.S. population was 100 million, with almost 30 percent of the labor force on the farm. The figures nowadays are 260 million, with less than 3 percent of labor on the farm. In sizing up contemporary problems, it is hard to know which will appear, ninety years hence, as threats to the Great Republic.

It behooves us to be tentative about the shortage that concerns us in this book—a shortage not of food but of trust. The former was prospective only; the latter is here and now. We must be tentative indeed about future consequences and their ultimate significance. But it is hard to overstate the present shortage.

Since the mid-1960s, trust in American institutions, and in government more than most, has declined precipitously and continuously, as measured by opinion polls, with but one partial, temporary upturn in the early 1980s. Government and politics are not to be distinguished in this matter. Indeed, politicians as a class now seem to be among the least trusted professional groupings in the country, right along with journalists, less even than lawyers.[2]

This loss of trust is matched by rather comparable trends in other advanced economies, and, indeed, I am told, in interpersonal relations generally throughout the developed world. Causes no doubt have dimensions that transcend single countries. But as we learned from 1968, when universities "blew up" in Western Europe as well as the United States, the all-important details of effective diagnosis and response were still shaped nationally. My guess is that the politics of mistrust is much the same. This chapter therefore concentrates on American phenomena.

Two questions at once suggest themselves: In the United States, what may have caused (or, anyway, exacerbated) that thirty-year decline of trust? And how much does it matter to the functioning of our peculiar form of democratic government?

The initial question I would answer, as a first approximation, by invoking Vietnam, Watergate, and stagflation in succession, and since then secular stagnation in the real incomes of two-thirds of our families, crowned by "downsizing." On that fearful combination, key voters—that is, "swing" voters—seemed to focus only with the unexpected stretch-out of the 1990 recession, even as the cold war faded away.[3] But focus then they did, and still are doing. Associated with these factors may be others, induced by alterations in society and in politics itself, affected deeply by the disappointed expectations drawn out of historical experience. The whole is a web of relationships to which I will return.

But before I do so, let me characterize my answer to the second question. The consequences I conceive as truly and continuously damaging for timely innovation in governmental programs, for thoroughgoing implementation of them, and for realistic expectations about them—hence for media approval and citizen satisfaction. By the same token, mistrust is of proven use in stalling or unraveling unwanted programs, and also in diverting public anxiousness from unmet needs. If mistrust were unfunctional from every point of view, contemporary politicians and reporters would be fighting it, not feeding it. And feed it they do.

Our government of separated institutions sharing powers is rigged at every level—intentionally, constitutionally—against acts of great consequence on minimal or transient majorities. Relative consensus is required to achieve much motion (although with enough consensus, motion can be fast indeed). Public trust, as such, cannot itself assure consensus among those who share in governing; mistrust, however, makes consensus harder to achieve or rules it out altogether. High levels of mistrust can help to render governance hard, frustrating and sluggish, something akin to traversing a field covered in molasses.

Those engaged may hate it. Observers may deplore it. Not everybody loses by it. Libertarians may think everybody gains.

Revolutionary this situation is not. Our constitutional system of Madisonian checks and balances at every level, entrenched in a most heterogeneous society, capitalistic in economy (and values), middle class in outlook if not income, continental in scale, has had but one civil war in 200 years. So it seems as near a proof against violent national regime change as a human system can be.

And it often has been subject in the past to levels of mistrust that were perhaps as high as those of today. Inching forward, or around in circles, knee-deep in molasses, seems to have been the fate of several of our presidents, most recently Harry S Truman during the Korean War and the McCarthy era. But predecessors run back as far as John Adams. Local violence there often has been, along with more wide-spread vituperation. Alienation falls and rises but in some degree is ever-present at the lowest social levels and the highest. Yet only in 1860, and in the South, has mass disapprobation of the system risen higher than dissatisfaction with the sitting government. Today, save for a fringe on the extreme right—"militia," superindividualists—the polls suggest that despite the distrust in government per se, the system and its symbols remain sacrosanct for most Americans. The Constitution and the Supreme Court still seem to be revered. Tourists still flock to the White House. Hardly anyone now burns the flag on television.[4]

History is an imperfect guide. The future may not quite be like the past. For nowadays the molasses contains some seemingly new ingredients, not present even as recently as Mr. Truman's time, and these make it uncertain that the gap between our citizens and government will ever again close, even to the degree we now recall (with some romance) in Dwight D. Eisenhower's time and John F. Kennedy's. What, then, will befall us if we should find ourselves confronting an unprecedented economic challenge on the scale of the Great Depression? Or a social challenge on the scale of the civil rights movement? Or an international challenge on the scale of the cold war? Or even such a lesser challenge as revalidating Franklin Roosevelt's legacy, the Social Security program? Or his pledge to house the United Nations with full honors in New York? Do perceptions and interpretations of the challenge lessen mistrust or inflate it further? At what point, if ever, does the gap in credibility, which now extends from presidents (and the Congress) to the government, as such, engulf the Constitution?

Answers depend on the causal weight one chooses to assign those extra ingredients. I myself think them of less significance in gumming up the works than do various younger colleagues. (Much depends, I think, on when one first came to the scene.) This is because I see so many near counterparts in earlier periods in which trust was also lacking yet was relatively readily restored, sufficing for the premier challenge of the day. So let me first lay out those "new" ingredients; then contemplate, historically, how similar is previous experience; then ask what differentiates the present from the past that may contribute to the government's condition, so much maligned, so sticky; and finally turn to what, if anything, might be done about it all.

In a brilliant 1997 essay, the political scientist Hugh Heclo, of George Mason University, identifies as a "legitimacy paradox" the fact that while public mistrust has rarely, if ever, been higher than now, members of the public have never been more closely watched, courted, and consulted by the very Washingtonians supposedly engaged in governing. The citizenry—especially prospective voters—are polled, addressed, cajoled, warned, and (if possible) aroused not only by elected politicians and their rivals but also by the plethora of interests organized to press causes upon them, and not only at campaign times but incessantly, responding to the rhythms of forever-sitting legislators and regulators. This, however, does not make the citizens feel connected to those Washingtonians (hence less mistrustful of them), and in truth they are not, for between them is a thickening array of public relations professionals, proliferating in the age of telecommunications. So Washington hovers, yet citizens hate: a paradox indeed.[5]

This condition Heclo attributes to a syndrome of four tightly interrelated developments in American politics. Other authors formulate these somewhat differently, but Heclo's version seems to me both representative and ingenious, so I take it as a handy guide to summarize in the following terms (the terms are mine, not his).

Heclo's first development is technological and managerial—the adaptation to our politics and public policy of scientific sampling, electronic media, computers, copying and fax machines, and now the Internet, deployed by one-time amateurs, or offshoots of the private sector's advertising industry, now become an industry themselves. These are the so-called political consultants—some specialized, some in full-service firms—who are fast taking over functions that not long ago were reserved for politicians and their parties or, more recently, their staffs, or, in the case of interest groups, to in-house staffs and law firms. These consultants can and do plan campaign strategy, sample opinion, select emphases, choose issues, manage media relations, stage "media events," write speeches, schedule tours, set meetings (and advance them), canvass voters (both by mail and phone—and on doorsteps if wanted), train and deploy volunteers (or substitute paid help), and organize the fund-raising to pay for it all. Consultants do not come cheap. Their fees and paid television time are the two biggest items of expenditure in current American politics.[6]

No wonder voters in the mass feel separated from Washington. They rarely even get to march in a parade, much less cheer one from the stands. They scarcely seem to have an active function even in their own manipulation. But that they are manipulated they can barely help but notice every time they read their mail or turn on their television sets. I take it Heclo thinks this adds to their mistrust.

If the government seems remote to citizens, they seem increasingly removed from it. For the traditional intermediaries, the journalists, have also changed their spots and their techniques, amounting to a change of generational styles even as technology transforms the media. Television now dominates transmission of the news and, as an increasingly commercialized entertainment medium, shapes it to suit. Journalists are college-educated now, and upper middle class, conforming to the canons of post-Watergate investigative reportage, ambitious to become television celebrities (which many do), and proud to think of themselves as the public's champions against the politicians, anointed as such by the First Amendment. Like most American professionals, they deem their own source of legitimization superior to popular election. So the reporters too, armed (and distorted) by technology, add to the layering between public and government, deepening mistrust not passively but actively.

And not reporters only. The electronic media are now in a revolutionary spin toward "narrowcasting," proliferating channels, replicating formats. News is disseminated nowadays not only by journalists but also by talk-show hosts—and guests! Perhaps a quarter of Americans rely on them as their primary source for news. Denouncing government is regularly part of their performance. Heclo does not make a point of these developments. Others do.[7]

The second factor that Heclo does distinguish he terms "structural," alluding to the pre-existing institutions of our politics, both partisan and legislative. The once dominant Democratic coalition of voters, assembled in the time of Franklin Roosevelt, so often labeled dead before, must finally be presumed so after 1994. We seemingly are on the verge of ultimate success for Richard Nixon's southern strategy. In terms of voters, this would not necessarily lead to an equally dominant Republican coalition, for party ties have loosened in the interim, while local party organizations, by and large, have less hold than before on any except dedicated activists. Nearly one-third of eligible voters claim to be "independent" (although fewer actually vote that way), and even the party activists are more nearly the capturers than captives of the local parties, owing their first loyalties to causes transcending politics.[8]

Republican activists, en masse, are evidently to the right and Democratic counterparts to the left of national majorities. This plays hob with the politics of nomination and tends to produce congressional parties more mutually opposed, and more antagonistic to the nationally elected president, regardless of party, than in the halcyon years (as we recall them) of bipartisan comity. The snarling and the partisanship are more open now, along with the uncertainty of party control after each future election. These are said to further offend citizen sensibilities and further reduce trust. They certainly reduce the prospects for cross-party consensus-building!

While congressional Republicans exhibit more internal party discipline than do congressional Democrats (and have had far less time, up to now, to learn how to abuse the privileges of majority status), members of each House are fundamentally in business for themselves, vulnerable to challenge both at primary and general stages of election by anybody who possesses or can raise the funds to buy consulting services and television time. Nowadays, a challenger with money can break through or past the local organization. If the money is privately owned, the Supreme Court, no less, says, "Sky's the limit!"[9]

So almost all incumbents feel impelled to crowd their schedules with their own fundraising, to run errands for (and listen to) contributors, and to invest substantial staff time in constituency services. Legislating necessarily comes last. This currently drives many thoughtful members of the Senate and the House to quit, taking their pensions with them. Journalists and less attentive publics seem oblivious to the indignities but conscious of the pensions—which does not add to trust.

Heclo's third development is the opening up of the system to varieties of "movements" previously expressed, if at all, through traditional parties, churches, community activities, or economic interest groups. Imitative of the civil rights movement, in an era of growth and high employment, and riding on the energy of the huge cohorts of baby boomers, there emerged in the 1960s and just after environmentalists and feminists—then, in reaction, right-to-lifers—along with a fast-widening array of minorities championing their uniqueness, in search at once of "roots," of recognition, and of affirmative action. In due course they were joined, or rather countered, from the religious right by increasingly sophisticated efforts, culminating in the Christian Coalition.

Like the temperance movement of the last century, all these mass movements promptly financed and staffed continuing organizations that took their places alongside (and sometimes far ahead of) the traditional economic interest groups. They lobbied not only legislators and regulators but also party nominating processes—and beyond lobbying, infiltrating. As they did so, many of them grew adept at turning the technology and the consulting firms to their account, rallying supporters while, and by, bashing opponents. In the process they have brought fresh interests and new faces into politics, but at the price of rendering consensus harder to achieve, effective coalitions harder to sustain. And those who had the playground to themselves before, or treasured an illusion that they did, are naturally resentful, and mistrustful, which only adds to the stickiness.

The fourth development Heclo describes is national perception of a universal realm for public policy, and a commensurate ascription to some government intent, or failure, of each social result in sight. Thus abortion, crime, drugs, education, employment, health care, homelessness, and so on down a long list—not excluding a wide category now lampooned as "corporate welfare" and another tagged as "populism"—are all considered subjects for the national government to do (or stop doing) something about, as a matter of course. On this, partisan activists from right to left seem to agree. So do the consultants, the reporters, the organized interests, and the talk-show hosts, to say nothing of faculties in schools of public policy. Since everything on such a list relates to everything else, the realm of policy knows no conceptual bounds.

Yet from the founding until well into the Great Depression, such a situation would have appeared absurd to a majority of Americans.

Heclo regards this as a cultural phenomenon associated with generational change, again attributable to the baby boomers. I, however, attribute it to the historical experience of the preceding generation, which lived through the extraordinary sequence of events from 1930 to 1960, remembering especially Roosevelt's early reassurances, together with the good things that had followed governmental rhetoric or action during and after World War II. Throughout the war, the government had run the national economy, superintending what it did not actually administer. The war had been a great success. Before its close, Roosevelt proclaimed an "economic bill of rights." Truman could not nail that down, but Eisenhower forbore to refute it, and the great postwar prosperity made it seem real enough.[10] An economic policy assuring such prosperity became accepted as, somehow, something Washington had and did. If the government could so confidently assume responsibility for the economy and the business cycle, then people could assume the government was ready to take on such responsibility for society and social policy too.

In Heclo's dire view, those four developments—constantly interacting and together constituting one big syndrome—put an end to governing as we knew it a generation or so ago, creakily Madisonian but working in its way. Instead we have the "Permanent Campaign," virtually its antithesis. For Heclo, writing as an American, governing amounts to nursing opposed interests into durable coalitions, so as to achieve effective compromises, nurtured by enough consensus to sustain them over time, with public acceptance anchored in realistic expectations. Those who achieve such compromises frame the expectations. They may blur the harsh edges and uncertainties somewhat, but not too much lest all come tumbling down.

What now goes on in Washington instead? Warfare among elites, waged since the 1960s in the name of causes, not compromises, fueled by technology, manned by consultants, rousing supporters by damning opponents, while serving the separate interests of particular candidates and groups at given times. President and congressmen and private organizations, and their massive staffs, all swirl around one another, seeking to manipulate public opinion and the media and one another for the sake of scoring points. They try incessantly to win a given election, to promote or to stop a given legislative provision, regulation, appointment, contract, or executive decision in diplomacy and defense. Increasingly, they all approach those givens with the same techniques consultants use, in roughly the same spirit: damn the torpedoes, full steam ahead, rouse your friends, trash the enemy, the long term's later, victory comes first.

Thus Heclo's permanent campaign. In all of that there's scant room for James Madison! Yet Heclo seems to think that it all is fastened on us irretrievably. This could be so, at least until the baby boomers pass from active life. For this is what they know; it's what they cut their eye-teeth on; it could be what they think is governance. (If so, God help us all.) That, at any rate, is the most pessimistic gloss to put on what Heclo writes, more so than his own words.

Relatively speaking, I'm an optimist. (Stress relatively.)

What makes me so is contemplation of three recent periods in American history, through all of which I lived, so I can conjure up the memory of a firsthand feel for context. Each of the three amounts to a winter snapshot of Washington, seen from the environs of the White House.[11] First comes 1938–39, second comes 1946–47, third comes 1950–51. None was a happy time, or easy, either from the standpoint of the governors or from that of citizens. On the contrary, frustration was piled high on either side, rather as now. All three snapshots show snarls, discouragement, unclarity, and what we now call "gridlock." That, of course, is why I chose them. Let me comment now on each in turn.

Early 1939 was assuredly the nadir of the Roosevelt administration. Congress, although nominally Democratic, was beyond the president's control. Both Houses now were in the hands of the so-called conservative coalition of Southern Democrats and Midwestern Republicans, which on domestic programs was to dominate the scene for the next quarter-century. The accompanying coalition of Southern Democrats and (mostly) Eastern Republicans, supporting postwar foreign policy was yet to come. So was the war. So was the policy. FDR may or may not have been sure that war was inevitable, with American forces necessary to a tolerable outcome, but he was saying nothing of the sort, and most of his fellow citizens preferred to hope that the Munich settlement would hold, or thought about war only with aversion.[12]

The country still was very inward looking, and most people evidently did not much like what they saw. Public opinion polls were both less common and far less reliable than now—the samples less careful and questions still looser—but impressions from the time and historical accounts agree about the widespread character of public dissatisfaction with American conditions, and, more moderately, with FDR as president. Such as they are, Gallup polls suggest that people blamed him less, for what ailed them, than "natural economic trends," and they blamed "government" not at all. Indeed, government evoked neither questions nor answers, while FDR and the economy were distinguished in a fine old-fashioned way unlikely to be understood today except by specialists and ideologues. Yet insofar as congressional elections serve to register public moods, November 1938 had been disastrous for Roosevelt, with a doubling of Republican representation in the House and in the Senate the return of a set of senior Democrats the president had rashly sought to purge at party primaries. There they still sat with their fellow southerners—in the committee chairmanships.[13]

The winter of 1937–38 had been a time of unexpected and severe recession. A year later, business recovery was under way, but employment was not. There remained some 10 million unemployed, perhaps one-fifth of the labor force, but public works had been cut back, and Congress was in no mood to enlarge them radically.[14] Those at work in industry were targets for the organizing drives of John L. Lewis's Congress of Industrial Organizations, fiercely resisted by major employers while both sides blamed Roosevelt for lack of support. Private investment was patchy, which Wall Street blamed on overregulation and the antibusiness atmosphere in Washington. Corporate managers positively hated FDR, the "traitor to his class," and naturally resented their own fall from public grace since the onset of the Great Depression. Hatred was also found well down the income scale, in attacks on the president and on his wife by certain radio commentators, notably Father Coughlin. Populist movements of more moment had been stalled by an assassin, Huey Long's fate, or blunted, as with Dr. Townsend, by timely legislation.[15] But the followings remained, along with the slow economy, on farms as well as in the cities.

Happenings abroad further soured the public mood at home. Europe's near escape from war in 1938 had aroused isolationist fears of Wilsonian entanglements, and Woodrow Wilson's assistant secretary of the navy was now in the White House. There followed the beginnings of organized isolationism, meant to tie Roosevelt's hands: this culminated in 1940 with "America First," a movement that proceeded with all the vigor and some of the intensity we now ascribe to the antiabortion cause.[16] Meanwhile, the ranks of Roosevelt's natural supporters for an interventionist course were split three ways, among those angry at him for not supporting the elected Spanish government against Francisco Franco, those aggrieved at his slowness to line up unequivocally against Hitler, and the relatively few who gave him credit for moving as fast as he could.

Credit was not much in evidence for FDR in 1939. Had Hitler's generals had their way, with war postponed until 1943, Roosevelt would have retired, at the end of his second term, as a well-regarded but failed president—eight years to cure an inherited depression and unable to do it.

This is not to say that the dissatisfactions of the time with the sitting president had much in common with today's mistrust of government. On the contrary, Roosevelt was beloved as well as hated, and by far more people. (For whatever it is worth, his Gallup poll approval ratings and their precursors never fell below 50 percent.) His infectious personal confidence in 1933 and the bipartisanship of his first two years had generated an enormous fund of trust in him among supporters, and respect among opponents, which trickled down to government as such. Besides, in 1939 the federal government was far less intrusive than now: fewer and lower taxes; few environmental, health, or safety regulations; few social welfare interventions (except old-age insurance, which was widely popular, even though no benefits had yet been paid). There was no financial aid to education. Federal housing programs were small. Agricultural production was controlled, but this had consent on the farm. Public jobs and public works were funded, on an unprecedented if declining scale, but these, while roundly criticized in conservative circles ("boondoggles"), were treasured by recipients. To be sure, Ronald Reagan probably first heard "Government's the problem" during Governor Alf Landon's campaign for the presidency in 1936.[17] But Reagan didn't vote Republican then. He joined two-thirds of the voters in casting his ballot for FDR.

The discontents of 1938–39 seem to have been more matters of dissatisfaction with the recession, or disappointment, or fear in private lives, than of sheer distrust for an abstract institution.[18]

That was the case again, except for louder gripes against the president, in 1946, my next winter-of-discontent, when Congress went Republican a year and a half after Truman had succeeded FDR at the triumphal close of World War II. According to the Gallup poll, the new man's popularity had slumped in that time period from 87 percent to 32 percent.[19] What had driven it down? Double-digit inflation, the slowness (compared with expectations) of demobilization, and upsetting adjustments during reconversion, which included strikes and shortages of consumer goods, especially meat (which farmers withheld at the start of the congressional campaign, successfully protesting price controls). Truman was so battered by September 1946 that the Democratic National Committee urged him not to campaign for congressional candidates, lest he hurt their chances. He didn't, but that hardly helped. The "terrible, do-nothing" 80th Congress, as he termed it two years later, came in due course, with Republicans controlling both the House and the Senate.

That such a pile-up of dissatisfactions should have followed the war may have been inevitable, and that it should have expressed itself in turning out the Democrats on Capitol Hill may have been no less so. Their majorities had been declining with every election since 1938. But that mistrust of government as such, apart from Truman and his hapless price controls, was at the root of it is countered by the evidence of what had gone before and what came after: on the one hand "the good war," as Studs Terkel has called it, and on the other the beginnings of the cold war, in the Truman Doctrine and the Marshall Plan.

World War II was indeed a "good war" for most Americans, casualties aside, and a good time, too, for almost all except the combat troops. After the dismal years of the depression, there were jobs for everybody, women included; money to be made and saved; stable prices (until the very end); rationing, to be sure (but that was for "our boys"); and above all production—an amazing, thrilling, and overwhelming outpouring of aircraft, ships, and tanks, pridefully demonstrative of what the country could do. And government had organized it all (or in the fine print supervised and subsidized it all). During the first postwar years, Democrats might be denounced, but not the government per se, especially not those parts of it in uniform. Trust in government, while never very high among Americans, may never have been higher than through those mid-1940s. And the same goes for confidence. One of the reasons that Washington and Wall Street took Stalin so seriously in those years was that we ourselves had run a "command" economy and saw what it could do.

The point is but confirmed by what ensued when Truman undertook to counter Stalin's outward reach with precedent-breaking measures from that "do-nothing" 80th Congress. Greek-Turkish aid in 1947, the Marshall Plan in 1948, and preparatory talks on NATO were pursued by the president with scrupulous bipartisanship. He also rather hid behind the screen of General George C. Marshall, army chief of staff in World War II and now secretary of state, and other wartime worthies like Robert Lovett of Wall Street.[20] But having done so, Truman succeeded. A bipartisan majority, that second coalition, passed those measures; the country accepted them; and the Republicans then nominated to oppose him for the presidency a convinced supporter of his European policy. Thomas Dewey's nomination was hard-fought, and by no means pleased everyone, especially not Senator Robert Taft, his party opponent. Seeds of trouble were planted, to sprout later. But the point is that the government's capacity to do these unprecedented things or not, as it might choose, was scarcely questioned—which is a monument to trust.

Yet only three years later, that trust seems to have dissolved. This had happened by the time of my third dire winter, 1950–51. It was a cheerless time for Truman and the country. The Chinese entered the Korean War in late November 1950, forcing the longest military retreat in American history, leaving uncertain whether we could stay on the peninsula at all, and raising specters in Washington minds of World War III. Not only had the war turned sour and stretched out, but two bouts of panic buying in the months since its inception, the preceding June, had raised consumer prices 10 percent, a frightening and angering experience for many, robbing Truman of his credibility as a persistent champion of price controls. By the time he slapped them on full force, in January 1951, most of the steam had gone out of price rises, leaving the controls as irritants. A recession in 1949 had been replaced by full employment just before the war broke out. Inflation, followed by controls, took much of the fun out of that.

And the war spoiled what chances remained for enactment of Truman's domestic legislative program, the Fair Deal, on which he had run and been narrowly elected in 1948, when Congress returned to Democratic control. The more controversial measures had been stalled or defeated during the first session. What was hoped for as the highlight of the second session, national health insurance, was defeated in the fall, shortly before the 1950 congressional elections reduced the Democrats to paper-thin majorities.[21]

Domestic anticommunism reared its head in those elections, and thereafter it did so more powerfully than before. A separate innovation had been interjection of the American Medical Association into campaigns to defeat proponents of health insurance, in a display of techniques long-anticipating Heclo's permanent campaign.[22] Its successes frightened politicians off from comprehensive health reform for more than forty years. "Socialized medicine" was the AMA's battle cry. It seemed to mesh effectively, although perhaps not deliberately, with older charges by the House Un-American Activities Committee and with newer charges by that fast-evolving demagogue, Senator Joseph

McCarthy, who had chanced on the Communist issue just four months before the Korean War began. The Korean war made McCarthy formidable, its harsh turn in November much more so. Nothing in contemporary politics is quite as nasty, nor are any manifestations of mistrust more palpable.

McCarthy's fellow Republicans might have repressed him early on, but they reportedly decided not to do so out of fury that the Democrats had unexpectedly (and inexplicably to them) retained the White House in 1948. They were sure it should have been theirs. Anticipating that outcome had stoked their earlier bipartisanship. Truman's election began its retraction. His wartime troubles, some of them of his own making, were too tempting not to exploit.[23]

And when, in March 1951, having recovered South Korea, Truman and his overseas allies chose not to press farther and sought to lay the groundwork for a compromise with Beijing, the minority leader of the House invited the commander in the field, General Douglas MacArthur, to comment. The latter promptly did so publicly, in writing. "There is no substitute for victory," he argued, and made plain his wish to vanquish the Chinese. Truman took this as a constitutional challenge to the commander-in-chief. MacArthur was promptly fired. He returned home to a rapturous reception from coast to coast—a national sentiment only gradually contained by a long set of Senate hearings that brought out the administration's logic, bolstered by support from a unanimous joint chiefs of staff. MacArthur faded away, but meanwhile Truman's Gallup poll approval rating touched bottom, at 23 percent (1 percent below Richard Nixon's lowest at the time he resigned).

Thereafter, mistrust centered on the president who had begun a war he would not "win" and could not stop. For the nearly two years he had left in office, Truman's approval rating never rose above 31 percent. This does not mean an equal lack of confidence in government—not anyway in the expanding part of government, the military, which grew fourfold in those years, or in our European commitments, which were enlarged by five divisions on the ground, along with General Eisenhower. State, Treasury, Justice, and the White House are another matter: the one accused of coddling Communists, the others of corruption.[24]

Eisenhower succeeded Truman at the White House in January

1953. A month later Stalin died, setting off a succession struggle in the Kremlin. For one reason or another, the Chinese chose to liquidate the Korean conflict, and the truce that had eluded Truman was agreed that summer. Thereafter, in this country, the snarly sense of crisis passed within a year, yielding place to the complacency of the mid-1950s. Still more remarkably, memories of the war and of the angers it evoked dropped out of national consciousness. Even the "never again club" of senior army officers, determined that there should be no more ground wars for Americans in Asia, disappeared within a decade, gone almost without a trace.

How do those three winters seem to differ from our present situation? The similarities are obvious, and it is they, of course, that make me a relative optimist. But it is differences that shed the most light on contemporary problems, aiding diagnosis. A few already have been noted. In what do the rest consist?

First, those previous bouts of discontent were shorter in duration than the present deep distrust, even if one dates that only from the 1990 recession and the remarkable defeat for reelection two years later of the president, George Bush, who had fought and won the Gulf War. But properly speaking, one cannot date it so. According to the polls, it had its beginnings in the Vietnam War, which the whole country came to think mistaken, half because it seemed immoral or un-winnable and the other half because we did not carry it to Hanoi and then win it.

"Vietnam," which could appear to non-Americans as simply a long and lost war, was felt in the United States as much more than that. The war was Americanized in 1965, just as this country tasted the first fruits of high prosperity without inflation, consequent on the income tax cuts that President Kennedy had sought and President Johnson had won in 1964. The Johnson Great Society program produced in 1965 and 1966 a wide range of innovative social legislation, raising expectations on every hand. Yet these were mostly underfunded later in the war, or otherwise ill-implemented, which produced no less wide-ranging disenchantments. In 1965, the civil rights movement peaked for the South with passage of the Voting Rights Act. Yet that summer and the next, unforeseen by whites, black urban ghettos in the North were rife with riots. Two years later, Martin Luther King, Jr., and Robert Kennedy were assassinated. Meanwhile, the first televised war in viewers' living rooms showed American soldiers dying, many of them black. The medium also focused on civilian youngsters, mostly white and evidently privileged, who burned the flag, fought the police, fouled their own collegiate nests, smoked "pot," and dodged the draft. In many living rooms, more substantial arguments against the war were overwhelmed by those pictures. Others, of course, cheered.

At the 1968 Democratic Convention, which nominated Hubert Humphrey, national television showed impassioned activists clashing with police. Four years later, a variety of youthful activists crowded the pictures from the convention that nominated the peace candidate, George McGovern.

A deep sense of domestic disorder took hold among both opponents and supporters of the war, and also a deep sense of division between them, compounded by differences of region, generation, class, and race.[25] The patriotic sentiments that, throughout two world wars, had bound most Democrats together frayed apart, and the new Republican president, Richard Nixon, took notice. Hence his appeal to a self-proclaimed, war-supporting "silent majority."

By the time Nixon took office, Americans were experiencing something novel and, for many, unpleasant—namely, sustained inflation, war-induced, of 5 percent to 6 percent a year on the Consumer Price Index. This had taken root in 1966, shown its full face in 1968, and—despite income-tax increases, once LBJ reluctantly reversed himself, and also despite recession in 1969—persisted year after year. It was very unlike the short, sudden spurts of 1946 and 1950, and the less palatable for that. Nixon, overriding most of his economists, slapped price controls on the economy in 1971 and brought the rate down below 4 percent before the 1972 election. At the same time, the Federal Reserve Board eased monetary policy, aiding the "feel good" factor. After his reelection, Nixon's economists, fearing cumulative distortions, persuaded him to lift controls. Prices surged. But that result got so mixed up with the effects of unrelated food shortages, which blended into the first oil shock, that earlier causes were overshadowed.

By then, at any rate, Nixon was embroiled in the unraveling cover-up of Watergate. By then, also, he had ordered the last U.S. combat troops out of the war. They all were home in January 1973.

But everything that went before (and one thing after, Saigon's surrender) is still encompassed for Americans now middle-aged or older in the term "Vietnam."

Returning to the differences between current mistrust and my earlier "winters," a second difference is that previous angers were vented on perceived external forces such as "natural economic trends" (before the expectations built into such things as the Employment Act of 1946), or, alternatively, on presidents in office, rather than on "government" per se.[26] The president-as-target is not unknown to us more recently (witness the fates of Jimmy Carter and George Bush— and also Bill Clinton's negatives). But those discontented winters had not been accompanied—year in, year out, for half a generation—by Heclo's syndrome as an alienating spectacle to citizens. Nor had those winters featured presidential condemnation of the government—a novelty with Carter, much embellished by Reagan, and echoed by Bush and Clinton. It amounts to shifting blame, and for some it has been successful.

Third, in those earlier instances, dissatisfactions in private life, which seem to be associated with disapproval of presidents, were eased by external forces rather quickly. Those winters have a transient quality: the Great Prosperity follows hard on the heels of the Great Depression. Postwar reconversion yields to high employment and coherent foreign policy. Eisenhower's peace follows Truman's war.

And what has happened since Vietnam? The Democrats deserted patriotism. The Republicans got tarred with Watergate. The young continued troubling lifestyles. The oil shocks of the 1970s produced stagflation and, indeed, the first double-digit inflation seen since 1946 (which was to be experienced together with the hostages in Teheran). Productivity slumped, unaccountably, in 1973, and workers ceased to gain a proportionate share of what remained. Trade unions decayed. Belying previous decades of steady growth, real family income stagnated, even with wives at work. Children got latch keys. Then downsizing![27] And all of this is to say nothing of crime, drugs, education, and immigration, or, for that matter, affirmative action, both as experienced and as portrayed on national television.

Here is a clue for us about our present and our future. For a full generation, two sets of people in this country have been doing worse, economically and socially, than in the past, or than they had come to expect. One set is urban ghetto youths, predominantly black, starved of stable families, schooling, jobs, or values linking them steadfastly to the rest of us. The other set is what we once called the blue-collar middle class, now joined by various white-collar counterparts, more white than black, and mostly male, whose fathers were prime beneficiaries of post–World War II prosperity; now these men are forced to recognize that they cannot keep pace, nor can their sons, without costly college educations.

The first of these two sets is relatively voiceless in our politics, except through crime and riots, since their vote is disproportionately low. But the second set does vote—and how! It includes the "hard-hats" on whom Nixon relied as the core of his patriotic "silent majority." It must be presumed to overlap, in large degree, with the "Reagan Democrats" who left the wimpish Carter for the nearest thing to John Wayne, then deserted Bush in 1992 when their long-lasting plight finally came home to them, then took it out on the House Democrats in 1994, when nothing further had been done for them, and, as I write, in August 1996, appear to be regarded by both major parties as keys to the coming election.

Here is the heart of the "anxious class" in our society—more properly of anxious voters—mainly heads of household in the family income bracket of $30,000 to $50,000 but with ranks now swelled by fears of downsizing to brackets below and above, and to those with white-collars as well as blue. Politically, there is something about them quite distinct from the disgruntled or scared voters of my prior winters. These contemporary voters not only have had reason to be anxious for a generation, but also, in the past six years, they have repeatedly been promised specific relief by presidents of one party or the other, and each time the promise has gone unkept. This still goes on today.

And all of these specifics were piled on top of the implicit promise that these men thought they had heard Reagan make but that he could not keep: "America's back" turned out to mean shadow, not substance, for them; it was not "pork chops" or remembered rising wages but rather rising payroll taxes for Social Security reform.[28] Perhaps this accounts more for the fall, after a short-run rise, of public trust in Reagan's years than does the savings-and-loan bail-outs or the Iran-Contra scandal.

Consider the specifics. To go no farther back than 1990, President

Bush let it be understood, and no doubt thought, that the oncoming recession would be sharp and short, like 1981–83. In 1991 and early 1992, he said that it was almost over. But it wasn't, or at least it didn't feel so to millions of voters until much later.[29] Bush, by then, was history. During the 1992 campaign, Clinton pledged a "middle-class tax cut." In office he felt that he could not deliver, and even had to obtain a tax hike instead, albeit mostly on higher incomes.[30] In 1992, again, he promised to make health care more secure for everyone. In 1993 and 1994, his elaborate plans to do so succeeded in scaring many and were junked on Capitol Hill. In 1995, both he and the Republican congressional leaders promised a tax cut anew, and quarreled spectacularly over its shape, to no avail. Nothing was enacted. In 1996, those promises and more are repeated as I write.

The only comparable thing in my three winters is FDR's recession of 1937–38, after he had bragged about recovery in 1936, asserting "We planned it that way."[31] But Roosevelt had behind him a great reservoir of trust—as Clinton does not—and ahead of him wartime prosperity. In 1996 one peers ahead in vain for any sign of economic changes likely to assuage those anxious voters. Apparently, all that can help them is tax relief and better social services. Looking at the records of both our political parties, amidst the hue and cry of permanent campaigning, it is scarcely to be wondered at that they mistrust their government. They may have other reasons also—reasons that are less specific, more sociological, or cultural—and more traditional—or bound up with the rhetoric of politics in recent times. But here's one set of reasons rooted in the most immediate sort of direct economic experience. By way of explanation, it alone could suffice.

So if my optimism is to be sustained, one of three things must happen. Those anxious voters must gradually become adjusted to their lot, no longer voting their anxieties but rather their wives' hopes, if some remain. (The wages of women still lag behind men, but they are relatively on the rise.) Or they must give up voting as a pointless exercise, and so drop out of political calculations, which would be a pity; our electorate is dwarfish as it is. Or they must get some closure from one party or the other, even if only inculcation in more realistic expectations, or educational assistance for the coming generation, or symbolic gestures like the capping of executive pay, or better, some of the tax breaks so long promised, or best, some means to share in productivity increases. For otherwise these people will continue to thrash around, politically, until they do real damage—for example, by surrendering to populist simplicities.

Why has it been so hard, for so long to give these voters either realism or satisfaction? The question brings me back to Heclo's syndrome. The answer seems to be that in this context our elective politicians have become too scared to vote consistently on anything more long-term, or more national, than funding sources and the polls suggest will help them to win reelection in home constituencies. This is something we have done to ourselves. Nowhere else among democratic regimes are the elected legislators forced to self-finance repeated runs for office on such a scale, with so little assurance of renomination and so much sheer badgering from well-heeled interests. In a fascinating book, *Running Scared,* another political scientist, the friendly British observer of our scene, Anthony King, contrasts the plight of U.S. representatives in these respects with the conditions of employment for British and German parliamentarians.[32] It is a very sobering comparison. It tempers my optimism as well as, of course, Heclo's.

What strikes me as the worst of it is that most of our politicians, careerists though they have become, do not rise in their own professional defense. Representatives do not press for longer terms, although the original justification for a two-year term has long since been outmoded by communications technology. Incumbents don't insist on public funding of elections or free television time, although they constantly complain that permanent campaigning ruins their lives. Nor do they shake themselves loose from the smothering array of staffs and consultants, who since Truman's time have come to dominate not only campaigning but also the legislative process, adding new layers of stickiness, previously unknown.

Emulating both Ronald Reagan and Jimmy Carter, many, perhaps most, of our politicians now routinely blame "the government" for causing the problem, whatever the problem may be. This is understandable, considering the spread of regulatory powers and their reach across so much of the economy since the Johnson and Nixon administrations: most private problems now do have some direct public aspect. Many segments of society, besides the two I single out earlier, have personal experience to feed dissatisfaction. But I suspect that nothing helps turn the dissatisfactions to mistrust more readily than such repeated rhetoric from politicians. They are presumed to know whereof they speak, because they, after all, are part of government (and themselves are mistrusted to suit).

So even if the future were to hold surprising economic benefits for one-time Reagan Democrats, or even, miraculously, for black ghetto-dwellers, mistrust of government can be expected to persist as long as our elected politicians actively encourage it while they fail to address their own plight. Some mistrust, of course, would persist even if they changed their tune—mistrust being an American tradition. It is not for nothing that the United States was founded in revolt against taxes for our own defense, forcing the "best people" to board ship for Halifax.[33]

Still, my three winters suggest that present levels of mistrust are actually, historically, unusual, at least in dragging on so long while cutting as deep as they appear to do. I grant that the appearance is an artifact of polls, and it could be superficial, like so many polling questions. Yet the practical behavior of our politicians up to now attests that they sense something deeper. Even relative optimists should take heed and beware—especially when politics and economics, combined, lack ready cures for what concretely ails so many of the disaffected.

Deep distrust does serve the purposes of some participants in public policy, limiting action, diverting attention, feeding the permanent campaign. But the result is less capacity for reliable consensus-building and for coalition maintenance than I, looking back but also trying to look forward, think prudent. In that, I am at one with Heclo. Regardless of what others do, or don't, about their comparable problems, we Americans are well advised to mitigate mistrust all we can. But if we are to do so, our elective politicians have to play their part, rallying genuinely in their own defense.

It probably asks too much of them to stand up and be counted all alone. For what seems to intimidate them is the Heclo syndrome, or, more precisely, aspects of it: the pervasiveness of polls, the commercialism of television, the lobbyists and staffs in swarms, the constituents on jets, the readiness of those who vote to split their ballots (or stay home), along with court decisions that promote the sovereignty of money. All these, I do not doubt, are heightened by the swagger of consultants and the righteousness of journalists, wrapped in their First Amendment. Unless the former grow more careful and the latter grow more humble, I fear my call will not be heeded by most politicians. I would find it hard to blame them, or at any rate them only.

So I am at best an apprehensive optimist and at worst a hopeful pessimist. Events that I cannot foresee conceivably might come to our assistance, as before. Or some new administration might show realism, probity, and dignity throughout, thus startling an unaccustomed public into almost Rooseveltian admiration. Or members of the public might draw realism from unaided observation, evoking more potential for consensus than elected politicians dare endeavor to induce themselves. Then all they have to do is ride an incoming tide. They should be capable of that.

Some contemporary commentators see such a tide approaching and are cheered by short-run indicators like Republican reluctance, as I write, to let their speaker of the House, Newt Gingrich, the triumphalist of 1994, show himself nationally in the campaign of 1996.[34] Others see the voluntary sector and the best-run states as sources of progressive innovation that perhaps can ease the pain of those whose economic plight fuels anger against "government" and otherwise do good as well. My three past winters lend some credence to such hopes, since we survived them—indeed, flourished afterwards by means few could foresee. But it is differences in lack of trust, not similarities, that feed my apprehension: the differences of long duration, of spread from presidents to government as such, and of slim chances for salvation by events. These differences trouble me the more because they come combined with Heclo's syndrome (which, taken by itself, would scare me less). That combination of clouds does not blot out but certainly hazes over every prospect for renewed trust in American government.

PART Three

Data on Public Attitudes toward Governance

Eight

Changing Attitudes in America

Robert J. Blendon, John M. Benson, Richard Morin,
Drew E. Altman, Mollyann Brodie, Mario Brossard,
and Matt James

Those who serve in government at the turn of the new century are likely to confront an important cultural phenomenon. As they seek to address the major domestic and international problems of this era, they will do so in an environment characterized by widespread citizen distrust of government and skepticism about its ability to solve the problems it seeks to address. This phenomenon is not only likely to be seen when discussing government's role as a whole, but also to be reflected in the relatively low levels of citizen respect and confidence shown to those who serve in both elective and appointed government roles.

This chapter traces in a practical way the evolution of this phenomenon as it emerged over the past thirty years in the United States. Our task is descriptive, helping to frame the issues discussed throughout the book. The data presented here grew out of a collaborative effort among researchers at the *Washington Post,* the Henry J. Kaiser Family Foundation, and Harvard University. The nature of this effort was twofold: (1) to examine and analyze the long-term trends in Americans' attitudes and knowledge about their government as reflected in a half-century of opinion surveys; and (2) to conduct an in-depth national opinion survey building on these earlier studies. Unless otherwise noted, the data in this chapter are drawn from this collaborative survey.[1]

The survey, conducted between November 28 and December 4, 1995, and released in the *Washington Post* in a six-part series starting January 28, 1996, examined public understanding, perceptions, and attitudes about the role of government. Its aim was to shed light on why Americans in the mid-1990s are so distrustful and cynical about the federal government and its ability to act effectively. The survey instrument was designed jointly by the three institutions involved in the project, with advice from a panel of academic experts. Interviews with 1,514 adults nationwide were conducted over the telephone by Princeton Survey Research Associates. The margin of error was ±3 percent.[2]

Public Trust in Government

Any effort to examine long-term public opinion trends about distrust in government is limited by the lack of available statistical data prior to the mid-1960s. As Ernest May reminds us in Chapter 1, this country was founded by individuals who were deeply distrustful of government power and those who sought to exercise it. Although Americans see an important role for government, the views held by our founding fathers have carried on in some form since the nation's birth. Unfortunately, we have no statistics to calibrate the ebb and flow of citizen confidence and trust during prior periods of our nation's history. The 1960s, when our measures of trust begin, may well represent a golden age of public support for the government.

In 1958, when the American National Election Study first asked about public trust, nearly three-fourths (73 percent) of Americans said that they trusted the government in Washington to do the right thing just about always or most of the time. The figure declined to 61 percent in 1968, to 36 percent in 1974, and finally to 25 percent in 1980. Public trust rose during the mid-1980s, but not to the pre-1970s level. By the early 1990s, only one in four Americans trusted the federal government.[3] In our recent *Washington Post*/Kaiser/Harvard

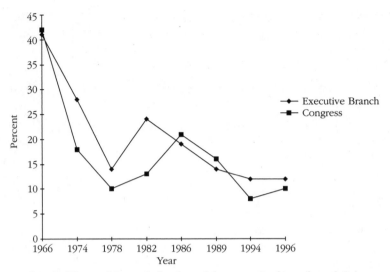

Figure 8-1. Public confidence in leaders of the executive branch and Congress: percent saying "a great deal"

Source: Harris Poll, 1966–96.

survey, the proportion who trusted the federal government stood at 25 percent, one-third the level of thirty years earlier (see Figure 3-1).

The decline in trust is mirrored in measures of public confidence in the leaders of the executive and legislative branches of the federal government. In 1966, Louis Harris and Associates found that four in ten Americans had a great deal of confidence in the people running the executive branch (41 percent) and Congress (42 percent). Confidence in the leaders of both institutions dropped sharply by 1974. As shown in Figure 8-1, currently, barely one in ten express a great deal of confidence in the people running the executive branch (12 percent) and Congress (10 percent). These trends have remained relatively constant regardless of which political party controlled the presidency or the Congress.[4]

Obviously, not all Americans hold identical views of their government, and this is reflected in the findings shown in Figure 8-2. Hispanic and African Americans, who have looked to the federal government to redress some of their grievances associated with historical and current inequalities, express higher than average trust in the federal

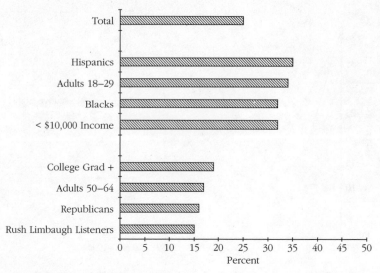

Figure 8-2. Trust in federal government to do the right thing; percent saying
"just about always" or "most of the time"

Source: *Washington Post*/Kaiser Family Foundation/Harvard University, 1995.

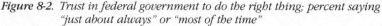

government to do the right thing. Those at the lowest end of the
income ladder, as well as young adults age eighteen to twenty-nine,
also express more trust than other Americans. Yet only about one in
three Americans in each of these groups report trusting the federal
government just about always or most of the time.[5]

Not surprisingly, Republicans, who since the New Deal have
typically argued against the enlargement of the federal government
and its powers, are less trusting of the federal government than other
Americans. Only one in six Republicans (16 percent) and adults age
fifty to sixty-four trust the federal government just about always or
most of the time. But the least trusting Americans are those who
regularly listen to the talk radio program of Rush Limbaugh, one of
the nation's most prominent politically conservative hosts.[6]

Asked which level of government they trust to do a better job in
running things, six in ten (61 percent) choose their own state government, while only one in four (24 percent) trust the federal government
more (see Figure 8-3). Among major demographic groups, only Jewish
Americans gave the federal government (44 percent) more trust than
state government (36 percent). African Americans, who have had

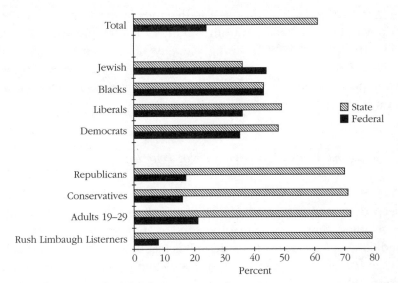

Figure 8-3. *Trust in the federal government of your own state government to do a better job running things*

Source: *Washington Post*/Kaiser Family Foundation/Harvard University, 1995.

historical reasons to distrust state governments, are nonetheless split evenly on which level they trust more. Even liberals and Democrats trust their state government more than the federal government. Republicans (70 percent), conservatives (71 percent), and Limbaugh listeners (79 percent) overwhelmingly side with state government. Interestingly, adults age eighteen to twenty-nine, who are among the groups most trusting of the federal government to do the right thing, trust state government over the federal government by more than a three to one margin (72 percent to 21 percent).

The advantage held by state governments in comparison with the federal government should not, however, be read as a strong endorsement of state governments. Only about one in three Americans say that they trust their own state government to do the right thing just about always (5 percent) or most of the time (30 percent). That is significantly higher than the level of trust accorded the federal government; however, 65 percent of Americans do not profess much trust even for their state governments.

The higher degree of trust in state governments is a dramatic reversal of attitudes at the height of the New Deal a half-century ago.

In 1936, a majority (56 percent) said that they favored a concentration of power in the federal government rather than in state governments (44 percent).[7] In 1939, a strong plurality (41 percent) thought the federal government was more honest and efficient in performing its own special duties than local (17 percent) or state (12 percent) governments.[8]

Reasons Americans Give for Not Trusting Government

The reasons underlying Americans' views about government have been discussed in preceding chapters and will be evaluated in the concluding chapter. Some of the reasons may be causally complex and difficult for citizens to express. It is instructive, however, to listen to the reasons Americans give for distrusting government. We asked exactly that in our 1995 survey, and the main reason Americans gave revolved around the way the federal government spends money. As reflected in Figure 8-4, eight in ten say that inefficiency and waste (80 percent) and spending money on the wrong things (79 percent) are major reasons for distrust. More than six in ten say that special interests

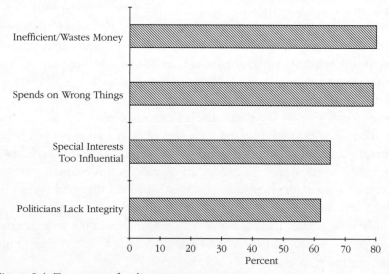

Figure 8-4. Top reasons for distrusting government

Source: *Washington Post*/Kaiser Family Foundation/Harvard University, 1995.

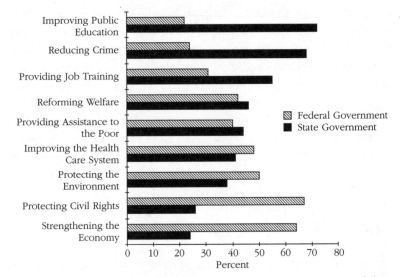

Figure 8-5. Americans' views of federal versus state government responsibilities

Source: NBC News/ *Wall Street Journal,* 1994–95.

having too much power (65 percent) and politicians lacking integrity (62 percent) are major reasons.

The preference for greater state responsibility does not rest alone on beliefs about better efficiency or public management at the state level. Rather, Americans see their own state governments as better reflecting their own regional or cultural preferences in setting government priorities. The principal reasons Americans give for trusting their state government more than the federal government in running things are that they see state government as being (1) more responsive to the needs of people like them (65 percent), (2) able to solve problems more quickly (64 percent), and (3) more likely to spend money on the right things (56 percent).[9]

In addition, although a majority of Americans trust their own state government more, the public still prefers that the federal government have more responsibility than state governments for certain problem areas. As reflected in Figure 8-5, about two-thirds think that the federal government should have more responsibility than state governments for strengthening the economy (64 percent) and protecting civil rights (67 percent). More Americans prefer that the federal government rather than state governments have responsibility for protecting the environment (50 percent for federal, 38 percent for states) and improving the health care system (48 percent to 41 percent). The main areas where Americans prefer state government responsibility are improving public education (72 percent states, 22 percent federal), reducing crime (68 percent to 24 percent), and providing job training (55 percent to 31 percent).[10] Similarly, more recent surveys have shown the public favoring more state responsibility in the area of welfare. Fifty-eight percent of registered voters favor state governments rather than the federal government (34 percent) having responsibility for food stamps and Aid to Families with Dependent Children.[11]

Public Confidence in Leaders

A review of thirty years of survey data shows a near collapse in public confidence in domestic leadership groups. Parallel to the decline in public trust and confidence in the federal government and its branches has been a sharp decline in confidence in the leaders of many other major institutions in American society. For instance, the proportion of Americans who say that they have a great deal of confidence in the people running universities and colleges has declined from 61 percent in 1966 to 30 percent in 1996; in leaders of the press, from 29 percent to 14 percent; and in leaders of medicine, from 73 percent to 29 percent.[12] (See Figure 8-6.) These declines suggest that the problem of public confidence is not unique to government but has been a broader societal phenomenon. After reviewing these trends through the mid-1980s, Seymour Lipset and William Schneider concluded that a combination of leadership failures and economic downturns could account for much of the decline in the public's evaluations of government and other institutions.[13]

On the other hand, the decline in confidence has not affected all institutions equally: confidence in the people running the military declined sharply during the Vietnam years—27 percent expressed a great deal of confidence in 1971, compared with 61 percent in 1966. Public trust rebounded, however, especially after the Gulf War. Currently about half (47 percent) of Americans express a great deal of confidence in the leaders of the military. The example of the military

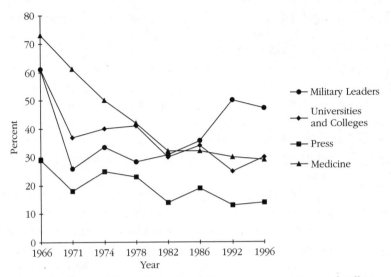

Figure 8-6. *Public confidence in leaders of the press, universities and colleges, the military, and medicine: percent saying "a great deal"*

Source: Harris Poll, 1966–96.

points out that perceived success of government in addressing visible problems can raise the public's confidence in an institution's leaders.[14]

Perceived Failures of Government

A key factor associated with declining Americans' trust in government is the public perception that the federal government has failed in its efforts to solve many of the nation's most serious problems. The *Washington Post*/Kaiser/Harvard survey found that fewer than one in five believe that things have improved over the past twenty years in any of six important areas in which the federal government has devoted major amounts of resources. Only 18 percent perceive improvements in air quality; 16 percent, in the economy; 15 percent, in poverty among people over age 65; 11 percent, in the income gap between the middle class and the wealthy; 3 percent, in children from single-parent homes; and 2 percent, in violent crime. These survey responses are striking when contrasted with the evidence Derek Bok presents in Chapter 2. Even when things (such poverty among the elderly) are—objectively—much improved, most Americans perceive things as getting worse, not better.

Asked more explicitly about the effect of *federal* programs, only a minority said that those programs had improved the situation in any of five key areas of federal spending. While 44 percent said federal programs had improved air quality, a much smaller proportion thought they had improved poverty among people over age 65 (23 percent), the income gap (11 percent), children from single-parent homes (11 percent), or violent crime (10 percent).

The perceived failure of the federal government to improve the economy is especially important. Our survey found that only 16 percent thought that the economy was getting better. Among those who said the economy was staying the same or getting worse, more than six in ten said that it was the fault of the federal government, either because of something the federal government has done (29 percent) or had not done (34 percent). The chief criticisms of those who blame the federal government are that it did not do enough to keep American jobs from going overseas (named by 70 percent as a major reason that the economy has not improved), did not do enough to create new and better jobs (68 percent), and did not reduce the federal budget deficit fast enough (67 percent).

Some authors have argued that the decline in public trust in the federal government is partly a result of media coverage of politics and government becoming more negative.[15] Indeed, Gary Orren in Chapter 3 argues that the media are critical in shaping citizen expectations of government and in judging performance. The *Washington Post*/Kaiser/Harvard data was not able to examine this issue. The survey does, however, reveal that most Americans (72 percent) report that they get their impression about the federal government from the media rather than from personal experience (18 percent) or from friends and family (8 percent).

Trust in the federal government does not vary much by principal source of a person's news about politics and government (see Table 8-1). Among those who get most of their news about politics and government from television, 26 percent trust the government just about always or most of the time. Trust is slightly lower among those who receive most of their political news from radio (21 per-

Table 8-1. Trust in the Federal Government to Do the Right Thing, by Media
Source and Frequency of Use

	Percent Who Trust the Federal Government "Just about Always" or "Most of the Time"
National	25
By Media Source	
Television	26
Radio	21
Newspapers	22
By Talk Radio Consumption	
Listen to talk radio daily	25
Regularly listen to Rush Limbaugh	15
By Frequency of Newspaper Readership per Typical Week	
7 days	21
5–6 days	34
3–4 days	32
1–2 days	24
0 days	24
By Frequency of Network TV watching per Typical Week	
7 days	22
5–6 days	30
3–4 days	26
1–2 days	22
0 days	27

Source: *Washington Post*/Kaiser Family Foundation/Harvard University, 1995.

cent) or newspapers (22 percent). Frequency of news consumption and attentiveness to news on television or in newspapers also
seems to have little relationship to trust. As we have seen, only
Rush Limbaugh listeners seem much different from Americans as a
whole.

The survey also found that although Americans are very critical
of government, they are not very knowledgeable about even its
broadest activities. For instance, despite the publicity that surrounded
the victory of the Republican party in 1994, only six in ten knew that
the Republicans controlled the U.S. Senate (62 percent) and House of
Representatives (61 percent). Moreover, only 53 percent knew that
Congressman Newt Gingrich was speaker of the House, and only 60
percent could name Al Gore as vice president. While 79 percent knew
that family-leave legislation had been enacted during the past three
years, only 10 percent knew that the annual federal deficit had declined during that period.

Trust in Individuals

Another cultural trend that occurred during the past thirty years is the decline in individuals' trust in others. Some researchers have suggested that an individual's personal experiences with other people might affect his or her trust not only in fellow citizens but also in the federal government.[16] In fact, trust in fellow citizens has fallen during the past three decades, paralleling the decline of trust in government, although not nearly as sharply. When asked in the *Washington Post/* Kaiser/Harvard survey whether most people can be trusted or if you can't be too careful in dealing with people, 35 percent said that most people can be trusted. This represents about a 20-point decline since 1964 (when 54 percent said most people can be trusted) and 1968 (56 percent).[17]

This snapshot of the American case raises puzzles and challenges, which are explored in the other chapters in this book. The figures presented here should give us pause. If the cultural factors we have discussed remain the same, Americans' overwhelmingly negative attitudes about government may place substantial limits on the ability of those in public service to act on major problems facing the nation. Tomorrow's public leaders may find themselves confronting an extraordinary dilemma. On one hand, the public will demand action on a number of national problems; on the other, they will be highly skeptical of government proposals and policies aimed at addressing them and suspicious of those who put them forth.

CHAPTER Nine

Postmateralist Values and the Erosion of Institutional Authority

Ronald Inglehart

During the past four decades, the American public has become increasingly convinced that their government is not to be trusted. In 1958, the vast majority of Americans felt that their national government was basically honest. When asked, "Do you think that quite a few of the people running the government are crooked, not very many are, or do you think that hardly any of them are crooked?", only 24 percent of the public said that "quite a few" of the people running the government were crooked. But the proportion who were distrustful rose steeply during the 1960s and 1970s, leveled off during the 1980s, and reached an all-time high in 1994, at which point an absolute majority—51 percent—of Americans polled said that quite a few of the people running the government were crooked.[1]

This massive erosion of trust in government has given rise to a good deal of scholarly discussion—including this book—since the condition was first noted by Arthur Miller in 1974. As we have seen in the preceding chapters, there is sharp disagreement about why it has occurred. It seems clear, keeping Derek Bok's caveats in mind, that good or bad performance is *part* of the story. For example, confidence in the U.S. military dropped to extremely low levels during the disastrous intervention in Vietnam, but it subsequently recovered and rose to fairly high levels after the relatively quick and successful operations in Grenada and the Gulf War. It clearly is not simply a matter of government performance, however, for the United States was experiencing peace, steady economic growth, rising real income, low inflation, and relatively low unemployment in 1994, when confidence in the national government fell to an all-time low. Governmental performance almost certainly influences public evaluations, but objective performance is always evaluated according to internalized standards—which, as Gary Orren reminds us, have changed in recent decades.

If one believed in a simple one-to-one relationship between objective performance and mass evaluations, one would assume that President Clinton must be the most inept and dishonest leader to have held office since these measurements began to be taken. That interpretation doesn't hold water. The historical record suggests that governmental corruption hasn't increased over the past generation; in fact, it has probably diminished. But regardless of whether that is true, evidence presented in this chapter indicates that the phenomenon goes beyond the United States: we are witnessing a downward trend of trust in government and confidence in leaders across most industrialized societies. In order to explain the findings, one would need to assume that practically all of the leaders in power in the early 1990s—from Clinton to Major to Mitterrand to Gonzales to Mulrooney to Andreotti to Hosokawa—happened to be among the most incompetent and dishonest leaders their countries had ever seen. This is implausible. Instead, it seems that the rules have changed, and that the publics of these countries are now evaluating their leaders and institutions by more demanding standards than were applied in the past.

Why is this true? I believe that it is linked with economic development: insofar as it gives rise to relatively high levels of existential security, it reduces the tendency for mass publics to defer to authority. Conversely, conditions of insecurity give rise to the Authoritarian Reflex—the tendency for mass publics to seek and idealize strong, authoritarian leaders.

In societies undergoing historical crises, a phenomenon has been observed that might be called the *authoritarian reflex*. Rapid change leads to severe insecurity, giving rise to a powerful need for predict-ability. Spurred by insecurity, the authoritarian reflex takes two forms:

- *Fundamentalist or nativist reactions* This phenomenon fre-quently occurs in preindustrial societies that are confronted with rapid political and economic change through contact with indus-trialized societies; it is often found among the more traditional and less secure strata in industrial societies, especially during times of stress. In both cases, the reaction to change takes the form of a rejection of the new and a compulsive insistence on the infallibility of old, familiar cultural patterns.
- *Adulation of strong secular leaders* In secularized societies, severe insecurity brings a readiness to defer to strong secular leaders, in hopes that superior individuals of iron will will lead their people to safety. This phenomenon frequently occurs in response to military defeat or economic or political collapse.

Thus, disintegrating societies often give rise to authoritarian and xenophobic reactions. Pogroms broke out in the declining years of czarist Russia, and after that country's collapse, power was seized by rulers who were even more ruthlessly authoritarian than the czars.

The publics of prosperous, stable, and democratic industrial so-cieties are more secure. The authoritarian reflex becomes latent, less evident in ordinary political discourse. These publics do not show higher levels of satisfaction with their political systems than do the publics of relatively poor, authoritarian countries—quite the contrary. Astonishing as it may seem, the publics of advanced industrial socie-ties show significantly less confidence in their leaders and political institutions than do their counterparts in developing countries. This reflects the fact that economic development brings gradual intergen-erational changes in basic values. When the point is reached at which most people take physical survival for granted, significant numbers of postmaterialists begin to emerge.[2] Although postmaterialists have higher levels of income, education, and occupational status than materialists, they do not manifest higher levels of subjective well-be-ing. Postmaterialists take prosperity for granted and focus on other aspects of life, such as politics and the quality of the physical and social environment. These domains are subjectively more important to postmaterialists than they are to materialists, and they apply higher, more demanding standards to them. Thus, although postmaterialists generally live in less noisy, less polluted neighborhoods than materialists, they register lower, not higher, levels of satisfaction with their environment.[3]

They also evaluate politics by more demanding standards. Although they live in the same political systems as materialists, and are more able to make these systems respond to their preferences (being more articulate and politically more active), they do not register higher levels of satisfaction with politics.

The rise of postmaterialist values is one symptom of a broader postmodern shift that is transforming the standards by which the publics of advanced industrial societies evaluate governmental performance. It brings new, more demanding standards to the evaluation of political life and confronts political leaders with more active, articulate citizens. The position of elites has become more difficult in advanced industrial society. Mass publics are becoming increasingly critical of their political leaders, and increasingly likely to engage in elite-challenging activities.

Long-enduring security paves the way for the reverse phenomenon: the public gradually sees less need for the discipline and self-denial demanded by strong governments. A postmaterialist emphasis on self-expression and self-realization becomes increasingly central.

Our findings contradict the widely accepted belief that the American public has become apathetic and disengaged from politics. *Voter turnout* has indeed declined, but this mainly reflects the diminishing ability of the established political parties to mobilize their supporters: the number of disciplined, unquestioning party loyalists is declining. But while electoral turnout is stagnant or declining, participation in more active, and elite-challenging forms of political action have been rising. Throughout advanced industrial societies, publics are becoming more likely to discuss politics and more likely to sign petitions, take part in boycotts, join issue-oriented groups, and engage in other forms of political activism.[4] Citizens have become increasingly critical of politicians and political parties and more willing to use noninstitutional forms of political action to pursue their goals. The evidence examined in this chapter suggests that we are witnessing a long-term trend that is weakening the authority of established institutions.

All societies depend on some legitimizing formula for authority: unless their leaders' decisions are seen as legitimate, they rest solely on coercion. A central component of modernization was the shift from religious authority to rational-bureaucratic authority, justified by claims that the governing institutions were conducive to the general good.

A major component of the postmodern shift is a turn away from all kinds of authority, because deference to authority has high costs: the individual's personal goals must be subordinated to those of a broader entity. Under conditions of insecurity, people are more than willing to do so. Facing threats of invasion, internal disorder, or economic collapse, people eagerly seek strong authority figures who can protect them.

Conversely, however, conditions of prosperity and security are conducive to pluralism in general and democracy in particular. This helps to explain a long-established finding: rich societies are much more likely to be democratic than are poor ones. This finding was pointed out by Seymour Lipset and has been confirmed most recently by Ross Burkhart and Michael Lewis-Beck.[5] Democracy is linked with economic development for a number of reasons, but one factor is because the authoritarian reflex is strongest under conditions of insecurity.

Some observers have interpreted the decline of trust in government as a sign of alienation and apathy. Pointing to declining rates of voter turnout, they argue that the American public has become disenchanted with the entire system and has withdrawn from politics completely. The empirical evidence flatly contradicts this interpretation. As we will see, although voter turnout has stagnated (largely because of weakening political party loyalties), Western publics have not become apathetic—quite the contrary. In the past two decades, they have become markedly more likely to engage in elite-challenging forms of political participation. Furthermore, the erosion of trust does not apply to all institutions: it is a withdrawal of confidence from authoritarian institutions specifically. During the same years when trust in political authority was fading, environmental protection movements rose from obscurity to attain remarkably high levels of public confidence: in the 1990–91 World Values survey of more than 40 societies, fully 93 percent of those polled approved of the environmentalist movement, with 59 percent approving "strongly." But support for certain types of institutions is sharply differentiated according to whether one has materialist or postmaterialist values, with materialists being much more likely to support authoritarian institutions. Authoritarian institutions have suffered from declining mass confidence throughout the history of advanced industrial society. This seems to be part of a pervasive development.

Norms Concerning Authority

Let us examine some actual changes that were predicted and observed in the two waves of the World Values surveys. These surveys were carried out in more than twenty countries in 1981–82 and in more than forty countries in 1990–91. We will examine trends in the twenty-one countries for which we have data from both time points. In the 1981 survey we found strong correlations between attitudes toward authority and materialist/postmaterialist values across nearly all countries. Materialists tend to support the proposition that "more respect for authority would be a good thing," while postmaterialists tend to reject it. Consequently, we predicted a gradual shift toward the values of the postmaterialists—that is, toward less emphasis on respect for authority.[6]

Figure 9-1 tests this prediction. It shows that from 1981 to 1990, emphasis on more respect for authority became less widespread in seventeen of the twenty-one countries for which we have data. The absolute levels of support for authority, and the size of the changes from 1981 to 1990, vary a good deal from country to country. But emphasis on respect for authority declined in most countries. Argentina, South Africa, Ireland, and South Korea were the only exceptions to this trend. We suspect that this pervasive decline in respect for authority has contributed to the erosion of institutional authority. Performance still counts, but the tendency to idealize national leaders has been growing weaker, and their performance is being evaluated with a more critical eye.

Our prediction that this shift would occur is based on a simple population replacement model: as the younger, more postmaterialist

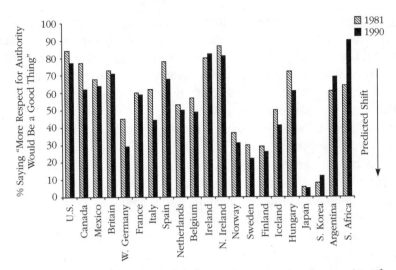

Figure 9-1. *Predicted and observed shifts: percentages saying "more respect for authority would be a good thing," in 1981 versus 1990, in twenty-one countries*

Source: 1981 and 1990 World Values surveys.

birth cohorts replace the older, more materialist cohorts in the adult population, we should see a shift toward the postmodern orientation. Moreover, because the size of the respective cohorts is known from demographic data, and because we have survey data on the attitudes of the various birth cohorts, we can also estimate the size of the attitudinal shift that population replacement should produce over a ten-year period. We do this by simply removing the oldest ten-year cohort from our sample and replacing it with a new ten-year cohort at the youngest end. In creating this new cohort, we assume that it will have values similar to those of the youngest cohort in the sample—a conservative assumption, given that younger cohorts usually show more postmodern values than older ones.[7]

When we perform this calculation, it indicates that, for most of these countries, we would expect to find a decline of only four or five points in the percentage favoring more respect for authority. This is a small shift. If we found it in only one case, it would be an unimpressive finding: a difference between samples of this size is statistically significant at only about the 0.05 level. But if we observed several such consecutive shifts over thirty or forty years, the finding would be highly significant, both statistically and substantively: over that time it could convert a 60:40 division of attitudes into a 40:60 split.

The same principle applies to a pattern of cross-cultural findings. Such a finding from only one country would hardly be worth mentioning. If we had data from three or four countries, however, and they all showed shifts of this size in the predicted direction, it would be highly significant. And if we found that the predicted shifts in values or attitudes generally held true across a score of societies, the probability of its being a random event would dwindle to the vanishing point. I have examined the shifts found with forty variables across twenty-one societies. Although the amount of change observed is usually small in any one case, the overall pattern is compelling and statistically significant at an enormously high level.[8]

With attitudes toward authority, our theory predicts a shift of only four or five percentage points per country during this nine-year period. This is modest. In the short run, the impact of current economic or political events (or even sampling error) could easily swamp it in a given society. Thus, it would be astonishing if our predictions did hold up in every case. They don't: instead we find that, in some countries, attitudes concerning authority moved in the predicted direction, while in others they didn't. Moreover, some countries show shifts in the predicted direction that are too large to be due to population replacement alone: in these cases, situation-specific factors are probably adding to the results of population replacement, exaggerating the shift.

We can predict only one component of what is shaping mass attitudes, so we cannot predict precisely what will happen in every country. Nevertheless, our predictive power across many societies should be considerably better than random. In the long run, over many countries, our predictions should point in the right direction. When examined empirically, it turns out that they actually do. Our theory predicts declining emphasis on authority, and in seventeen of these twenty-one countries we find it.

Let us examine some evidence from the 1981 and 1990 World Values surveys that demonstrates the claims we have just laid out. Across nearly all of our societies, materialists place more confidence in their country's hierarchical institutions—especially the armed forces, police, and church—than do postmaterialists. These findings are consistent with our argument that a sense of insecurity tends to motivate support for strong institutions and for strong political authority in particular. Having experienced a relatively high sense of economic and physical security throughout their formative years, postmaterialists feel less need for strong authority than do materialists. Moreover, postmaterialists place relatively strong emphasis on self-expression—a value that inherently conflicts with the structure of hierarchical bureaucratic organizations.

The value-related differences point to the possibility of a shift over time, toward the outlook of the younger and more postmaterialist respondents. Do we find it? The answer is yes. In most countries, we find lower levels of confidence in government institutions in 1990 than those that existed in 1981.

Our respondents were asked how much confidence they had in a dozen national institutions. Postmaterialists show lower levels of confidence in most established institutions than do materialists, and in three cases the correlations were high enough to meet our criterion of "reasonably strong": postmaterialist values are especially strongly linked with low levels of confidence in their country's police, armed forces, and church. Consequently, we predict that confidence in these institutions will decline.

As Figure 9-2 demonstrates, from 1981 to 1990, confidence in the given society's police declined in sixteen of the twenty countries for which we have data. Confidence rose only in Ireland and Iceland, and in Argentina and South Africa, two of the three societies in our sample that were undergoing regime changes (1981 data are not available for Hungary, the third such society).

Confidence in the country's armed forces shows a similar pattern (see Figure 9-3). It declined in seventeen of the twenty countries for which we have data and rose only in Northern Ireland and, again, in Argentina and South Africa. As I noted earlier, U.S. data from a longer time span show increasing confidence in the military, but this seems to reflect recovery from an abnormally low level that was linked with the war in Vietnam. Confidence in one's country's church also moved on the predicted trajectory; it fell in fourteen of the twenty cases in which changes occurred. Confidence in the churches rose only in the United States, Ireland, and Northern Ireland, and in Hun-

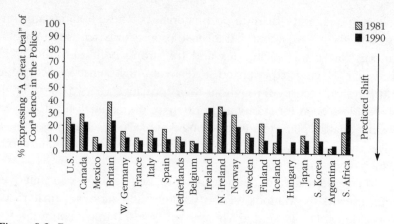

Figure 9-2. *Percentages expressing "a great deal" of confidence in their country's police forces, in 1981 versus 1990, in twenty countries*

Source: 1981 and 1990 World Values surveys (1981 data not available for Hungary).

gary, Argentina, and South Africa, the three countries undergoing regime changes.[9]

Data from a number of other sources confirm the thesis that confidence in hierarchical institutions is declining throughout advanced industrial society. The National Opinion Center at the University of Chicago has been measuring confidence in U.S. national institutions every year since 1973. These institutions include Congress, the executive branch, the press, the military, organized labor, the Supreme Court, television, education, and organized religion. Nearly all of these institutions (with the notable exception of the post-1980 military) have suffered some decline since 1973. And in a number of cases, the 1993 levels of confidence were the lowest ever recorded during this twenty-year period. This was true of the American public's rating of Congress, the press, television, education, and organized religion. The decline in confidence was substantial. For example, in 1973, only 15 percent of the public said that they had "hardly any" confidence in Congress; in 1993, 41 percent said they had "hardly any" confidence. Similarly, although 1993 was not the low point of confidence in the executive branch (that was registered in 1974, when President Nixon resigned), there was an overall downward trend here too: in 1973, only 18 percent of Americans said they had "hardly any" confidence in the

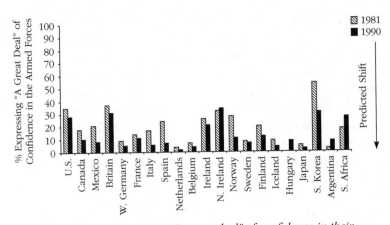

Figure 9-3. Percentages expressing "a great deal" of confidence in their country's armed forces, in 1981 versus 1990, in twenty-one countries

Source: 1981 and 1990 World Values surveys (1981 data not available for Hungary).

executive branch; in 1993, 32 percent said they had "hardly any" confidence.[10]

Another manifestation of the collapse of public faith in politicians is the recent emergence of massive support for term limitations on elected representatives in Congress, and in some cases, in state legislatures as well. Although they probably are not constitutional, such proposals have been passed in every state where they have been on the ballot. Obviously, voters already have the right to limit the terms of their representatives by simply not reelecting them. But the mass mood seems to reflect a widespread perception that the incumbents have become a self-perpetuating privileged class, and the only safe way to curtail their power is by placing formal limits on their tenure of power.

The old standards for evaluating elites no longer apply. A record that once would have ensured reelection is now insufficient. More than seven years after he had led allied forces to victory in World War II, a grateful nation elected Dwight Eisenhower president by a landslide margin. By contrast, shortly after the cold war had come to a sudden and (from an American perspective) astonishingly successful conclusion, and immediately after a swift and (from an American perspective) almost bloodless victory in the Gulf War, and with an economy that was actually in relatively good shape, George Bush failed to win reelection in 1992. This was not just a failure of charisma on Bush's part, for within two years his successor had become massively unpopular, and his party lost control of both the House and the Senate. This happened even though the economic indicators looked better than they did under Bush. It has become clear that, in the realm of political behavior, the standard economic indicators no longer explain as much as they once did. Postmodern publics evaluate their leaders by different and more demanding standards than those applied throughout most of the modern era.

This phenomenon is not limited to the United States. Since 1973, the publics of the European Union countries repeatedly have been asked, "Generally speaking, are you satisfied or dissatisfied with the way democracy is working in your country?" Although, as one would expect, these ratings tend to rise and fall with the economic cycle, they also show a long-term downward tendency. Thus, in the recessions of the early 1970s and the early 1980s, "dissatisfied" ratings became nearly as numerous as "satisfied" ratings among the combined European Union publics. But during the recession of the early 1990s, for the first time, negative ratings became more widespread than positive ratings. In 1993, dissatisfaction reached the highest level ever recorded.

How deep does this dissatisfaction run? The respondents in the World Values surveys were asked how proud they were to be French, Mexican, Japanese, and so forth, answering on a scale that ran from "very proud" to "not at all proud." Evidence of ethnic conflict around the world has made it commonplace to assert that this is "an era of rising nationalism."

But is it? The reality is more complex. In light of the evidence of a widespread decline of confidence in national institutions, one might expect pride in the nation itself to decline as well, as national pride is strongly correlated with confidence in national institutions and with the strength of one's religious convictions. Furthermore, we find that postmaterialists express lower levels of national pride than do materialists (and the correlation is "reasonably strong"). Hence, we would predict a decline in feelings of national pride.

The traditional form of nationalism is rising in many settings, but not in most advanced industrial societies. There has been a rising

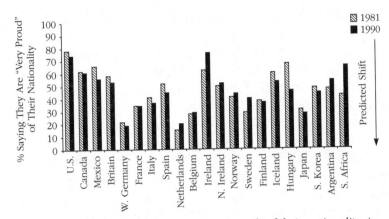

Figure 9-4. *Percentages saying they are "very proud" of their nationality, in 1981 versus 1990, in twenty-one countries*

Source: 1981 and 1990 World Values surveys.

tide of one form of "nationalism"—that is, of xenophobia linked with insecurity—in poorer and less secure societies: it has had dramatic and tragic consequences in India, Sri Lanka, Azerbaijia, Armenia, Sudan, Nigeria, Rwanda, the former Soviet Union, and the former Yugoslavia. In advanced industrial societies, however, we are witnessing a quite different phenomenon: we find demands to transfer authority away from the existing nation-states to smaller, more immediate units having greater cultural coherence: from Spain to Catalonia, for example, or from Canada to Quebec. The partisans of such movements tend to be postmaterialists, motivated by concerns for cultural autonomy and a sense of community. Very confusingly, this completely different phenomenon is also called "nationalism." The fact that the term "nationalism" is used to denote both hyperloyalty to the nation-state and withdrawing one's loyalty away from it to smaller units has given rise to a good deal of confusion and misunderstanding; two quite different (indeed, almost opposite) things are lumped together as "rising nationalism." This usage equates contemporary Quebecois autonomists with the xenophobic nationalists of the nineteenth century. They are not at all the same thing. In advanced industrial societies, ethnic separatist movements generally do not involve an inward-looking parochialism. Instead, they represent a shift of focus away from the hierarchical nation-state in two directions: on the one hand you have a greater emphasis on community and local autonomy; on the other you have a growing openness to broader ties. Thus, the Quebecois separatists tend to be more favorable to North American free trade than are Canadians in general, and the Catalan "nationalists" tend to be partisans of European unification.

From 1981 to 1990, feelings of national pride tended to move on the same trajectory as did the other elements of this syndrome, but the results are mixed: in twelve out of nineteen countries, we find a decline in the percentage expressing strong feelings of national pride, as Figure 9-4 demonstrates. The results move in the predicted direction in 63 percent of the cases in which change occurred. But there are a number of exceptions. In addition to the usual countertrends in Argentina and South Africa, national pride rose in Ireland, Northern Ireland, Norway, Sweden, the Netherlands, and Belgium. We do not find a simple split between secure and insecure societies.

Our predictions show a success rate of 63 percent; this is better than random, but it is not doing as well as with most political variables. It raises an interesting question: Why is national pride not declining as much as we would expect in advanced industrial societies? We suspect that two major contemporary events are involved.

The first is a West European reaction against massive non-European immigration. The immense disparity between living standards in Western Europe and developing countries, coupled with wide-bodied jet aircraft, has brought a large influx of visibly different immigrants into societies that never before had large numbers of them. Suddenly, most of these countries find themselves with large minorities of ethnically distinct peoples, often coming from very far away. Interacting with the insecurity owing to the recent recession, this has given rise to a wave of xenophobia—and the tendency to reemphasize one's traditional ethnic identity.

The other factor is the push toward European Union, which (like most major changes) has also given rise to a traditionalist reaction in many countries.

An increase in feelings of national pride did not take place in North America during this period, despite the fact that the United States and Canada have had larger immigrant inflows than any West European society. But more recently, the United States also has experienced strong pressures to limit further immigration.

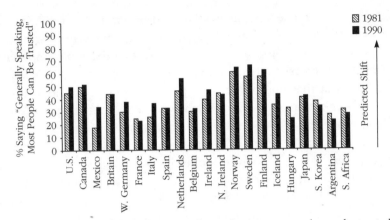

Figure 9-5. *Percentages saying "generally speaking, most people can be trusted," in 1981 versus 1990, in twenty-one countries*

Source: 1981 and 1990 World Values surveys.

The decline of confidence in established institutions and of trust in government does not represent a broad withdrawal of trust concerning people in general: it is specifically a withdrawal of confidence from authoritative institutions. Interpersonal trust is strongly linked with postmaterialist values; consequently, we would predict rising, not falling, levels of interpersonal trust. As Figure 9-5 demonstrates, this prediction is confirmed: interpersonal trust rose in thirteen of the nineteen countries in which change was observed. The exceptions include France, Northern Ireland, and South Korea and the three societies undergoing regime change, Hungary, Argentina, and South Africa. National Election Study and General Social Survey data from the United States demonstrate that there was a significant downward movement in interpersonal trust from 1964 to 1994, but the United States is exceptional in this respect. In the majority of countries examined here, mass publics are coming to trust people more but hierarchical institutions less.

Moreover, there is one striking exception to the decline of mass confidence in established institutions: during the period 1981–90, confidence in "major corporations" did not decline. Although it started from relatively low levels in 1981, confidence in corporations showed a rising trend in most societies. During this era, the collapse of state socialist economies helped to make private enterprise look good by contrast. And in a sense, this is a logical reaction to the pronounced decline of trust in government: if the state is coming to be seen as the problem rather than the solution, it becomes all the more important to have a strong countervailing force to offset its power. In any case, it seems clear that one of the most pervasive defining tendencies of the modernization era—the tendency to look to the state as the solution to all problems—has reached its limits.

Throughout advanced industrial democracies, voter turnout is stagnant or declining. In most countries, established political party machines are losing their grip on voters. Party membership has fallen to about half the level it had a few decades ago. And although plenty of people still identify with some political party, their behavior is much less influenced by party loyalty than it was in the past; split-ticket voting has increased markedly. Electoral volatility has increased. And political parties that had dominated their societies for decades—from the Liberal-Democratic party of Japan to the Christian Democratic party of Italy—have lost their hold on power (as the Democratic party has lost its seemingly permanent dominance of the U.S. Congress).

One frequently hears claims that mass publics have become apathetic, based on the fact that voter turnout rates have declined. As I will demonstrate, these allegations of apathy are misleading: mass publics are less heavily influenced by the old-line oligarchical political organizations that mobilized them in the modernization era, but, far from being apathetic, these same publics are becoming *more* active than ever in a wide range of elite-challenging forms of political participation.

Samuel Barnes et al. and I predicted that elite-challenging political participation would rise in the long term, as a consequence of changing values and rising skills levels, as intergenerational population replacement takes place.[11] These predictions were published more than a decade before the data for the 1990 World Values surveys were collected. They contradict the conventional wisdom that focuses on declining voting rates and concludes that citizens are losing interest in politics and the prevailing trend is toward mass apathy. But voting turnout largely reflects the parties' ability to mobilize their supporters, and it is a misleading indicator of real mass interest and involvement. The World Values survey data show strong correlations between materialist/postmaterialist values and the more active forms of political participation (though not with voting). Accordingly, we would expect to find rising, not falling, levels of mass political participation. Let us examine the evidence.

Evidence from the twenty-one countries surveyed in both 1981 and 1990 indicates that, although they may vote less regularly, most publics are not becoming apathetic—quite the contrary. They are becoming increasingly interested in politics. Political interest rates rose in sixteen countries and fell in only four. The findings are unequivocal, and they contradict the conventional wisdom about mass apathy. Another good indicator of political interest is whether or not people discuss politics with others. Here, too, the predicted rise in conventional participation is taking place, as Figure 9-6 indicates. The proportion of the population that discusses politics rose in seventeen countries and fell in only three (with one country showing no change).

Another, more active form of conventional political participation also shows the predicted increase: as Figure 9-7 demonstrates, from 1981 to 1990 the percentage reporting that they had signed a petition rose in sixteen countries and fell in only four. When we examine trends over a still longer time period, the results are even more dramatic. Four of the countries that were included in both World Values surveys were also surveyed for the 1974 Political Action study.[12] The data for these countries (the United States, Britain, West Germany, and the Netherlands) are included in Figure 9-7. In all four cases, we find even larger increases from 1974 to 1990 than we do from 1981 to 1990. In the United States, the percentage reporting that they had signed a petition rose from 58 percent in 1974 to 68 percent in 1981 to 71 percent in 1990; for Britain, they rose from 22 percent to 62 percent to 75 percent; for West Germany, the figures are 31 percent, 43 percent, and 56 percent; and in the Netherlands, the rise was from 21 percent to 37 percent to 50 percent.

This is dramatic evidence of rising mass political activism. How do we explain declining rates of voter turnout and falling political party membership in the light of these findings? The confusion over whether participation is rising or falling arises from the fact that we are dealing with two distinct processes: elite-directed participation is eroding, but more autonomous and active forms of participation are rising.

This decline in voter turnout reflects a long-term intergenerational

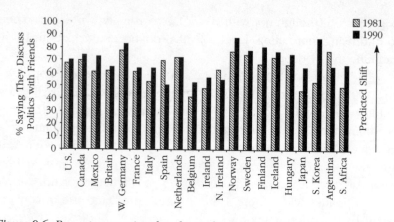

Figure 9-6. *Percentages saying that they "often" or "sometimes" discuss politics with friends, in 1981 versus 1990, in twenty-one countries*

Source: 1981 and 1990 World Values surveys.

decline in party loyalty. Although the younger, better educated birth cohorts show higher rates of political interest, political discussion, and so forth than their elders, they have lower levels of party loyalty. Surveys from a number of West European countries reveal that the postwar birth cohorts have considerably lower rates of political party loyalty than the older cohorts.[13] This finding parallels a pattern of intergenerational decline in party identification that has been found among the American electorate during the past two decades.[14]

Although their higher levels of education and politicization predispose them to identify with some political party, the younger and relatively postmaterialist cohorts have less incentive to identify with any specific political party among the available choices. The traditional political parties were established in an era dominated by social class conflict and economic issues, and they tend to remain polarized along these lines. For the older cohorts, religion and social class still provide powerful cues in establishing one's political party loyalties. But the younger cohorts' loyalties are less strongly influenced by social class and religion. Moreover, in recent years, a new axis of polarization has arisen based on cultural and quality-of-life issues. Established parties have had difficulty in reorienting themselves in relation to this axis. The established political party configurations in most countries today do not yet adequately reflect the most pressing

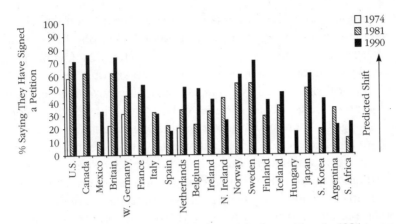

Figure 9-7. Percentages saying that they have signed a petition, in 1981 versus 1990, in twenty countries

Sources: 1981 and 1990 World Values surveys (1981 data not available for Hungary); 1974 figures for the United States, Britain, West Germany, and the Netherlands from Barnes et al., 548–49.

contemporary issues, and those born in the postwar era have relatively little motivation to identify with the established political parties.[15]

But partisan loyalties and party organizations were the main reason for the high electoral turnout of earlier years. Hence, we find two divergent trends: on the one hand the bureaucratized and elite-directed forms of participation such as voting and party membership have declined, and on the other the individually motivated and elite-challenging forms of participation have risen.

These processes have implications that both are alarming and encouraging. Established institutions that have shaped industrial society for generations seem to be losing their authority over the average citizen. Public confidence is declining, not only in key governmental institutions such as parliament, the police, the civil service, and the armed forces but also in political parties, churches, educational systems, and the press. We even find a weakening sense of attachment to that most basic of all Western institutions, the nation-state itself. The danger of this evolution is that societal institutions could become too atrophied to cope with a national emergency. But there are positive aspects as well. In societies characterized by too much respect for authority, this shift is conducive to democratization, for the erosion of state authority has been accompanied by a rising potential for citizen intervention in politics. This is partly due to a shift in values, with a weakening emphasis on the goals of economic and physical security that favor strong authorities; but another factor that favors rising citizen intervention is the long-term rise in educational levels and in mass political skills that have characterized all industrial societies. In the long run, industrialized societies of both East and West must cope with changes that are making their publics less amenable to doing as they are told and more adept at telling their governments what to do.

The rise of postmodern values brings declining respect for authority and growing emphasis on participation and self-expression. These two trends are conducive to democratization (in authoritarian societies) and to more participatory, issue-oriented democracy (in already democratic societies). But they are making the position of governing elites more difficult.

Respect for authority is eroding, and the long-term trend toward increased mass participation is not only continuing but has taken on a new character. In industrial societies, the masses were mobilized by disciplined elite-led political parties. This was a major advance for democratization, and it resulted in unprecedented numbers of people taking part in politics by voting—but mass participation rarely went much beyond this level. In postmodern society, however, the emphasis is shifting from voting to more active and issue-specific forms of mass participation. Mass loyalties to long-established hierarchical political parties are eroding; no longer content to be disciplined troops, the public has become increasingly autonomous and elite-challenging. Although voter turnout is stagnant or declining, people are participating in politics in increasingly active and more issue-specific ways.

Public Trust and
Democracy in Japan

Susan J. Pharr

A half century ago, Japan emerged from an era of imperialism, fascism, and war to embrace democratic institutions closely modeled on those of the West. Despite a postwar economic miracle under the leadership of the conservative Liberal Democratic party (LDP) that transformed postwar Japan from a World Bank loan recipient as late as 1966 to its current standing as the world's number-two economic power and technological wunderkind, Japan today is in the grip of deep-seated malaise about government. Virtually every recent survey establishes that public trust in political leaders and institutions is low. Civic disaffection with government and those who lead it is, of course, a widespread phenomenon today in the advanced industrial countries. The preceding chapters have explored its sources in the American context. This brief chapter enlarges the scope of inquiry to include Japan. At a minimum, weighing Japan's experience challenges easy assumptions about what ails contemporary democracies.

Disaffection in Japan has several quite distinctive features. First, in contrast with the United States and many European democracies, Japan has not seen public trust plummet from more halcyon days in the 1950s and 1960s; instead, disaffection with politics *has been endemic in the postwar era*. Despite stability and prosperity under LDP rule, the polarized nature of the early postwar political system and a civic tradition of deference to authorities left a substantial portion of the electorate alienated and detached from political life. Even LDP supporters were critical of the "money politics" that kept the party in power. Reporting the results of numerous surveys conducted by Japanese newspapers and polling organizations in the 1950s and 1960s, Richardson concluded, "Majorities of respondents showed either little satisfaction or outright dissatisfaction with the way politics is conducted."[1] As for government itself, although Japan's elite bureaucracy enjoyed high prestige, confidence in the responsiveness of officials to citizen concerns was low. For example, asked in a 1966–67 cross-national study directed by Sidney Verba if they thought their point of view would be given serious consideration if they visited a government office, only 6 percent of Japanese respondents said yes, in contrast to 48 percent in the United States.[2] Survey results suggest that even after the national income–doubling decade of the 1960s, Japan in the mid-1970s, along with Italy, had the lowest levels of trust in politics among seven industrial nations (see Table 10-1). Since the 1970s (except for a brief interlude around the mid-1980s), from around one-half to two-thirds of the Japanese public, depending on the survey, have said that they were dissatisfied or somewhat dissatisfied with politics (see Figure 10-1). With regard to political leaders, some studies suggest that public distrust easily surpasses levels in the United States. According to a 1989 binational survey on ethics in government, for example, a dismally low 10 percent of the Japanese respondents

Table 10-1. Percentage of Political Trust and Orientation in Seven Countries

	Japan	Britain	Germany	Netherlands	Austria	United States	Italy
Trust in Politics[1]	27	45	69	58	71	31	22
Interest in Politics[2]	49	45	63	58	54	69	21
Efficacy[3]	27	37	27	44	28	59	28

[1] Respondents answering that "the people" rather than "big interests" run politics.
[2] Respondents answering they were interested in politics "all of the time" or "sometimes"; missing data are excluded from calculations.
[3] Respondents answering that people have a "say" in what government does.
Source: Data are for 1976. Adapted from Bradley M. Richardson, "Japanese Voting Behavior in Comparative Perspective," in Scott C. Flanagan, Shinsaku Kohei, Ichiro Miyake, Bradley M. Richardson, and Joji Watanuki, *The Japanese Voter* (New Haven, Conn.: Yale University Press, 1991), 25, Table 1.3. Data are from the 1976 Japan Election Study conducted by the scholars listed above (referred to as the "JABISS" study, an acronym comprised of the first initial of each team member) and the ICPSR "Political Action" Study code book.

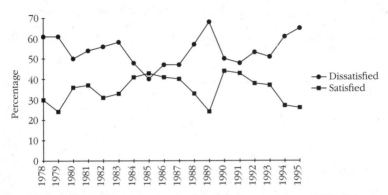

***Figure 10-1.** Political dissatisfaction and satisfaction in Japan, 1978–95*

"Dissatisfied" records the percentage of those who said they were "dissatisfied" in response to the question "In general are you satisfied with politics today, or are you dissatisfied?" "Satisfied" records the total percentage of those who said they were either "satisfied" or "somewhat satisfied." "Don't know/No answer" responses ranged from 6 to 17 percent. Results from annual surveys conducted in December, with the exception of 1989 (March) and 1991 (September). Sample size: 3,600 individuals. Nationwide, selected two-stage stratified random selection method. First stage: 345 national statistical areas were classified by age structure, industrial structure, and population. Second stage: persons are randomly selected from one randomly selected election district in each area and are interviewed in person by university student volunteers. Response rates around 75 percent.

Source: Asahi Shimbun, Tokyo Morning Edition.

(in contrast to 61 percent of the Americans polled) considered the ethical standards of their country's legislators to be "very high" or "somewhat high."[3] In 1992, an astonishing 74 percent of Japanese in a major study endorsed the view that "many dishonest people" were running their country (see Table 10-2).

Nor did the end to almost four decades of virtually uninterrupted LDP rule inspire greater public trust in leaders and government. After a surge of corruption scandals in the late 1980s and early 1990s, the Liberal Democrats in July 1993 lost their majority, ushering in a new era in Japanese politics. In the face of widespread public pressure for political reform, an eight-party opposition coalition government headed by Prime Minister Morihito Hosokawa pushed through, in January 1994, a major reform package aimed at curtailing "money politics" and improving the quality of political life. Japan's multimember, medium-sized electoral-district system that weighted rural votes

Table 10-2. How the Japanese Public See Those Who Run the Country: "Do you think there are many dishonest people among those who manage our national politics, some dishonest people or no dishonest people at all?"

	1976	1983	1992
Many Dishonest People	44.3%	44.2%	74.1%
Some Dishonest People	46.8	42.9	21.5
No Dishonest People	1.8	3.2	0.7
Don't Know/No Answer	7.1	9.7	3.7

Source: Data for 1976 are JABISS (lower house election) (see Table 10.1 for explanation); data for 1983 are from the 1983 Japan Election Study (JES) (upper house election); 1992 data are from a survey conducted by Ikuo Kabashima and others, the results of which appear in his "Seiron to seiken koudai" [Public Opinion and the Alternation of Power], in *Dai seiben* [The Big Political Change], ed. Tōru Hayano, Yasunori Sone, and Kenzō Uchida (Tokyo: Tōyō Keizai Shinpōsha, 1994), 178.

over urban ones and, critics held, drove up the cost of politics by pitting members of the same party against one another for the multiple seats available, was replaced with a Lower House electoral system that combines new and smaller single districts with proportional representation.[4] A new law provides 30.9 billion yen ($280.9 million at 110 yen to the dollar) in public funds for campaigning, to be distributed among the parties. Furthermore, in a frontal attack on money politics, the reform package set new limits on company donations, reducing the maximum for contributions to 500,000 yen ($4,545) per politician per year, with further scaling down ahead.[5]

All these reforms, in a larger sense, were intended to revitalize Japanese democracy and to restore public trust in leaders and government. But if anything, citizen disillusionment and cynicism are higher today than before. Just 26 percent of people questioned in a 1994 survey agreed that national policy reflects the will of the people well or to some extent (see Table 10-3). In a December 1995 *Asahi Shimbun* (a Japanese newspaper) survey, 65 percent of those questioned reported being "dissatisfied" with politics, a rate that is one of the highest recorded in *Asahi* surveys since 1978 (see Figure 10-1). In another leading newspaper's survey the same month, only 29 percent subscribed to the view that democracy in Japan was functioning well, while 61 percent disagreed.[6] Whatever their long-term effect, the reforms, so far, have done little to rebuild public trust; in fact, it is quite likely that raised—but unfulfilled—expectations over what an

Table 10-3. Japanese Trust in Government and the Political Process: "How well do you feel that national policy reflects the will of the people?"

	1982	1983	1984	1985	1987	1988	1990	1991	1992	1993	1994
Reflects It Well or to Some Extent (%)	24.4	30.7	34.0	36.4	35.7	26.8	30.1	32.6	23.4	30.8	25.6
Not Very Well	48.0	43.9	40.9	37.8	42.2	48.3	47.7	48.2	49.3	62.8	52.6
Hardly at All	15.6	10.4	10.2	8.2	10.6	15.5	11.7	12.8	20.8		15.2

Source: Prime Minister's Office, *Public Opinion Survey on Society and State* (Tokyo: Foreign Press Center, selected years). This survey is administered more or less annually to a sample of over 7,000 persons 20 years and older in December. Thus the figure for 1993, for example, reflects opinion five months after the July 1993 watershed lower house election. For 1993, 62.8 is the combined figure for "not very well" and "hardly at all." Columns do not total 100 since "don't knows" and nonresponses are omitted.

end to one-party dominance might bring, constituted a whole new source of public distrust. After five prime ministers and three varieties of coalition governments since the start of 1993 and yet more scandals, voters gave the Liberal Democrats a near majority (238 out of 500 seats) in the first Lower House election under the new electoral system on October 20, 1996, reflecting their frustration with the transition era.

A second distinctive feature of disaffection in Japan is that for most of the postwar era public distrust in Japan *has centered on politicians and politics, not bureaucrats and bureaucracy.* Japan's elite bureaucracy, drawn from the top national universities and tested by one of the world's toughest higher-civil-service-exam systems, has commanded a high level of respect and trust. A trend of the past few years, however, is declining public trust in bureaucrats as well. In the mid-1990s, scandals involving various combinations of money-for-favors and bureaucratic ineptitude—quite rare in the past—were at center stage in Japan, and administrative reform was the issue of the hour. In a December 1995 survey, 70 percent of citizens questioned answered "no" when asked if they had confidence in legislators; 65 percent similarly distrusted central government bureaucrats, an astonishing comedown for the public officials who, among other things, were the engineers of postwar economic growth.[7] On the top rung of the ministry prestige ladder is the Ministry of Finance (MOF); its standing has been such that until 1975, no bill originated by MOF had ever been tabled in the legislature, or Diet.[8] In 1995, for the thirty-first year in a row, its retirees outstripped those of all other ministries to capture the largest number of postretirement private-sector posts, in the Japanese practice of *amakudari,* or "descent from heaven."[9] Despite this exalted status, however, criticism of MOF in the mid-1990s had become rife; indeed, in 1996, MOF bashing in Japan rivaled Clinton bashing in America.

A third characteristic of public distrust in Japan is the degree to which it has *been directed at national-level as opposed to local officials.* Prefectural and local officials are trusted more in Japan, and this overall trend continues: the closer the proximity to the voter, the more the trust. The persistence of this relationship has been measured by local election studies conducted regularly by one of the country's leading public watchdog survey groups, the Clean Election League

(Akarui Senkyo Suishin Kyōkai). If we ask why widespread distrust of national politicians and politics over the entire postwar era has not been more of a problem in Japan, higher confidence levels in local representatives and officials (and in the national bureaucracy) is an important part of the answer. Recently, however, trust in local leaders, like trust in other institutions, has declined. The December 1995 *Japan Economic Journal* survey found, for example, that only 12 percent of people questioned were prepared to say that local government was "quite responsive" or "somewhat responsive" to "people's opinions and wishes."[10]

A final feature of public distrust is that it has tended to be *highest in urban areas and among better-educated people and also among the young*. With well over a majority of the public voicing dissatisfaction with various aspects of political life at almost any point over the post-war period, distrust in government and in public officials obviously is not confined to particular subsets of the population. In general, however, disaffection levels typically have been highest among these groups. In Japan, in the anomaly reported by Joji Watanuki many years ago,[11] electoral turnout is highest in rural areas, where voters are passive and parochial in their political orientation and choose their representatives on the basis of "personal vote" factors—that is, service to the district or to the candidate and personal ties with the candidate—rather than party or actual issue positions.[12] Turnout is lower in urban areas, where people in the high and middle range in socioeconomic standing, while interested in politics and relatively more efficacious and active in their basic political orientation, but are cynical with respect to national political life. The same holds true today; farmers and owners and employees of small businesses remain far more likely to have positive feelings toward national politics, while urbanites and salaried workers are the most negative.[13] Recently, more and more voters have the "modern" mix: an active, efficacious orientation toward politics that does not get translated into active political behavior when it comes to elections because of cynicism and distrust. When it comes to age, recent survey data reveal that levels of alienation from politics are exceptionally high among the younger citizens, who also have low levels of attachment to the political parties (including the new ones that have emerged since the 1993 shake-up).

Are the Japanese really as disaffected as survey data suggest? Some observers would say no, and might make two arguments. First, some hold that disaffection is more or less cyclical. Thus it could be argued that disaffection levels around the time of the Lockheed scandal (1976), in which former Prime Minister Kakuei Tanaka was accused, and later convicted, of taking a $1.8 million bribe from Lockheed, were exceedingly high, and that by the mid-1980s voters had more or less returned to normal and were—for Japan—feeling more optimistic and trusting of public officials, institutions, and the democratic process. With the Recruit (1988) and Sagawa Kyubin (1992) scandals—both involving purported exchanges of money for favors between service sector firms and leading politicians—ire rose again, contributing to the LDP's loss of its majority in the 1993 election, but things will settle down once more, once the current political situation stabilizes—or so the argument goes. The January 1996 strong showing of support for LDP prime minister Ryūtaro Hashimoto (who was then presiding over an LDP-led coalition that included the Social Democrats plus a smaller party) supports the back-to-business-as-usual interpretation; a 54 percent approval rating for the Hashimoto cabinet at the start of his administration, in contrast to a 30 percent approval rating for the Socialist-led cabinet in 1994, also lends credence to such a view. Second, those sceptical about the high level of disaffection might claim that political distrust is not deeply held. Thirty-eight years of one-party dominance, so this argument goes, established a pattern in which voters sounded off about the LDP secure in the knowledge that it would stay in power; indeed, voicing disapproval of both the party and the political system with which it came to be synonymous was a perfectly reasonable way of checking LDP excesses, but it makes survey evidence of disaffection suspect.

These lines of argument ultimately are not very compelling, however. High disaffection levels over the entire postwar era cast doubts about the validity of any "cyclical" interpretation. Furthermore, if signals of disaffection and disapproval were really voter strategies in a system of one-party rule, then we might have expected to see greater confidence in government restored after 1993, particularly in the wake of reforms that voters themselves had sought. As Figure 10.1 indicates, however, there has been no such upswing: far from declining, disaffection appears to be spreading to new targets. Finally, relatively high approval ratings for any particular cabinet should not be taken as evidence of more general satisfaction with politics. It is noteworthy in this regard that while the overall support level for the Hashimoto cabinet was at 53 percent according to a study released May 29, 1996, only 21 percent of those questioned said that they trusted Hashimoto.[14]

Doubters imply that expressions of trust or distrust in government in Japan do not reflect deeply held views. There is substantial evidence, however, that the quality of political life is of considerable importance to people. In a 1987 survey, 65 percent of citizens asked whether improving politics had any relation to their own lives said that it did; only 14 percent saw no meaningful connection between the two.[15] There is overwhelming evidence today that Japan's better-educated and more nationally oriented electorate want more from their leaders and from their democracy.

Is Japanese Democracy Different?

How, then, are we to explain the high levels of public distrust among Japanese citizens? Some would hold that disaffection in Japan has an altogether different meaning from the kind found in Western countries, and that it signals basic ills with Japanese democracy itself. Over twenty years ago, a report of the Trilateral Commission on the state of health of industrial democracies saw Japan as something of a laggard in comparison with the United States and Europe; because Japanese citizens were somewhat less efficacious and active in their orientation toward politics than their industrial-society counterparts, democracy there, the report implied, was somewhat more fragile.[16] In a rash of widely read books in the late 1980s and since of the so-called revisionist school, which has seen Japan as unique rather than "Western," journalists Karel van Wolferen and James Fallows, among others, similarly cast doubts about the state of Japanese democracy.[17] Survey data fail to support such a conclusion, however. Indeed, data over past decades on changes in the civic culture show a steadily deepening acceptance of the values associated with democracy. In Japan, for example, a key index is whether people are prepared to defer to authority, as in the prewar era, or to adopt a more participatory stance. Data collected over a fifty-year period by the Clean Election League reveal that citizens have moved steadily away from a belief that leaving things to leaders is preferable; they believe, far more than in the past, that they should be actively ("debating among themselves") making policy choices rather than passively accepting what leaders do. Similarly, following from top-down patterns of authority in prewar Japan, early postwar generations saw voting as a duty rather than a right. Among younger people in Japan today, however, voting over-whelmingly is seen as a right; in the 25–29 age group, for example, 57 percent in one study saw voting as a right, while only 35 percent said it was a duty.[18] In this sense, Japanese democracy has matured, and the lag once described has virtually disappeared. Indeed, if dis-affection has moved to higher levels in the 1990s, ironically it may be that Japan is catching up with the other industrialized democracies in that respect as well.

Economic Malaise as a Cause

Numerous observers of rising political dissatisfaction levels in advanced industrial democracies see economic dislocations and a resulting sense of economic insecurity as root causes. The economic ills themselves vary, from chronic unemployment in many European countries to a decline in real wages in the United States over more than two decades. Japan, too, has had its share of economic problems, especially since the onset in 1991 of the longest recession in the country's postwar history. But other signs of a modest economic ratcheting-down can be detected before that time. Japan has long been a society in which the overwhelming majority of people—over 90 percent since 1970—see themselves as middle class, but the sense of perceived *relative* prosperity within that class has undergone subtle change. A regular survey conducted by the Prime Minister's Office tracks these shifts. From the high growth decade of the 1960s, as the benefits of high growth filtered down to create greater prosperity for individuals, there was a gradual increase in the percentage of Japanese who said they considered themselves "middle" middle class as op-posed to "lower" middle class. But on the eve of the 1980s, the trend began to reverse itself, especially as the "bubble era" of the late 1980s, which inflated the value of land and stock, created a perceived gap between those who owned assets and those who did not. The percentage of people considering themselves middle middle class fell from 60.6 percent in 1979 to 53.6 percent in 1992, while the percentage who considered themselves lower middle class correspondingly rose from 22.2 percent to 26.2 percent over the same period.[19] The difference in income between these two groups was quite small; the most significant difference was in the floor space of their homes: under fifty square meters for the self-identified lower middle class and seventy-five square meters for the middle middle class.[20] If people's relative sense of well-being is relevant for how they judge their government and leaders, however, then relatively minor shifts of that kind potentially matter.

Still, it is important not to overstate the importance of these modest shifts, particularly in light of other facets of Japanese perceptions. In any assessment of expectations, a crucial factor is where one is coming from as well as where one is going. A 1995 international Gallup poll found that the Japanese, like citizens in fourteen out of seventeen countries surveyed (but, interestingly, unlike people in the other three Asian countries included), are pessimistic about the future, in the sense that more of them believe that things will be worse for the next generation than believe that things will be better.[21] But among the trilateral countries, the Japanese public, with 58 percent believing that the next generation will be worse off, was less pessimistic than the public in Germany (70 percent), Canada (64 percent), the United Kingdom (63 percent), and the United States (60 percent).[22] Furthermore, when asked to compare the world today with the one their parents grew up in, the Japanese respondents were totally unlike their America counterparts (see Table 10-4). Even if the Japanese doubt greater prosperity in the future, their lives represent a vast improvement over the deprivation and hardship that their own parents experienced growing up—which is a perspective that relatively few Americans share. At any rate, the endemic nature of disaffection in Japan, which persisted and even rose during those years between the 1950s and 1980s when people saw major improvements in economic well-being, casts doubts on economic factors as central causes of political distrust.

Table 10-4. Public Perceptions of Today Compared with the Past: "How is the world you live in today compared to the world your parents grew up in?"

	Better	Worse	Same
Japan	60%	23%	13%
Germany	46	25	24
France	43	40	16
United Kingdom	36	45	9
Canada	35	46	16
United States	35	52	10

Source: International Gallup Poll conducted in April 1995 (in May in the case of France). "No opinion" responses are excluded.

"Video-legitimation" vs. Videocracy

Much recent work highlights the purported negative effects of the media and particularly of television on public trust.[23] As one of the planet's most media-saturated countries, which also has high distrust levels, Japan obviously invites study on this score. Japan's per capita newspaper circulation is the highest in the world, and more than twice the U.S. level.[24] Indeed, even in the 1960s, according to one major cross-national study, Japanese outstripped Americans as consumers of the media.[25] Today, one study shows, 59 percent of Japanese watch two or more hours of television a day, in contrast to 53 percent of Americans.[26] Furthermore, Japanese citizens, like people elsewhere, to a great extent get their political information from television rather than newspapers, despite the fact that Japan boasts five national dailies with huge circulation figures.

There is no obvious reason, however, to assume that the media operate in the same way in Japan, or with similar effects, as they do elsewhere. In contrast to the situation in a number of other countries, for example, newspapers are one of Japan's most trusted institutions, along with the police and prosecutors and hospitals (see Table 10-5). And while television is the particular target of many scholars today looking for sources of public disengagement and distrust, it can be argued that in Japan, newspapers have fostered their own kind of cynicism and public detachment from politics. In reaction to a prewar

Table 10-5. Trust in Institutions in Five Countries: "Among the following domestic organizations and public institutions, which is the most trustworthy?"

	Japan 1993	Japan 1995	United States	England	Germany	France
Prime Minister or President	9%	3%	29%	8%	17%	23%
National Congress	6	6	14	11	17	18
Police and Prosecutors	27	42	22	31	26	19
Courts	30	29	12	15	24	20
Military Forces	6	10	25	36	19	18
Churches or Temples	8	10	59	21	20	18
Central Government Offices	4	4	9	3	16	9
Local Government Offices	—	9	16	11	16	16
Schools	14	17	32	26	23	41
Hospitals	21	35	40	26	35	46
Newspapers	34	34	13	7	11	11
Television	15	16	12	12	9	7
Large Enterprises	2	2	7	5	6	8
Labor Unions	5	5	14	12	17	18
Nothing in Particular	25	14	16	26	29	14

Source: Yomiuri Shimbun, June 22, 1995. From Gallup and Yomiuri Joint Poll, May 1995. The Japan 1993 survey was conducted in September, after the July 1993 upset lower house election.

legacy of censorship and coerced support for state goals, the leading newspapers as a matter of policy do not endorse candidates and maintain a posture of strict neutrality in which they have seen themselves as more or less unrelenting critics of whatever government is in power. Thus partisan promotion of policies and leaders of a kind common in Europe—the kind that stirs strong allegiances to political parties and may mobilize readers to action—is largely absent in Japan, except in the mass-circulation Japan Communist party newspaper *Akahata (Red Flag)* and the mini media.[27]

Media effects on public trust await further study, but, based on research to date, they appear to be mixed. In a major study drawing on 1976 data, Scott Flanagan found that media exposure, among other things, had (1) increased citizens' political knowledge and their ability to translate information into informed choices at election time; (2) boosted their awareness of issues, their interest in politics, and the likelihood that they would discuss politics with others; (3) helped to open up party competition (and in that sense, worked against one-party dominance by the LDP); and (4) given a higher profile to both party leaders and national (vs. local) issues.[28]

Some recent observers similarly portray positive media effects, at least in the area of television coverage of political candidates. Because of legal constraints, television became a major force in political campaigning in Japan only in the election of 1993, wherein candidates seized the electronic loophole represented by TV talk shows and other soft-news programs to increase their visibility. Some argue that in a country in which much electioneering in the past and today has been based on personalistic networks, television—especially talk shows and debates—has given voters a new type of exposure to candidates that brings the public further into political life and increases their interest in politics.[29] If these accounts are correct, then the media, including television, would appear to promote greater political interest and engagement.

Other evidence raises doubts about this conclusion, however. As Ellis Krauss shows in a recent study, an inordinate amount of news coverage on NHK—Japan's public channel that, for most of the post-war era, has been the principal source of television news—portrays the state as both authoritative and distant. In contrast to American television coverage—which ignores bureaucracy and official pronouncements in favor of personalities, the input side of politics, and conflict—NHK news emphasizes the administrative state, and it is apt to portray the state as conflict manager.[30] One consequence is "video-legitimation";[31] but another, one could easily conclude, is to foster quiescence. In addition, Japan's press-club system, which binds print and broadcast journalists into close relations with their sources, and patterns of ownership in which the leading newspapers each have their own television station, constrain what gets reported. The result, some claim, is a "cartelization of information" that limits public discourse.[32]

Similarly, there are some signs, particularly in recent years, of problems much studied in other countries. Saturation television news coverage in Japan of bizarre events easily rivals its American counterparts; as one example, television coverage of a March 1995 sarin gas attack in the Tokyo subway, and of the subsequent hunt for the Aum Shinrikyo religious sect members responsible and the ultimate trial of the group's leader, ballooned into a soft-news drama and morality tale on a scale not unlike that of the O. J. Simpson trial in the United States. Between March 20 and mid-June 1995, over 500 hours of Aum coverage on television held viewers transfixed, pushing aside other social, political, and economic news.[33] Opinion journalism on television (in the Japanese case, particularly of anchor-entertainers in soft-news formats) is also on the rise, with the danger that it whips up public outrage and does little to foster the serious weighing of issues.

Precisely how the media today, and notably television, may be affecting ordinary people's trust in their leaders and government—and, indeed, their bonds with the community around them—is a topic that warrants much further research, and Japan presents itself as a leading arena. It is possible that, overall, Japan's newspapers and television (especially NHK) have fostered support for the administrative state and have thereby contributed—until recently—to public trust in bureaucracy but, at the same time, have aroused desires and expectations for a quality of political life that went unmet, thus fostering distrust of politicians and politics. Certainly any notion that television is the culprit behind postwar political malaise is highly suspect in the Japanese context. Heavy television viewing—of the three-plus-hours-daily variety—is less common in Japan today than it was twenty years ago (and less common than in the United States[34]); furthermore, distrust in politics significantly predates the spread of television. Still, for explaining why disaffection remains as high as it is today and why it has spread to new targets, television may be a part of the puzzle.

Conclusion

Obviously Japan does not hold all the answers for why disaffection is as widespread as it is among the industrial countries. But its experience and example should deter us from explanations that travel no farther than Washington's Beltway, and at the same time open up inviting avenues for exploration. A number of scholarly activities under way in Japan hold considerable promise for contributing to the debate.[35] High disaffection levels in Japan throughout that country's astonishing economic rise in the 1960s, and when national wealth began to trickle down to improve the lives of individuals in the 1970s, and in the boom years of much of the 1980s, should give pause to those who are quick to assume that economic malaise is the ultimate key to how people feel about politics and those who lead them. Lockheed in Japan, along with the surge of corruption scandals there beginning in the late 1980s, are reminders alongside Watergate of the potential importance of watershed events—boosted today in significance by saturation media coverage—in deepening or otherwise shaping public orientations toward politics for successor generations. Similarly, the persistence of disaffection and distrust of leaders over many decades casts doubts about the causal power of recent factors like the end of the cold war in explaining lack of confidence in government. For those who believe that "positive" news reporting alone might rebuild confidence in government, the coexistence of "video-legitimation" and political distrust in Japan is instructive. Meanwhile, given newspaper neutrality, coupled with the "cartelized" nature of traditional print and broadcast news coverage in Japan, the rise of soft-news formats and opinion journalism on television may be increasing political information and interest in ways that open up political life to citizens, even if the effects of videocracy on political distrust are not yet clear. Disaffection in Japan, a country far newer to democracy than most of its trilateral partners, challenges any notion that Western countries have a monopoly on postindustrial malaise. Sorting out both the common and distinctive features of public distrust in Japan and their sources should illuminate the larger inquiry.

Conclusion: Reflections, Conjectures, and Puzzles

Joseph S. Nye, Jr., and Philip D. Zelikow

Modern life is "everywhere complicated, but especially so in the United States, where immigration from many lands, rapid mobility within the country itself, the lack of established classes or castes to act as brakes on social changes, the tendency to seize upon new types of machines, rich natural resources and vast driving power, have hurried us dizzily from the days of the frontier into the whirl of modernisms which almost passes belief." This, at least, was one of the conclusions that the President's Committee on Social Trends arrived at after surveying American society for four years.

The committee further found that America needed to face up to the "outstanding problem" of comprehending "the interdependence of the factors of our complicated social structure," and coordinating them for a new era of national growth. The report shows more than a touch of nostalgia, as the President's Committee recalled the wartime period when the country saw "the rapidity and the success with which a people can recast its basic institutions at need."

The committee's comments reflect views that are widely held today. Indeed, they are as widely held today as they were when the report was issued, by President Herbert Hoover's committee, in 1933.[1]

The report expressed a profound unease widely shared by intellectuals and the general public alike: "The sense that a new society, turbulent, full of different sorts of people, problems, and ideas, had come into being was as widespread as the awareness that big business, consumerism, and new technology were creating a new economy. Regardless of their place on the ideological spectrum, thinkers and doers sought to cope with this overriding social reality."[2] In decades to follow, most Americans thought their government had adapted, more or less successfully, to the challenges of a new society. Large majorities told pollsters that, most or even all of the time, the federal government could be trusted to do what is right.

Large majorities of Americans do not say this anymore. New social upheavals have been accompanied by widespread discontent with the federal government. Many think government does too much; almost equal numbers think government is not doing enough.[3] Whatever government is doing, people are far less sure that it is right. Again, thinkers and doers try to cope. The scholars who have joined in this project and this book share an unease about the current circumstances of governance in the advanced industrial democracies. As the Introduction explains, this volume begins a larger research enterprise by examining the most obvious symptom of discontent—expressions of public distrust in and dissatisfaction with government.

Much of the evidence cited in the chapters comes from public opinion polls, but the project (and this volume) are not primarily about survey research. Surveys are just an instrument to observe a symptom of more complex public attitudes about governance that are, themselves, only part of a diagnosis for democratic governance as it adapts to the tasks of a new century. Unfortunately, there are few automatically generated measures of how people translate their attitudes into behavior, so we fall back on survey research as a first approximation. As noted in the Introduction, different questions produce different answers, and the context of a poll can affect even the most scientifically selected samples. Some polls ask about trust, some about confidence, and some about satisfaction.

Thus we are suspicious, for example, about the absolute levels of confidence that are reported. One of the most important surveys (the National Election Study) has long asked, "How much of the time do you think you can trust the government in Washington to do what is right—just about always, most of the time, or only some of the time?"

Neither of us would say that we trust the federal government to do the right thing "just about always." The response "some of the time," although commonly treated as an expression of relative distrust, is still consistent with confidence in government (and perhaps very high confidence in its performance of certain activities). For example, if "only some of the time" is added to "a great deal," then Congress and the executive branch of the federal government receive some approval from about 60 percent of the public.[4]

What cannot be dismissed, however, is the consistent and quite dramatic downward shift in answers to the *same* questions. Notwithstanding some oscillation in the early 1980s and in recent years, the trend has been apparent for three decades for most institutions in *all* polls of American opinion. It is replicated by the results of focus groups.[5] There is a similar downward trend in some other developed countries. Obviously, something is happening that is more than an artifact of polling questions or brief fads that affect the context of a few polls. Moreover, some behavior—such as voter turnout, party membership, and protests like the 1970s tax revolt or the current term limits movement—suggest that the issue of trust in government is also not merely a reflection of fads or sloppy polling.

This volume focuses mainly on the national government of the United States, although some attention has been paid—and will be paid here as well—to the situation in other countries. The book was structured in three parts. First we stepped back and examined some sets of existing conditions: the scope of government, its apparent performance by various measures, and the way this performance is being perceived by American citizens. That was Part One. Then, in Part Two, we reviewed some major explanations for these conditions—social, economic, and political. Finally, in Part Three we offered, for those who are interested, some deeper probes into the data that have been gathered about public attitudes toward governance in the United States, Europe, and Japan.

The chapters by Gary Orren and Robert Blendon et al. both offered a portrait of public attitudes. Satisfaction with government is not just a function of how government performs relative to the expectations that people have for it. It is a function of *perceived* performance. The federal government is the most distant from most citizens' daily experience. It is thus the most dependent on indirect perceptions mediated by the press and television.

Blendon and Orren's pictures of negative subjective attitudes contrast sharply with Derek Bok's description of objective performance. Bok explained how hard it is to find any truly objective, or neutral, way of evaluating government performance. Public opinion is inadequate for this purpose partly because public beliefs about performance are a product of shifting expectations and partly because large parts of the public are demonstrably ill-informed about many aspects of government performance. Program performance is hard to measure, especially in situations where the performance cannot be calibrated using meaningful numerical criteria.[6] Instead, Bok picked a set of policy areas and measures various indicators of American progress since 1960, then also compares these indicators with the parallel achievements of other advanced democracies that share broadly similar goals in these policy areas.

Using such measures, we can see that American government has moved ahead toward commonly shared goals in almost all policy areas. Judged by Bok's yardsticks, performance has not become demonstrably worse during the past fifteen to twenty years, having slowed in some areas but quickened in others. If he is correct, then the straightforward explanation that diminished confidence in government reflects diminished performance by government is wrong. In addition, such an explanation would not account for the simultaneous decline in confidence in other major institutions (unless one could demonstrate that all of them had also turned in worse performances).

At the same time, America's record is disappointing when compared with that of other advanced democracies. Comparing the level of achievement of more than sixty common objectives, the United States is below average in roughly two-thirds of the cases and at or near the bottom of the list in more than half. Where American performance lags behind that of other advanced democracies, government appears to be a key factor but more because of general policy choices and policy designs than because of inferior management by civil servants. Where money is wasted, it tends, again, to be the product of bad policies more than bad management. Because no extraneous factors exist that could account for America's meager performance, at least part of the explanation would appear to reside in the formation and implementation of our government policies and programs.

One way of accounting for this apparent contradiction between subjective opinion and objective performance is some historical perspective on the broadening scope of what government now tries to do. Ernest May reminded us that, traditionally, governments had vast authority over secular and spiritual life. For many centuries the limitations of power were more practical than philosophical. The era of limited government is relatively modern. Indeed, the powers of government have almost never been as limited as they were in the England of the late seventeenth and early eighteenth centuries, the very time at which the intellectual chromosomes of English governance were transferred so indelibly to the American colonies. These chromosomes figured in the genetic structure of the national government chartered by the U.S. Constitution and Bill of Rights.

May described renewed assertions of government power as reactions to the social and economic transformations associated with the first and second industrial revolutions. During the first, government gave new forms of support for private capitalists, assumed new responsibilities for public safety in the growing cities, and began providing comprehensive public education to train citizens and workers. During the second industrial revolution, government became the counterweight to the feared power of private capitalists, attempting to regulate and control their activities. Government also revived in new form its historic role in shaping national economies through more intensive preparations for war and assumed quite new roles in redistribution of income for social welfare and ambitious efforts to control the business cycle itself. The twentieth century witnessed efforts to come to terms with the expanded scope of government by cooperative relationships between government and private interests and, alternatively, control of private interests by government.

At the national level, the United States was slower to adopt the enlarged features of government power. Yet since the depression and World War II, America, too, strengthened the scope of central, federal power and took on large roles for shaping the national economy and providing social benefits.

Having conditioned readers to continuing ups, downs, and ups in the scope of governance, May invited us to consider the nature of the next phase. If a third industrial revolution is under way, with new transformations of culture and society related to information and accompanying technologies, then he wonders if governance must change in equally fundamental ways—as it did in the past. Recall the observations of thoughtful Americans early in the century, quoted at the beginning of this chapter, about the need to respond better to the new challenges they faced. May's argument hints at a possible linkage between public discontent and forms of government that are increasingly outmoded or ill-suited to the times. He called particular attention to a possible turn away from the modern emphasis on purely material well-being and back to older notions of government assertiveness in the moral or spiritual status of citizens. He also noticed, with others, the growing doubts about just how older notions of government sovereignty over national economies and regulation of capitalist activity will be reconciled with a more global organization of the world's commerce.

The next set of chapters explored possible causes for dissatisfaction. Robert Lawrence found that there has been a relative deterioration of economic performance in the advanced economies since the mid-1970s. While some economists argue that the decline is exaggerated by the difficulty in measuring long-term changes in productivity, Lawrence said that the deterioration is real and defies either good explanation or ready policy solution. In any event, there is a perceived decline in growth and productivity. Such a condition could well stimulate underlying dissatisfaction with government. But Lawrence pointed out that any simple economic hypothesis is undermined by two problems: (1) trust in government starts falling in the mid-1960s, while economic performance is still strong, and (2) trust in government falls among rich and poor citizens alike, with little correlation to their disparate economic experience. Given worsening trends in income distribution that have accompanied the information revolution over the past two decades, this is a striking finding. Confidence in government declines for winners and losers alike.

Jane Mansbridge canvassed hypotheses about the significance of broader changes in American society and culture. Social problems have grown, and she singled out the related phenomena of crime and more children in poverty (and the linked breakdown of the traditional family) as major sources of unease. Consistent with May, she noted how the expectations for government have risen. Governments have claimed and are now granted much responsibility for the state of the economy. Government is increasingly responsible for health care and for old-age pensions. Government has become a major agent of multiracial and multicultural assimilation. The ancient public duty of providing collective defense against external enemies seems less pressing in the advanced democracies. So demands for material security and public safety take precedence. These common expectations may not, however, be accompanied by strong norms for common behavior. Instead, Mansbridge illustrated the rising concern about a culture that, to some, seems centered on individual rights and material entitlements established and secured by the government.

Mansbridge distinguished between the way that changing social attitudes directly affect confidence in government and the way that social changes—by creating problems that make governance more difficult relative to rising expectations—indirectly affect that confidence. Like Orren, she stressed the importance of rising expectations, and observes that satisfaction often seems to derive not directly from performance but from the ratio of performance to expectations. She concluded that Robert Putnam's alleged decline in voluntary association membership is probably not sufficiently strong to be a major cause of declining trust in government. Nor is the decline in the nuclear family a direct cause of distrust in government except for those people who attribute this critical social trend to government involvement. At the same time, indirectly, the decline of the nuclear family creates problems related to education and crime that make those broadly accepted tasks of government more difficult. Mansbridge believes that many of the discontents with government arising from social change will not be resolved unless citizens are involved in institutions that make them weigh for themselves the complex trade-offs that are required.

David King concentrated on party politics as the mechanism that links society and its collective aspirations to the institutions of government. If the American public is having trouble defining what it wants to achieve collectively, it is hard to imagine how government institutions could perform well in delivering those desires. Alternatively, the distortion may reside in the party system. King argues that the parties have changed more than the electorate.

While Democrats still possess a slight majority in self-identification in the American electorate, the Republican position has greatly strengthened because of the collapse of the New Deal coalition and the shift of southern and some ethnic northern white voters to the Republican party. But measured by a series of issues, the national electorate has become only slightly more conservative regarding the appropriate scope of government. Asked every two years whether government should provide fewer services in order to reduce spending, about 20 percent favor cuts and 15 percent oppose them, with the rest in between. Americans simultaneously demand lower taxes and higher spending. The majority of the electorate, including self-identified independents, remains at the center of the spectrum on most issues, but party activists and the parties in Congress have shifted outward to the left and right. This more inflexible partisanship has reduced compromise and has been corrosive of institutions. Yet, and this is one of King's more significant observations, it is the party loyalists—Democrat and Republican—that have the greatest trust in government. The decline in trust can be linked to the declining role of parties as the mediating force between governments and citizens.

As King argues, the demise of the New Deal coalition, the shift of the South, the declining fidelity to party labels, and the rising partisanship in Congress "all point to a growing gap between the interests of political elites and the preferences of average Americans." That gap is not filled by third parties because our electoral system makes that difficult. Instead, the gap is being filled with cynicism and mistrust.

Richard Neustadt concentrated on the capacity of the political system to satisfy the needs of our changing society. He again brings in the historical perspective. Ominous forecasts are not new. Is there anything novel in the current situation? Perhaps. Playing variations on a theme suggested by Hugh Heclo, and consistent with King's findings, Neustadt singles out (1) the technological and marketing developments that have transformed the American electoral process; (2) the structural decline of traditional political institutions like the major parties; (3) the replacement of such older organizations with direct political participation by "movements" and single-interest groups of all kinds, which weakens the consensus-building role of mediating institutions like the parties; and, consistent with May and Mansbridge, (4) the seemingly universal claims of modern public policy (inevitably producing disappointment).

Neustadt balances this dispiriting analysis with the assurance that periods of sagging trust have existed before. He offers brief sketches of the hard times of 1938–39, the grumbling of 1946–47, and the gridlock of 1950–51. But these previous winters of discontent lasted for a season, not a generation. Anger was more narrowly focused on leaders rather than government as a whole. Now the discontent with government seems longer and deeper. To explain this, Neustadt invokes the factor of economic deterioration. He can explain the rise of dissatisfaction in the 1960s, as he associates this with a complex of events that fall under the loose heading of "Vietnam," but he guesses that, whatever its origins, the distrust persists thanks largely to the lasting economic sluggishness that Lawrence describes.

At this point, however, Neustadt's views diverge from Lawrence's observation that polls show that trust in government does not vary significantly among disparate demographic or income groups. Neustadt adds the observation that discontent may be most concentrated among a specific segment of anxious voters that might be called middle class or working class. Wealthier voters have always mistrusted government more, and their ideological preferences may have increasingly outweighed their pocketbook experience in the aftermath of Vietnam and Watergate. If so, this would be another instance of general perceptions outweighing personal experience. A further explanation is rising educational levels over three decades. Wealthier and better-educated voters may have become more sophisticated and skeptical over time. At this stage, however, there is no received wisdom, and the puzzle persists.

Government has earned public dissatisfaction, Neustadt argues, by promising to remedy these economic and social problems and then not being able to keep the promises. Again, expectations play a major role. Politicians, running scared, keep making the promises and yet are unable to fulfill them. They respond by attacking the government institutions they represent. The media may play an important role. It provides most of the political views that people hear, and the views have become increasingly negative over the past three decades. Though past experience cautions him against indulging in fateful predictions about American democracy, Neustadt—like the rest of our authors—finds ample cause for concern.

Although our primary focus is on America, we can learn from the attitudes of citizens in other advanced democracies of the industrial world. For instance, Susan Pharr's chapter on Japan showed that dissatisfaction with politicians has been high throughout the postwar period. Lately the discontent has expanded to include the once-venerated civil servants. At the same time, belief in democracy as a system of government remains strong in Japan, and has even gained strength. In this third dimension—confidence in democracy as a regime—the United States and Japan are similar. In expressing opinions about political leaders or institutions, Japan differs from the United States in the constant low confidence for leaders throughout the postwar period and in the more recent onset of mistrust in the bureaucracy.

The outstanding feature of the Japanese data on leaders seems to be its overwhelming and consistent quality. The only other advanced democracy that has exhibited such long-standing pronounced distrust for political leaders in the central government, by so many measures, is Italy. Interestingly, both countries emerged from postwar occupation and the onset of the cold war with central governments dominated for decades by a single political party. And the mistrust of leaders developed despite strong economic performances in both countries.

There are many reasons that Japan has taken its particular path of postwar political development, yet the results suggest a political hypothesis. The Japanese people may be so dissatisfied with their politicians because Japanese politics at the top (like Italian politics) has long been perceived to be deeply corrupt. Pharr documents the Japanese public's extraordinary constant disgust with the responsiveness and ethics of their legislators.[7] Orren shows that Americans also believe that their government and leaders have become more corrupt since the 1960s, but the situation in Japan (and Italy) has been far worse. An added challenge, for Japan, is to explain why mistrust has spread recently from political authorities to bureaucratic institutions. One major change in the 1990s was the prolonged recession in Japan. Perhaps economic unease, coupled with scandal, has contributed significantly to weakening respect for institutions that had previously received at least the credit for managing Japan's earlier economic success.

Ronald Inglehart's chapter looked at a wider range of countries that were surveyed in 1981 and 1990.[8] He argued that conditions of prosperity and security are conducive to "postmaterialist" values of individual autonomy and diminished deference to authority, but that this does not mean diminished political participation or alienation. It does mean less deference to established institutions in developed societies. Evidence from the World Values surveys in forty-three countries shows that peoples of low-income societies accept authority more readily than do citizens of advanced societies. Therefore the task of governing in rich countries may be more difficult, at least in some ways.

Western Europe presents a complex picture, and the survey questions have often differed from those asked in the United States. Aggregated ratings of satisfaction with "the way democracy is working" in European Union (EU) countries have tended to rise and fall with economic cycles. As Inglehart pointed out, in the recessions of the early 1970s and early 1980s, "dissatisfied" ratings became nearly as numerous as "satisfied" ratings, and in the recession of the early 1990s, for the first time negative ratings overtook the positive ones until 1994. Yet, if we go beyond Inglehart's data, we find that by 1994 an uneasy balance had returned. For the past few years Europeans in EU countries have been divided about equally between those who are satisfied with their governments and those who are not.[9]

An attempt to correlate the European declines in satisfaction with economic performance runs into the same sort of problem that Lawrence found with the American opinion data. Lawrence argued that economic explanations were weakened because there was so little variation by income group in American opinion about trust in government. European survey data also appear to reveal little variation in opinion about satisfaction with democracy in the respondents' country among income groups, except for somewhat lower satisfaction among the lower middle class.

Opinions within Europe also vary too much to allow for ready generalizations about the causes of the ups or downs. In a pair of polls about confidence in institutions in EU countries taken in 1981 and 1990, confidence in the armed forces, police, legal systems, parliaments, and the civil service declined overall. (The education system was the exception among public institutions.) Of the eleven countries with adequate data, confidence in government institutions declined in six (Norway, Sweden, Belgium, France, Italy, and Spain), was mixed in four (Germany, Ireland, Britain, and the Netherlands), and rose in Denmark. Private institutions showed a similar pattern, except for major companies, which showed a nine-point increase (from 41 percent to 50 percent).[10]

Denmark also stands out on the Eurobarometer questions about the working of democracy. Eighty-three percent of Danes were satisfied with the way democracy was working in their country in March 1996; only 11 percent of Italians shared the sentiment. Opinion in Western Europe thus presents useful puzzles. Some of the trends are similar to those in the United States, especially the decline in attachment to traditional political parties. This presents important opportunities for new insights if we can understand more about why some European countries and institutions have earned or held the satisfaction of their citizens better than others.

Problems of Explanation

The chapters in this volume suggest that the decline of confidence in government in the United States is a complex phenomenon touching economic, social, and political behavior. While it would be surprising if there were one simple explanation, we need to prune away as much of the undergrowth as we can so that we can identify the best trees to provide the lumber to build remedies. Without a better understanding of causation, some remedies will be feckless or even counterproductive. The Introduction surveyed a wide range of suggested causes and the prima facie evidence that has been adduced for them. In selecting which of the many hypotheses to prune away, we suggest five key criteria.

1. *Timing.* A good explanation should fit the onset and the persistence of the behavior. For example, the end of the cold war may have exacerbated the problem of mistrust by removing the external threat, but it fails to explain either the onset or the persistence of the behavior in the 1960s. The Vietnam and Watergate explanation fits very well with the onset. As Orren shows, the sharpest drop, 16 percent, occurs from 1972 to 1974. But these explanations fail to address the persistence and later variation. They need an auxiliary hypothesis to rescue them. Neustadt suggests one: the economic slowdown after 1974. But

alone, Vietnam and Watergate are not enough. Similarly, as Lawrence shows, a simple economic hypothesis that explains everything in terms of the slowdown and compression of wages also fails by a decade to explain the onset of the decline. As we will see, economics plays a role, but it is not a sufficient explanation, at least in its simple form.

Another auxiliary hypothesis that can be used to shore up the Vietnam/Watergate explanation is the argument that Vietnam destroyed the consensus called "cold war liberalism" that justified government in the 1950s and early 1960s. Brian Balogh argues that "the blistering critique of the war in Vietnam and its bipolar rationale leveled by all the social movements of the Sixties destroyed cold war liberalism's outspoken source of solidarity. Americans continue to search for it even today."[11] This would explain the persistence of mistrust long after the event, and possibly some of the revival during the early Reagan years.

2. *Other institutions.* A good explanation should tell us something about the decline in confidence in other institutions as well as government. Failure to notice the generality of the phenomena would be like explaining the rise in car prices by behavior in the automobile industry without noticing that a general inflation was raising all prices. Thus explanations that confidence in government has declined because of the growth of its scope or it its poor performance have prima facie plausibility, but they were not borne out by the opinion data that Blendon and King provide, nor by Bok's assessment of performance. But even if these assessments are mistaken, the scope and performance explanations are also suspect on more general grounds unless one can prove that other institutions suffering a similar decline have also outgrown their appropriate scope or suffered a severe decline in performance. In fact, however, antigovernment and antibusiness sentiment rose together from the 1950s to the 1980s, with business slightly worse in the first half and government slightly worse in the second half of the period.[12]

3. *The experience gap.* A good explanation should also address the gap between what people report as their personal experience and their general attitudes. Experience and attitude differ in a wide range of areas. Many people have no confidence in the public school system

but like their local school.[13] They distrust Congress but like their local representative. According to a study in the 1970s, when the sharpest declines occurred, "persons who had direct dealings with government agencies, both federal and state, were found to be satisfied with their 'bureaucratic encounters.' . . . Such judgments are in sharp contrast with general evaluations of government agencies."[14] Daniel Katz suggests that people organize their cognitions both at the pragmatic empirical level and at a more general ideological level. Thus many people report a gloomy view of the direction of the country even when they report that their personal circumstances are quite good. This interpretation might explain the striking anomaly that Lawrence reported: the absence of variation in views of government between those who have done well and those who have suffered economically. The well-off are making their general judgments on information other than personal experience. In this indirect way, the economic slowdown, wage compression, globalization, and the middle-class layoffs could affect general confidence in government.

How do people get their information about politics and government if not from personal experience? As Blendon et al. show, 72 percent say that they rely primarily on the media rather than friends or personal experience. While one must be careful of self-reported behavior, Seymour Lipset and William Schneider concluded in *The Confidence Gap* a decade ago that "confidence in institutions seems to be more a social than a personal judgment." The major source of information on the condition of the country is the mass media.[15] As Thomas Patterson and others have shown, and Orren argues in Chapter 3, the role of the media has changed over the same period as the decline in confidence in institutions—roughly since the 1960s. Both the press and television have become more intrusive, editorial, and negative in their reporting.[16] This would explain why close observers of Congress report that that body has become less venal over the past three decades while public perceptions of congressional venality have increased.[17] It would also explain why perceptions of increased crime in such communities as Levittown, New York, rose despite declining crime rates. Obviously, it is far too simple to blame the decline in confidence in institutions on the media alone. After all, confidence rose in the early Reagan period without the media changing their approach. But this point does suggest the importance of the media as an explanation for the experience gap in relation to a wide range of institutions, including government.

4. *Cross-national variation.* To the extent that what is happening in the United States is reflected in the experience of other countries, we should be suspicious of explanations that rely on American exceptionalism. If we are simply seeing a cycle of traditional American attitudes, why would it appear in other countries? After all, Japan has no Jeffersonian tradition. Although there is variation in attitudes toward government among the relatively affluent democracies and between developed and less-developed countries, there are some common trends across most of the developed democracies (such as declining attachment to traditional political parties). Some of these trends could be consistent, at a higher level of abstraction, with the social and cultural effects associated with a third industrial revolution. One could expect the United States, at the forefront of the information revolution, to show such effects somewhat earlier than other developed countries. A particular aspect of the information revolution is the technological transformation of communications, first in television broadcasting and lately in narrowcasting via cable and the Internet. The full implications are not yet understood, but the effects should show up and be subject to study in a cross-national context.

A similar cross-national explanation that bears closer examination is the secular decline in authority in wealthy societies, particularly its acceleration since the "youth revolutions" of the 1960s. To the extent that behavior is cross-national, this would lead us to rely more heavily on explanations that have transnational dimensions.

5. *Anomalies.* A social science truism is that one cannot explain variation with a constant. Good explanations should account not only for cross-national variation but also for anomalies among American institutions. One such anomaly that we noticed is the rise of confidence in the military even before its performance in the Gulf War. Some might explain this in terms of the military role in patriotic endeavors. But this is a constant. One explanation might be that the military as an institution, despite its large bureaucratic nature, adapted very successfully to troubling social problems such as illegal drug use or race in the 1970s. Another explanation, consistent with the media hypothesis, is that the military is one of the few parts of government

able to market itself through recruiting ads. This fits the timing of the end of the unpopular conscription system in the 1970s. Few other government agencies, except perhaps the post office, have been able to so consistently present positive advertisements about themselves over the past two decades.

Anomalies encourage humility.[18] They provide challenging tests of hypotheses. Moreover, they should also stimulate new research programs.

Looking over the seventeen or so hypotheses that started this project and are outlined in the Introduction, our five criteria have allowed us to discard or downgrade nearly half as powerful causal explanations. For the United States at least, the most promising survivors are enlarged, illusory expectations of what government can do (particularly for the World War II generation); the changed role of the media in shaping perceptions; the pervasiveness of more libertarian or postmaterialist values that question authority; and political processes that have created a gap between political elites and the general public.

The set of events we associate with Vietnam and Watergate played precipitating roles. The apparent failures of government in dealing with rising crime and family instability had an impact. Less directly, and often through the vicarious experience of media reports and perceptions, economic changes played a background role. At a higher level of abstraction, the onset of the transnational information revolution might also be important.

These causes are more than enough to *over*determine the results, unless the different factors affect one another. They probably do, and they can be combined into a variety of narratives, some more plausible than others. But not everything goes, as the rough judgments in Table 11-1 illustrate.

Combining Causes into a Single Explanation

Humility is the beginning of wisdom. At this point, we know too little to draw a single conclusion about what has happened to confidence in government (and other institutions) over the past three decades. Stories can be constructed out of a fusion of the more

Table 11-1. Initial Hypotheses about Decline in Confidence in Government

Hypothesis	Rating	Comment
1. Scope grown too fast (as measured by GDP).	Low	Scope increased from 3% to 20% but largest growth is in programs that are popular (Social Security, Medicare). Does not explain other institutions.
2. Scope grown too intrusive (measured by new subjects).	Low/Mixed	Divided views on cultural issues. Popularity of environment and safety regulation. 40% say "interfering too much." Does not explain other institutions.
3. Performance has weakened.	Low/Mixed	81% say "wasteful and inefficient," but Bok disputes net change; also does not explain decline in other institutions.
4. End of cold war.	Low	Largest decline is 1964–74.
5. Vietnam and Watergate.	Mixed	Fits with onset, but needs auxiliary hypothesis to explain persistence. May affect all institutions.
6. World War II effect.	High	1950s seems abnormally high. May affect all institutions.
7. Political realignment and polarization of elites.	High	Fits timing of onset. Explains growth of conservative coalition. Does not explain other institutions.
8. TV effects on politics (party decline, negative marketing).	High	Fits timing and persistence. Distancing of elites.
9. Changed role of media.	High	Fits timing of onset and persistence. Fits other institutions.

plausible hypotheses. We will sketch one that we think is plausible and may possibly prove valid. There may be other stories, or quite different ways of describing the factors we mention. All we can say is that, measured against our five criteria, this story is plausible.

Most complex social phenomena have multiple causes, and it would be surprising if this one did not. In combining explanations, it is often useful to see them in terms of chains of causation with some links in the chain being more proximate and others more remote from the events being explained. For instance, if one asks why the lights are on in a room, the precipitating cause would be that someone flicked the switch, an intermediate cause was that the room was wired and fitted with electric bulbs, and a deeper structural cause was the

Table 11-1. (continued)

Hypothesis	Rating	Comment
10. Increased corruption/ dishonesty.	Mixed/Low	Little evidence of increase, but perception grows and Vietnam, Watergate, and aftermath had effects.
11. General economic slowdown.	Mixed	Some variation with unemployment and inflation, but does not fit timing of onset.
12. Rising economic inequality.	Low	Does not show variation by winners and losers.
13. Globalization and loss of control.	Mixed	Affects general mood, but effects indirect and timing unclear.
14. Third Industrial Revolution.	High	Explains changes in the economy and communication, but direct causal links unclear. Fits other institutions and transnational.
15. Decline of social capital (measured by voluntary groups).	Low	Evidence in dispute; causal links to government unclear.
16. Decline of social capital (measured by family cohesion).	Mixed	Timing about right regarding onset and persistence, but causal link is somewhat indirect. Unclear relation to other institutions and countries.
17. Authority patterns and postmaterialist values, particularly since 1960s.	High	Fits all institutions and countries. Does not explain all variations.

discovery of electricity. We will use a similar device to order the explanations in our preferred story about decline of confidence in institutions since the 1960s.

The precipitating causes, at least in the United States, seem to have been the experiences of Vietnam and Watergate, which the polls show caused the two most dramatic drops in confidence in government. And these two events in which presidents deceived the public came after a period of perhaps abnormally high confidence in the first postwar decades. But why does the mistrust persist? It persists, in part, because some political sins of deception have become habits for politicians and are now a constant topic for media attention. But why did these corrosive developments also affect other institutions? Why do there seem to be some analogues in other countries? As a counterfactual exercise, one could ask if confidence would have declined even without Vietnam and Watergate. If by those terms we mean the particular historical events rather than a syndrome of social change (discussed later), then the answer is almost certainly yes. Because of the deeper causes, one would likely have a decline in confidence, albeit without such a sharp onset.

At the deep, structural level, two changes prepared the ground. One was the transformation in the economy that we have described as the third industrial revolution. As argued earlier, the process of creative destruction that accompanies major technological changes disrupts existing social patterns. This in turn creates anxiety and dissatisfaction in large parts of the public. This anxiety has been reinforced by the transnational dimensions of the change, the greater sensitivity of the economy and society to global effects, and the sense of loss of control. Some people benefit and some lose from these changes, but the sense of anxiety about change is experienced by nearly all. In terms of timing, the information revolution and the greater globalization of the economy accelerate in the 1960s and 1970s.

The second deep structural change is in social-cultural attitudes. As argued earlier, there has been a long-term secular change in the balance between the individual and the community that has been going on for centuries in Western culture. This trend toward the individual undercuts the authority of all institutions, not just government. This sociocultural trend accelerates in the United States with the youth revolutions of the 1960s, but it takes place in Europe and Japan as well. While protest against the Vietnam War played a large exacerbating role, the social dimensions went far beyond the antiwar movement. The changes began with civil rights and involved race, gender, family, and most institutions. Government was seen, for the first time, as a new arbiter of social relations, especially race relations and the role of families. Government intervention against racial discrimination, as well as government intervention in gender relations and widespread change in the laws governing divorces, made the federal government a lightning rod for social concerns from every point on the compass. In the words of Brian Balogh, "the centrifugal force of individual rights overpowered more abstract appeals to community. . . . Starting close to home with the authority of parents, college administrators, and local officials in the South, social movements challenged the legitimacy of virtually all forms of social hierarchy."[19]

Hugh Heclo likens the 1960s to earlier periods of moral fervor that have been called "Great Awakenings" in American history: "The Awakening of the Sixties created a central paradox. Institutional authority was challenged throughout American society at the same time as demands and expectations on government were multiplied. . . . Everyday Americans find their lives entangled in a regime of activist government and activist antigovernment politics that they can little understand, much less sense they are controlling."[20]

Of course, the movements of the 1960s were not just limited to the United States, but that is consistent with the broader trends outlined by Mansbridge and Inglehart, and it helps to explain the decline of confidence in other institutions besides government. When combined with the idea that confidence in government and other institutions was abnormally high in the first two decades after World War II, one might have expected a conflict with the long-term trend toward questioning authority just as earthquakes relieve tensions in slowly moving tectonic plates. The result, according to this account, was the moralistic movements, both left and right, after the mid 1960s.

Many blamed government for the upheaval in the traditional social order. Expectations of government performance always included public safety and the administration of justice. They have risen to include prosperity and various norms of social stability. Many Americans feel, with excellent cause, that public safety and the administration of justice have deteriorated sharply in the last generation. Families are also notably less stable than they were a generation ago, with far higher rates of divorce and births out of wedlock (a perception borne out by data about both white and black Americans and true of many other countries as well).

A September 1994 Gallup poll found that most Americans believed the changes in values that began in the 1960s had been bad for the country. Most Americans have heard or experienced distress about crime, family breakup, and disturbance in traditional relations between people of differing race and gender. Citizens no longer believe that government has credible policy answers to the challenges that bother them most.[21] Politicians hasten to agree. According to Robert Kuttner, "For the first time in a century, both parties are effectively committed to the proposition that major social and economic ills are beyond government's capacity to remedy."[22]

We see, then, how these deeper changes can be linked to more proximate, intermediate changes in American political processes. As described by Neustadt and King, the New Deal coalition collapsed in the 1960s with the defection of the South and parts of the ethnic urban electorate from the Democratic to the Republican party, the displacement of party organizations by movements and single-issue groups that weaken consensus-building, and the rise of marketing consultants. While the majority of the electorate remains at the center of the political spectrum, party activists and parties in Congress shifted to more inflexible partisanship that was corrosive of institutions and accentuated the gap between political elites and the electorate. Party elites (activists and those based in Washington) get stronger, but parties as organizations mobilizing and connecting with the public get weaker. The effects of television campaigning and the role of money in the political process increase the sense of distance between the citizens and the politicians. The "distancing effect" accentuates populist mistrust of political elites, and often for good cause. As a *New York Times* story reported about the 1996 senate race in New Jersey, "Both Mr. Zimmer and Mr. Torricelli say that they don't really have time to spend with voters. There are too many donor calls to make, too many breakfast shows to appear on, too many editorial boards to meet and too diffuse an electorate."[23]

Since the mid-1970s, negative advertising has increased, and more politicians have run against Washington. The result is the systematic "demarketing" of government and a political culture that fosters a popular belief in bad, disconnected government. Cynicism about government becomes the new conventional wisdom. Those who believed that "the government is pretty much run by a few big interests looking out for themselves" rather than for the benefit of all the people has risen from 29 percent in 1964 to 80 percent in 1992. Substitute the word "country" for "government" and you might capture a typical public attitude of 1896, not 1996. In 1896, though, big business was the villain.

Big business is still unpopular, yet the regulation of capitalism has become a marginal subject in contemporary American politics. Antitrust policy is now the arcane preserve of specialists. The Democratic party's current leaders, the Republican party's leaders, and Ross Perot all proclaim themselves as pro-business and extol the application of successful corporate management practices. The lively public debate about containing the power of corporations has become a lively debate about containing, devolving, or privatizing the activities of government agencies.

As government becomes so greatly magnified in the public mind, and as nationalism is muted as a force in public life throughout the developed democracies, sentiments of resentment or even alienation are more easily displaced from big business onto big government. This observation seems especially credible if we also consider (1) May's point that Americans have traditionally been wedded to local governance despite its faults and (2) the dispiriting nature both of federal money politics[24] and the representations of governance in the national media.

This raises the second major intermediate change in the political process since the 1960s—the more intrusive and negative coverage by the press, both print and television. As noted earlier, when people offer opinions about the federal government as a generic entity or about the general performance of Congress (as opposed to their U.S. representative), 72 percent say that they rely on the impressions they receive from the mass media. National media coverage offers largely negative portraits of governance, and these have become notably more negative during the last generation. Media coverage of the national government is now dominated by the opinions of journalists rather than the words from or substantive details about the subjects they are covering. In fact, Vietnam and Watergate (as well as commercial considerations as television news became "infotainment") helped to produce this change. Thomas Patterson has measured the change starting in the 1960s—not just in the United States but in several European countries as well.

An obvious rejoinder would be that the media do no more than hold up a mirror to the actual behavior of government officials. If people are unhappy with what they see, the press is not at fault. It is always a mistake to kill the messenger bringing bad news, but it is also important to ask if the messenger is reporting faithfully or having an independent distorting effect. While the media are holding up a mirror to political reality, some analysts have shown that their mirrors used since the 1960s are more often like those found in carnivals. The figures are recognizable, but they appear in strange, entertaining shapes.

It is also possible that the media are not a prime cause. The negative portrayals of conspiratorial government in films has also been corrosive. The media are merely supplying the public's demand for the type of news (and entertainment) that is reported. The political changes may have come first, and the media merely followed and exacerbated them. Kenneth Newton argues that the strongest media effects on politics seem to be in the early links in the chain of causality—those consisting of the framing and substance of news rather than the last links such as voting turnout, or governability. He notes, for example, that election turnout in Europe has not generally fallen over the decades since television has come into its own.[25] On the other hand, controlled experiments by Joseph Cappella and Kathleen Hall Jamieson directly implicate media framing of political news in activating, if not creating, cynicism about campaigns, policy, and governance: "We do not believe that the news media are the only or even the primary source of public cynicism about institutions. Yet our data show—in ways that could only be suggested by previous commentators—that the way in which the news media frame political events stimulates cynicism."[26]

Politicians bear part of the blame. Controlled experiments by Stephen Ansolabehere and Shanto Iyengar show that negative television ads are effective, and politicians are in a prisoners' dilemma regarding their use. The effect of negative ads is to increase cynicism and to depress turnout among independent voters in the middle of the political spectrum.[27] Whether changes in the political process or the nature of media coverage came first matters less than that the interaction of the two is mutually reinforcing. Changes in the electoral process, the increased role of television, and new trends in the way government is portrayed in the media and films have combined to produce a popular belief of bad government. Politicians recognize the culture, appeal to it, and thereby reinforce it. The culture produces a prevailing fashion in which confidence in government seems at odds with conventional wisdom, silly, and naive. This in turn affects how the news is reported and how the public expects the news to be reported—perhaps even how people respond to questions in polls. The few institutions to resist the fashion seem to be those that have their own independent anchors in popular culture, such as the armed forces and the post office.

The short form of this story is that historical events in the 1960s and early 1970s (Vietnam and Watergate) precipitated a drop in confidence in the U.S. government, but the effects (as well as the cross-national analogues) have been broader and long-lasting because of (1) long-term secular changes in sociocultural attitudes toward authority and traditional social order that came to a head in the 1960s; (2) profound economic changes caused by the information revolution and globalization; (3) changes in the political process that increased the distance between the political activists and the public; and (4) a more consistently negative approach by the press to government and other institutions. Together, these changes have reinforced a popular culture of bad government. How much each factor contributed is difficult to judge. Indeed, some factors no doubt cut in the opposite direction, without which trust in government might be even lower.

This narrative is not an apologia for the federal government. The culture of bad government has a firm base in real failures and real problems in the way our politicians now practice their trade. Yet these changes in the political process and the press help to explain how these problems can acquire a singular breadth and persistence in public attitudes, a cultural phenomenon with a distinctive momentum of its own.

But Does Mistrust Matter?

As we discussed in the Introduction, a certain level of mistrust of government is a long-standing and healthy feature of American life. We gave reasons to believe that too much trust may be a bad thing for our liberties, but too little may mean a government incapable of performing well the tasks that most people want government to do. What is the optimal level, and what has it been historically? If the recent decline of trust in American government is partly linked to the breakup of the New Deal coalition, which raised it higher than normal in the context of the depression and World War II, then we might be returning to the attitudes toward government that were prevalent earlier in the century. How did people think about government back then?

Reliable national surveys only begin in the 1930s, but historians tell us about earlier periods of discontent. One such period was at the end of the last century, as the second industrial revolution and the rise of big business transformed a decentralized agrarian nation into an urban industrial economy. In that context, Americans in the Progressive era turned to the federal government to balance the feared power of big business. At that time, Americans often had jaundiced views of state and local politicians—they considered them machine bosses or corrupt rascals in the service of one or another special interest. Such disdain for state legislatures and local governments helped to drive the original expansion of federal power. And dealignment from the traditional two-party system is also not a new phenomenon. The cause of "progressivism" and political reform fueled the most powerful third-party movement of this century, reaching its high points in the national elections of 1912 (with Theodore Roosevelt leading the Republican dissidents and "Bull Moose" progressives) and 1924 (with Robert LaFollette leading the Progressive party).

Yet we are not returning to the past. Today's government is much larger, and it makes much larger demands on the people. In the past, the three levels of American government did not oblige their citizens to hand over more than one-third of the country's gross domestic product (GDP). Any authorities that claim such resources need to possess a healthy degree of legitimacy just to contain the inevitable dissatisfaction.

Absent such legitimacy, citizens may begin to withdraw voluntary compliance with the system, including voluntary compliance with other laws, and thus set in motion the downward spiral of worsening performance and more withdrawal from collective action of all kinds. American government might come to resemble that of Italy, which has the lowest level (20 percent) of satisfaction with government of any European country. Despite the tax revolt of the 1970s, and discounting the actions of fringe groups, there is not yet notable evidence that such a downward spiral has begun, although political scientists have been writing about the coming "crisis of democracy" for more than twenty years.[28] As for the quality of democracy discussed in the Introduction and the dangers of moving from a deliberative to a "thin democracy," there are some changes in the political process described by Neustadt and King that raise concern, but Sidney Verba and his colleagues have shown that overall political participation (writing letters, going to meetings, staging protests, and so forth) remains more robust than voting behavior.[29] Confidence in democracy as a form of government seems to remain strong in the United States as well as in other advanced countries.

Why, then, should there be any concern? The honest answer is that we are uncomfortable with uncertainty about something that matters so much—the health of our institutions of democratic governance as we enter a new century. Perhaps the American system is going through an adaptive cycle akin to that experienced at the end of the last century. We are unsure.

For example, we do not know enough about the ways in which loss of trust in one aspect of governance may be transmitted to another. Modifying distinctions suggested long ago by David Easton, one can imagine five levels of common life of a people.[30] Most basic is the sense of national community—pride in being an American. There, measured by polls and migration data (such as the millions of foreign citizens who want to become Americans), the evidence shows little problem. The next most general level is the belief in democracy and the American constitutional system as a political regime. Here, too, there is little erosion of traditional support. Institutions are the third, intermediate level. At this level, however, we have found a marked decline in trust over the past three decades. The next level is the electoral process that connects politicians to the institutions in a democracy. At this fourth level, focus groups, polls, and voter turnout again show an erosion of public support. Finally, the fifth level is that of the particular leaders holding authority at a given moment. Polls show diminished confidence in leaders of nearly all major institutions.

We do not know just when or how loss of confidence at one level affects attitudes at another. In Japan, where leaders were unpopular for a long period, loss of confidence in the key bureaucratic institutions did not follow until four decades later, and confidence in democracy has grown stronger. We simply do not have enough evidence to answer these questions about American governance.

Perhaps, as some pessimists argue, we are on a long, slow slide away from the Madisonian deliberative democracy that was established two centuries ago. Can we envisage incremental changes that would restore a condition of equilibrium? Or are we on the brink of requirements for dramatic changes in governance, such as occurred in Europe, Japan, and America sixty to one hundred years ago as a response to the social and economic forces associated with the second industrial revolution?

Borrowing a metaphor suggested to us by Richard Zeckhauser, we feel a bit like doctors who have encountered a patient with an irregular heartbeat. We do not know if the problem is really threatening. We do not know if it will be self-correcting, will require medication, or will require more severe intervention. We do know that the symptom commands attention, and that we ought to investigate possible causes more before we prescribe a remedy.

There are two ways of replying to these uncertainties. *First we must develop a research agenda that reduces the unknowns.* We will never have complete answers to complex social phenomena, but we can reduce the uncertainties. This book has made progress in that direction, but we are acutely aware of how much remains undone.

- The first fruitful direction for further research is cross-national. To the extent that we find common behavior in other nations, we should place more emphasis on the transnational causes. Where we find differences, we should explore them so that we understand their causes. We need to do more to relate the work on Europe and Japan to that in the United States by asking common and more refined questions in our survey research.
- Second, we should conduct in-depth studies of the anomalous cases, for they are the best substitute we have for a laboratory when dealing with complex social behavior. Why has confidence gone up in Denmark when it has declined elsewhere? We need a careful study of how the military rose in confidence after the 1970s—one that goes beyond the speculations offered here. We need to understand the experience of comparable institutions like the police and the FBI. We need to look for other anomalies. How are some of the less well-known institutions such as the Federal Reserve system and the Securities and Exchange Commission and the Environmental Protection Agency regarded?
- Third, we need to explore patterns of confidence relating to nongovernmental institutions, both here and in other countries. Why did public confidence in business rise in Europe in the 1980s? What has happened to nonprofit organizations like the Red Cross here and abroad? What about scientific organizations? What patterns exist, and how do they lead us to refine our current view of causes?
- Fourth, we need to move from research on attitudes to more study of actual behavior. Is there evidence that distrust affects important

political behavior? What behavior should concern us? Voter turn-out has dampened in America, but the current decline is not at an all-time low. Other indicators of political participation have not shown a clear decline. Further work could examine other areas of collective behavior, such as voluntary payment of taxes or reliance on the legal system. Some especially interesting insights might emerge from the cross-national studies.

Second, we should examine the possibility that the increasing disability of government may leave countries unable to accomplish some vital public ends. To sustain such a contention, some outline must be offered of a public agenda that may place new and critical demands on our processes of governance and the levels of public support for them. That is one of the major tasks of this project. What will be the challenges of the twenty-first century, and what roles should government, private enterprise, and the nonprofit sector play in meeting them? Like commentators during the early part of this century, we can see indications that contemporary social changes may have outstripped some fundamental capacities of the current political system. As indicated in the Introduction, the information and biologi-cal revolutions and the globalization of the world economy are raising problems for our collective lives—problems that pose new tasks for governance, and possibly new relationships among the three sectors.

Again, readers may have their own list of challenges, or think we have exaggerated either the concerns or the opportunities for action. Our principal worry is that a system encumbered by profound public distrust and alienation will become so "sticky" (to borrow Neustadt's metaphor) that problems may become insoluble. Insolubility will not make the problems disappear. Instead, answers may be forced on us in a period of crisis, when choices can become frantic and the reme-dies can become more severe than we might wish. As Neustadt points out, cynicism and stickiness prevent innovation and implementation of responses. The public as a whole may suffer, but some interests may benefit from the absence of response. One's stand on immobilism may depend on where one sits.

In this sense, public dissatisfaction with government can matter a great deal. Yet in tackling policy problems, we can tackle them with forms of governance that may ease alienation rather than compound it. We have already referred to the third sector and to the new forms of devolved government. We can also, as May and Mansbridge mentioned, reevaluate the engagement of government in the realm of our values and ideals, not just of our pocketbooks.[31] Some changes may involve entirely new forms of participatory democracy; others may involve less direct political participation.

Responding to the first and second industrial revolutions, the answer of the developed democracies was: more government. That answer is now engulfed in a rising tide of public distrust and distance from institutions. Responding to the new challenges associated with a third revolution in commerce and society, our project must next focus on how to understand and give another answer: different governance.

Introduction: The Decline of Confidence in Government

1. *Washington Post*/Kaiser Family Foundation/Harvard University Survey Project, 1996; Harris Poll, 1996; Hart-Teeter Poll for the Council for Excellence in Government, reported in the *Washington Post,* March 24, 1997. See also Seymour Martin Lipset and William Schneider, *The Confidence Gap* (Baltimore: Johns Hopkins University Press, 1987).

2. Harris Poll, 1966–96. There are some exceptions. For example, confidence in science remains strong, and in Europe, confidence in business has risen.

3. Hans-Dieter Klingemann and Dieter Fuchs, eds., *Citizens and the State* (New York: Oxford University Press, 1995); Michael Adams and Mary Jane Lennon, "Canadians, Too, Fault Their Political Institutions and Leaders," *The Public Perspective* 3 (September–October 1992):19.

4. Susan Pharr, "Confidence in Government: Japan," paper prepared for the Visions of Governance for the Twenty-first Century conference, Bretton Woods, New Hampshire, July 29–August 2, 1996. See also Everett Carl Ladd and Karlyn H. Bowman, *Public Opinion in America and Japan* (Washington, D.C.: American Enterprise Institute, 1996).

5. Alice Rivlin, *Reviving the American Dream: The Economy, the States and the Federal Government* (Washington, D.C.: Brookings Institution, 1992), 50.

6. Klingemann and Fuchs, chapter 11.

7. Robert Samuelson, *The Good Life and Its Discontents: The American Dream in the Age of Enlightenment, 1945–1995* (New York: Times Books, 1995).

8. Thomas Patterson, *Out of Order* (New York: Vintage Books, 1993).

9. In a 1995 poll, one-third of adults under age thirty said they would consider a job in government service at some point in their career (Hart-Teeter Poll, 21). In 1945, 24 percent said they would like to see their son to go into politics (a subset, perhaps a less attractive subset, of the careers alluded to by the 1995 question); yet even this rose to 36 percent in 1965. See Robert Lane, "The Politics of Consensus in an Age of Affluence," *American Political Science Review* 59 (December 1965):894.

10. On deliberative democracy, see Amy Gutmann and Dennis Thompson, *Democracy and Disagreement* (Cambridge, Mass.: Harvard University Press, 1996); for evidence on political participation, see Sidney Verba, Kay Schlozman, and Henry Brady, *Voice and Equality: Voluntarism in American Politics* (Cambridge, Mass.: Harvard University Press, 1995).

11. Theda Skocpol, *Protecting Soldiers and Mothers: The Political Origins of Social Policy in the United States* (Cambridge, Mass.: Harvard University Press, 1992).

12. *Post*/Kaiser/Harvard Survey, 1996. The 1995 Hart-Teeter Poll concludes that "America has not given up on government, but rather wants better management. . . . [E]ven among conservatives, the proportion who believe it is inevitable that the federal government will be ineffective is just 28 percent" (18). As Republican pollster Frank Luntz concluded, "The American people are not ideologically anti-government. They do see a limited role for government that goes beyond defense and foreign policy to protecting the poor and elderly" (*The 1996 ARMPAC Communications Dictionary,* 7).

13. Hart and Teeter report that on a long list of items, a majority of Republicans and conservatives also believe that it is necessary for government to monitor business. Survey conducted for the Council for Excellence in Government, March 1995, 15.

14. Steven Rosenstone, *Forecasting Presidential Elections* (New Haven, Conn.: Yale University Press, 1983); Ray Fair, *Testing Macroeconometric Models* (Cambridge, Mass.: Harvard University Press, 1994).

15. See Michael Sandel, *Democracy's Discontent: America in Search of a Public Philosophy* (Cambridge, Mass.: Harvard University Press, 1995).

16. Derek Bok, *The State of the Nation* (Cambridge, Mass.: Harvard University Press, 1996).

17. Theodore Marmor, "The Politics of Medical Care Re-form in Mature Welfare States: Fact, Fiction and Faction," paper prepared for Four Country Conference on Health Care Reforms and Health Care Policies in the United States, Canada, Germany, and the Netherlands, Amsterdam, February 23–25, 1995. Robert Blendon et al., "Who Has the Best Health Care System? A Second Look," *Health Affairs* 14, no. 4 (Winter 1995); 220–30.

18. *Washington Post,* January 29, 1996. When asked to guess, people believe that foreign aid accounts for 26 percent of the federal budget. In fact, foreign aid accounts for less than 2 percent of the budget.

19. *Washington Post,* January 31, 1996.

20. Harris Poll, 1996.

21. Gallup Polls (1992 and 1993) for the Advisory Commission on Intergovernmental Relations.

22. *Post*/Kaiser/Harvard Survey, 1996.

23. Lane, *APSR,* 877.

24. Jeffrey G. Madrick, *The End of Affluence: The Causes and Consequences of America's Economic Dilemma* (New York: Random House, 1995).

25. Figures compiled by Bureau of Labor Statistics, reprinted in Jack Beatty, "What Election '96 Should Be About," *Atlantic Monthly,* May 1996, 115; Robert Lawrence, "The End of the American Dream?," paper prepared for the Visions of Governance for the Twenty-first Century conference, Bretton Woods, New Hampshire, July 29–August 2, 1996.

26. Robert Lawrence, "The End of the American Dream?" and George Borjas, "Economic Slowdown and Attitudes towards Government." Both papers prepared for the Visions of Governance for the Twenty-first Century conference, Bretton Woods, New Hampshire, July 29–August 2, 1996.

27. Joseph Alois Schumpeter, *Capitalism, Socialism, and Democracy* (New York: Harper & Brothers, 1942).

28. *The OECD Jobs Study: Facts, Analysis, Strategies* (Washington, D.C.: OECD Publications and Information Center, 1994), 9–12.

29. E. J. Dionne, *They Only Look Dead: Why Progressives Will Dominate the Next Political Era* (New York: Simon & Schuster, 1996).

30. Ken Newton points out that school, family, and work may provide more training in reciprocity and trust than organizations. "Social Capital and Democracy in Modern Europe," unpublished paper, 1996.

31. Robert D. Putnam, "Bowling Alone: America's Declining Social Capital," *Journal of Democracy* 6, no. 1 (January 1995): 65–78: Putnam, "The Strange Disappearance of Civic America," *The American Prospect,* no. 24 (Winter 1996): 34–48. See also Seymour Martin Lipset, *American Exceptionalism* (New York: W. W. Norton, 1996).

32. Verba, Schlozman, and Brady, *Voice and Equality.* Also, Everett Ladd, "The Data Just Don't Show Erosion of America's 'Social Capital,'" *The Public Perspective,* 7, no. 4 (June–July 1996).

33. Ronald Inglehart, "The Erosion of Institutional Authority and the Rise of Citizen Intervention in Politics," paper prepared for the Visions of Governance for the Twenty-first Century conference, Bretton Woods, New Hampshire, July 29–August 2, 1996.

34. Frederick Schauer, "Allocating the Costs of Rights," paper prepared for the Visions of Governance for the Twenty-first Century conference, Bretton Woods, New Hampshire, July 29–August 2, 1996.

35. William Mayer points out that as the 1960s began, American liberalism was still largely defined by its economic philosophy, but over the next two decades

it staked out social and cultural positions never envisioned by the New Deal. *The Changing American Mind: How and Why America Public Opinion Changed between 1960 and 1988* (Ann Arbor: University of Michigan Press, 1920), 322. See also Ben Wattenburg, *Values Matter Most* (New York: The Free Press, 1995); Daniel Yankelovich, "Restoring Public Trust," *Mother Jones,* November–December 1995, 29.

36. University of Michigan National Election Study (NES), 1958–92.

37. See, for example, Suzanne Garment, *Scandal: The Culture of Mistrust in American Politics* (New York: Doubleday, 1991).

38. See Walter Dean Burnham, "Dialectics of System Change in the USA: The 1990's Crisis as a Case Point, " paper delivered at the American Political Science Association, September 1996.

39. Patterson, *Out of Order.*

40. *Washington Post,* February 1, 1996.

41. See Peter F. Drucker, *Managing in a Time of Great Change* (New York: Truman, Tally/Dalton, 1995); James P. Pinkerton, *What Comes Next?* (New York: Hyperion, 1995).

Chapter 1, The Evolving Scope of Government

1. John Kenneth Galbraith, *The Culture of Contentment* (Boston: Houghton Mifflin, 1992), 27.

2. Reagan, quoted in Jacob Weisberg, *In Defense of Government: The Fall and Rise of Public Trust* (New York: Scribners, 1996), 43; Galbraith, 180.

3. Primarily in *The Human Condition,* 8th ed. (Chicago: University of Chicago Press, 1973).

4. Patricia Crone, *Pre-Industrial Societies* (Oxford: Basil Blackwell, 1989), 39–40.

5. *Leviathan,* ed. C. B. Macpherson (London: Penguin Books, 1985), 227.

6. See J. A. W. Gunn, *Politics and the Public Interest in the Seventeenth Century* (Toronto: University of Toronto Press, 1969).

7. "Of Seditions and Troubles," in *Essays or Counsels, Civil and Moral* (1625), in *The Oxford Authors: Francis Bacon,* ed. Brian Vickers (Oxford: Oxford University Press, 1996), 369.

8. Reprinted from the first edition of 1664 (Oxford: Basil Blackwell, 1928), the book had actually been written much earlier in the century by a Dutchman, but its publication and popularity came later.

9. Adam Smith, *An Inquiry into the Nature and Causes of the Wealth of Nations,* ed. R. H. Campbell, A. S. Skinner, and W. B. Todd, 2 vols. (New York: Oxford University Press, 1979), 2:626–27.

10. *Capital: A Critique of Political Economy,* trans. Samuel Moore and Edward Aveling (New York: The Modern Library, n.d.), 823.

11. Henry, Lord Brougham, *Historical Sketches of Statesmen Who Flourished in the Time of George III,* 2 vols. (Paris: Baudry's European Library, 1839), 1:22.

12. Smith, 2:687.

13. W. L. Burn, *The Age of Equipoise* (New York: W. W. Norton, 1964), 289.

14. Peggy Noonan, *What I Saw at the Revolution: A Political Life in the Reagan Era* (New York: Random House, 1990), 102.

15. Thomas McCraw, "How Did the First and Second Industrial Revolutions Affect the Nature of Governance?," paper prepared for the Visions of Governance for the Twenty-first Century conference, Bretton Woods, New Hampshire, July 29–August 2, 1996.

16. Jan de Vries, "The Industrial and the Industrious Revolution," *Journal of Economic History* 54, no. 2 (June 1994):249–66.

17. Theodore M. Porter, "Rigor and Practicality: Rival Ideas of Quantification in Nineteenth-Century Economics," in *Natural Images in Economic Thought: "Markets Read in Tooth and Claw,"* ed. Philip Mirowski (New York: Cambridge University Press, 1994), 128–70.

18. Peter Mathias, *The First Industrial Nation: An Economic History of Britain, 1700–1914,* 2d ed. (London: Methuen, 1983), 192–93.

19. Gellner in, among other works, *Nationalism* (Cambridge: Cambridge University Press, 1988). Pointing to the fact that nationalism was in evidence before industrialism, notably in Tudor England, Leah Greenfield argues that its primary impulse was rationalization of devotion to regimes not legitimized by divine right (*Nationalism* [Cambridge, Mass.: Harvard University Press, 1990]). See Eric Hobsbawm, *Nations and Nationalism since 1780: Programme, Myth, Reality* (New York: Cambridge University Press, 1990).

20. Mathias, 190.

21. William Letwin, "American Economic Policy," in *The Cambridge Economic History of Europe,* ed. M. M. Postan et al., vol. 8 of *The Industrial Economies,* eds. Peter Mathias and Sidney Pollard (Cambridge: Cambridge University Press, 1989), 641–90.

22. Oscar Handlin and Mary Flug Handlin, *Commonwealth, a Study of the Role*

of Government in the American Economy: Massachusetts, 1774–1861, rev. ed. (Cambridge, Mass.: Harvard University Press, 1969), 52.

23. See Louis Hartz, *Economic Policy and Democratic Thought: Pennsylvania, 1776–1860* (Cambridge, Mass.: Harvard University Press, 1948).

24. Handlin and Handlin, 192–93.

25. Handlin and Handlin, 203.

26. Orestes Brownson, quoted on p. 76 of Michael B. Katz, "Education and Inequality," in *Social History and Social Policy,* eds. David J. Rothman and Stanton Wheeler (New York: Academic Press, 1981), 57–102.

27. McCraw, "How Did the First and Second Industrial Revolutions Affect the Nature of Governance?"

28. Gordon A. Craig, *Germany, 1866–1945* (New York: Oxford University Press, 1978), 150ff.

29. Quoted on p. 87 of E. P. Hennock, "The Origins of British National Insurance and the German Precedent, 1880–1914," in *The Emergence of the Welfare State in Britain and Germany,* ed. W. J. Mommsen (London: Croom Helm, 1981), 84–106. See also Jürgen Tampke, "Bismarck's Social Legislation: A Genuine Breakthrough?," 71–83.

30. Marc Allan Eisner, *The State in the American Political Economy: Public Policy and the Evolution of State-Economy Relations* (Englewood Cliffs, N.J.: Prentice-Hall, 1995), 86. The estimate regarding gross investment comes from Sidney Ratner, James H. Soltow, and Richard Sylla, *The Evolution of the American Economy: Growth, Welfare, and Decision Making* (New York: Basic Books, 1979), 326–27.

31. See Handlin and Handlin, chapter 10.

32. James Leiby, *A History of Social Welfare and Social Work in the United States* (New York: Columbia University Press, 1978), 99.

33. F. M. Scherer and David Ross, *Industrial Market Structure and Economic Performance,* 3d ed. (Boston: Houghton Mifflin, 1990), 153–55.

34. See Dorothy M. Brown and Elizabeth McKeown, *The Poor Belong to Us: Catholic Charities and American Welfare* (Cambridge, Mass.: Harvard University Press, forthcoming).

35. See Theda Skocpol, *Protecting Soldiers and Mothers: The Political Origins of Social Policy in the United States* (Cambridge, Mass.: Harvard University Press, 1992).

36. Arthur M. Schlesinger, Jr., *The Crisis of the Old Order, 1919–1933* (Boston: Houghton Mifflin, 1957), 578.

37. Edward D. Berkowitz, "How to Think about the Welfare State," *Labor History* 32, no. 4 (Fall 1991):489–502. The quotation is from p. 497.

38. David Vogel, "The 'New' Social Regulation," in *Regulation in Perspective: Historical Essays,* ed. Thomas K. McCraw (Cambridge, Mass.: Harvard University Press, 1981), 155–85. The quotation is from p. 161.

39. Al Gore, "Toward Commonsense Government," *Jobs and Capital,* 5 (Winter 1996): 3–7.

40. Anne Markusen, Peter Hall, Scott Campbell, and Sabina Detrick, *The Rise of the Gunbelt: The Military Remapping of Industrial America* (New York: Oxford University Press, 1991), 3. The authors explain their title by writing, "In their general shape, superimposed on the map of America, these new military-industrial regions . . . resemble the belt around the hips of the solitary sheriff . . . in an old western movie. The southwestern states, Texas, and the Great Plains make up the holster; Florida represents the handcuffs . . . ; New England is the bullet clip" (3–4)

41. Philip G. Cerny, "The Dynamics of Financial Globalization: Technology, Market Structure, and Policy Response," *Policy Sciences* 27, no. 4, (1994):319–42. The quotation is from p. 329. Joseph Finkelstein, ed., *Windows on a New World: The Third Industrial Revolution* (New York: Greenwood Press, 1989), has chapters on microelectronics, new materials (such as ceramics, polymers, plastics, and semiconductors), lasers, biotechnology, biophysics, telecommunications, computerized manufacturing, and new management techniques.

42. See McCraw, ed., *Regulation in Perspective.*

43. Tocqueville, *Democracy in America* (The Henry Reeve text, corrected and edited by Phillips Bradley; 2 vols.; New York: Alfred A. Knopf, 1984), vol. 1, 316.

44. See Philip K. Hitti, *Islam: A Way of Life* (Minneapolis: University of Minnesota Press, 1970), and Mark Elvin, *The Pattern of the Chinese Past* (Stanford, Calif.: Stanford University Press, 1973).

45. Cerny, 320.

46. *Financial Times,* June 6, 1996, 12.

47. Simon Kuznets, *Modern Economic Growth: Rate, Structure, and Spread* (New Haven, Conn.: Yale University Press, 1966), 9.

48. See I. Bernard Cohen, "Newton and the Social Sciences, with Special Reference to Economics, or, the Case of the Missing Paradigm," in *Natural Images in Economic Thought,* 55–90.

49. See Weber, *The Protestant Ethic and the Spirit of Capitalism,* English translation (London: Allen & Unwin, 1930); *The Religion of China: Confucianism*

and Taoism, English translation (New York: The Free Press, 1951); for a recent interpretation, John P. Diggins, *Max Weber: Politics and the Spirit of Tragedy* (New York: Basic Books, 1996); Arendt, in Jürgen Habermas, *The Structural Transformation of the Public Sphere: An Inquiry into a Category of Bourgeois Society,* English translation (Cambridge, Mass.: MIT Press, 1991); and Craig Calhoun, ed., *Habermas and the Public Sphere* (Cambridge, Mass.: MIT Press, 1992).

50. Sen, most accessibly in *On Ethics and Economics* (Oxford: Basil Blackwell, 1987); Sandel, *Democracy's Discontents.* On the "communitarian" school with which Sandel is sometimes linked, see Robert Booth Fowler, *The Dance with Community: The Contemporary Debate in American Political Thought* (Lawrence: University Press of Kansas, 1991).

Chapter 2, Measuring the Performance of Government

1. In trying to evaluate the "performance of government," we need to distinguish carefully between appraising the performance of public officials and assessing the effectiveness of government policies and programs. The former is sometimes carried out by looking at particular programs, much as the General Accounting Office does, and trying to ascertain how effectively officials have performed in carrying out assigned tasks. But this is a much narrower undertaking than assessing the performance of the government as a whole, which requires us to study policies and programs and to decide how effective they have been in achieving broad social objectives. The success of policies and programs involves much more than the competence of public officials. For example, the record of health care policy in the United States is affected only slightly by the work of the Public Health Service; it represents the outcome of many forces—congressional decisions, judicial rulings, interest-group pressures, public opinion, and the ideas of experts, among others. Because this paper grows out of a broad review of governance in the United States, I have proceeded on the assumption that the focus should be primarily on the performance of government as a whole and not simply the work of its officials.

2. The conclusions that follow, together with supporting data, are set forth in detail in Derek Bok, *The State of the Nation* (Cambridge, Mass.: Harvard University Press, 1996).

Chapter 3, Fall from Grace:
The Public's Loss of Faith in Government

I am grateful to Kristin Bunce, Jeremy Mindich, Peter Schworm, and Mark Sedway for their help in preparing this chapter.

1. Of course, this is not a new complaint. In the early and late nineteenth century, perceptive observers who visited the United States pondered why Americans

rarely elected their most talented citizens to high public office. Alexis de Tocqueville, *Democracy in America* (1835), vol. 1 (New York: Vintage Books, 1945), 207–09; James Bryce, *The American Commonwealth*, (1888), vol. 1 (New York: Macmillan, 1910), 77–84.

2. Cited in Susan Tolchin, *The Angry American: How Voter Rage Is Changing the Nation* (Boulder, Colo.: Westview Press, 1996), 6.

3. On the substantial public support for (and more limited popular opposition to) Adolf Hitler's regime, see Detlev J. K. Peukert, *Inside Nazi Germany: Conformity, Opposition and Racism in Everyday Life* (New Haven, Conn.: Yale University Press, 1987).

4. Seymour Martin Lipset and William Schneider, *The Confidence Gap: Business, Labor, and Government in the Public Mind* (Baltimore: Johns Hopkins University Press, 1987), 27–29, 375–92; Stephen C. Craig, *Malevolent Leaders: Popular Discontent in America* (Boulder, Colo.: Westview Press, 1993), 49–50.

5. Jack Citrin, "Comment: The Political Relevance of Trust in Government," *American Political Science Review* 68 (1974):973–88.

6. Samuel P. Huntington, "Americans and Their Government," and Mickey Edwards, "Three Considerations Concerning the Scope of Government," both papers prepared for the Visions of Governance for the Twenty-first Century conference, Bretton Woods, New Hampshire, July 29–August 2, 1996. As one journalist recently put it, "Instead of seeing cynicism as a warning that the country is falling apart—or instead of denying the existence of the phenomenon altogether—we might begin viewing it as a permanent, but not disabling, feature of a mature democracy. Under this analysis, citizen discontent is something that America must learn to live with, much in the way that Europe has. In fact, in some cases, disenchantment can even be seen as a sign of health. . . . Cynicism may simply represent the nation's wrinkles and worry lines—not always attractive, but hardly life-threatening." Anthony Flint, "Has Democracy Gone Awry?," *Boston Globe Magazine*, October 20, 1996, 49.

7. Calvin Trillin, *Remembering Denny* (New York: Warner Books, 1993), 6.

8. Robert Lane, "The Politics of Consensus in an Age of Affluence," *American Political Science Review* 60 (1965):874–95.

9. Wendy Rahn shows that trust, confidence, and responsiveness are reciprocally related and tap similar underlying beliefs. Accordingly, I use the words "confidence" and "trust" interchangeably in this chapter. See Wendy M. Rahn and Virginia Chanley, "A Time Series Perspective on Americans' Views of Government and the Nation," paper prepared for the 1996 Annual Meeting of the American Political Science Association, San Francisco.

10. John R. Hibbing and Elizabeth Theiss-Morse, *Congress as Public Enemy* (New York: Cambridge University Press, 1995), 22–61.

11. See Frank J. Thompson, "Critical Challenges to State and Local Public Service," in *Revitalizing State and Local Public Service: Strengthening Performance, Accountability, and Citizen Confidence,* ed. Frank J. Thompson (San Francisco: Jossey-Bass Publishers, 1993), 10–14. The same pattern remains true in 1997. Peter D. Hart and Robert M. Teeter, "Findings from a Research Project about Attitudes Toward Government," unpublished for the Council for Excellence in Government, March 1997. Confidence in government is low for all levels, but especially for the federal government.

12. The three principal longitudinal monitorings of public attitudes in the United States toward nongovernmental institutions have been conducted by the Harris Poll (since 1966), the Gallup Poll (since 1973), and the General Social Survey of the National Opinion Research Center (since 1973). Compilations of these trends can be found in *The Gallup Poll,* vol. 61, no. 6, June 7, 1996, 1–4; *The Harris Poll,* no. 10, February 12, 1996, 1–5; and *The American Enterprise* 4, no. 6 (1993). An extensive analysis of this data appears in Lipset and Schneider, *The Confidence Gap,* esp. 41–96.

13. Trust in institutions has fallen in many of the advanced industrial countries of Europe, North America, and Asia. After reviewing the relevant data, Robert Putnam concluded that "the last two decades have witnessed a widespread increase in cynicism about politics and government and an equally widespread decline in confidence in political leaders, in established parties, and in government more generally" although "the onset and depth of this disillusionment vary from country to country." Robert D. Putnam, Jean-Claude Casanova, and Seizaburo Sato, "Introduction: Troubled Democracies," in *Revitalizing Trilateral Democracies: A Report to the Trilateral Commission,* unpublished manuscript, April–October 1995, 9.

14. Or, as one study that concentrated on the period from 1980 to 1988 concluded, "because the social characteristics of a population change very slowly, demographic variables cannot help explain sizable attitudinal shifts like those observed for trust." Arthur H. Miller and Stephen A. Borrelli, "Confidence in Government during the 1980's," *American Politics Quarterly* 19 (1991):154. The same basic pattern described in Table 3-1 applies to the intervening years between 1964 and 1994. See Lipset and Schneider, 97–125; Stephen C. Craig, ed., *Broken Contract: Changing Relationships between Americans and Their Government* (Boulder, Colo.: Westview Press, 1996), 51–54; and Miller and Borrelli, 153–56.

15. Robert E. Lane, *Political Life: Why and How People Get Involved in Politics* (New York: The Free Press, 1989), 164–66; Joel D. Aberbach, "Alienation and Political Behavior," *American Political Science Review* 63 (1969):86–99.

16. Richard Morin and Dan Balz, "Americans Losing Trust in Each Other and Institutions," *Washington Post,* January 28, 1996, A1, A6–A7.

17. Lipset and Schneider, 108–09; Craig, *Broken Contract,* 27–29; Citrin, 974.

18. Robert D. Putnam, "Tuning In, Tuning Out: The Strange Disappearance of Social Capital in America," *PS: Political Science and Politics* (December 1995):664–83. See Table 3-1 for an indication of the cross-generational decline in political trust.

19. The direct and indirect connections between social capital and political trust, including the dispute over whether the supply of social capital in the United States has declined or not, are discussed by Jane Mansbridge in Chapter 5. The relationship between personal economic circumstances and trust in government is, though modest, relatively consistent. People whose financial situation has worsened voice less trust in government, as do people who offer negative evaluations of the state of the economy as a whole. Lipset and Schneider, 63–65, 156–58; Craig, *Broken Contract,* 43–44; Jack Citrin and Donald Philip Green, "Presidential Leadership and the Resurgence of Trust in Government," *British Journal of Political Science* 16 (1986):438; Miller and Borrelli, 163–64. At the aggregate level, while it is clear that some decline in public confidence can be traced to adverse economic conditions, Robert Lawrence shows that such conditions are not a powerful explanation for changes in confidence over time (Chapter 4). Since 1964 levels of trust in government have not correlated strongly with trends in economic health. Political trust has declined when the economy was strong and growing, and increased during economic downturns.

20. Putnam, "Introduction: Troubled Democracies," 21.

21. V. O. Key, Jr., *The Responsible Electorate: Rationality in Presidential Voting, 1936–1960* (Cambridge, Mass.: Harvard University Press, 1966), and Donald E. Stokes, "Some Dynamic Elements of Contests for the Presidency," *American Political Science Review* 60 (1966):19–38.

22. Huntington, "Americans and their Government," 1. See also Samuel P. Huntington, *American Politics: The Promise of Disharmony* (Cambridge, Mass.: Harvard University Press, 1981), esp. 31–60; and James A. Morone, *The Democratic Wish: Popular Participation and the Limits of American Government* (New York: Basic Books, 1990). For a different interpretation of American political culture, see Aaron Wildovsky, "A World of Difference—the Public Philosophies and Political Behaviors of Rival American Cultures," in *The New American Political System,* 2d ed., ed. Anthony King (Washington, D.C.: American Enterprise Institute, 1990), 263–86.

23. Daniel Bell, *The Coming of Post-Industrial Society: A Venture in Social Forecasting* (New York: Basic Books, 1976); Ronald Inglehart, *Modernization and*

Postmodernization: Cultural, Economic and Political Change in 43 Societies (Princeton, N.J.: Princeton University Press, 1997).

24. Philip E. Converse, "The Concept of a Normal Vote," in *Elections and the Political Order,* eds. Angus Campbell, Philip E. Converse, Warren E. Miller, and Donald E. Stokes (New York: John Wiley & Sons, 1966), 9–39.

25. Bok finds that the United States has performed poorly relative to other industrial nations in health care, education, poverty, and crime. Few Americans are aware of such comparative shortfalls, however, and even fewer routinely rate their well-being against their European counterparts.

26. Thompson, 13.

27. Most Americans say government has not been particularly successful in reducing poverty, crime, and drug abuse (Hart and Teeter, "Findings," pp. 4–8). For one empirical confirmation of this at the local level, see Daniel Katz, Barbara A. Gutek, Robert L. Kahn, and Eugenia Barton, *Bureaucratic Encounters: A Pilot Study in the Evaluation of Government Services* (Ann Arbor, Mich.: Institute for Social Research, 1977), 117–32, 175–78, 186.

28. Key, *The Responsible Electorate;* Lipset and Schneider, 399; Craig, *Broken Contract,* 42.

29. Arthur H. Miller, "Political Issues and Trust in Government: 1964–1970," *American Political Science Review* 68 (1974):961–63.

30. Miller and Borrelli, 169.

31. Walter Bagehot, *The English Constitution* (1867; London: Fontana Press, 1993), 63–68.

32. Lipset and Schneider, 74–79.

33. Gordon S. Black and Benjamin D. Black, *The Politics of American Discontent: How a New Party Can Make America Work Again* (New York: John Wiley & Sons, 1994), 107.

34. This view was expressed in a national survey conducted by the *Washington Post,* the Henry J. Kaiser Family Foundation, and Harvard University in 1995. The respondents were asked, in an open-ended question, what was the main reason they did not trust the federal government. Another survey (conducted for the Council for Excellence in Government by Peter Hart and Robert Teeter) asked a national sample of Americans in 1997 why they thought public confidence in government had declined. The respondents mostly cited weaknesses in government leaders and politicians: public officials pursued their own self interests, failed to keep promises, were influenced by special interests, and had low ethical standards.

35. According to Suzanne Garment, "There is simply no persuasive evidence that the increase in scandal has taken place because of a corresponding rise in corrupt official behavior. Today's myriad scandals come in much larger part from the increased enthusiasm with which the political system now hunts evil in politics and the ever-growing efficiency with which our modern scandal production machine operates," (*Scandal: The Crisis of Mistrust in American Politics* [New York: Times Books, 1991], 6). See also Larry Sabato, *Feeding Frenzy: How Attack Journalism Has Transformed American Politics* (New York: The Free Press, 1991).

36. Hibbing and Theiss-Morse, 14, 47–49.

37. Jeffrey B. Abramson, F. Christopher Arterton, and Gary R. Orren, *The Electronic Commonwealth: The Impact of New Media Technologies on Democratic Politics* (New York: Basic Books, 1988).

38. Over the years I have argued, as summarized in this paragraph and the next, that "media effects" are often exaggerated because of our failure to distinguish between instances in which the media convey information about events and instances in which the media shape perceptions about those events by the nature of their coverage. William Mayer also develops this argument in *The Changing American Mind: How and Why American Public Opinion Changed between 1960 and 1988* (Ann Arbor: University of Michigan Press, 1992), 277–98, distinguishing between the "informational" and "packaging" effects of the media.

39. V. O. Key, Jr., *Public Opinion and American Democracy* (New York: Alfred A. Knopf, 1961), 552.

40. Key, *Public Opinion and American Democracy*, 537–38.

41. Stephen Ansolabehere and Shanto Iyengar, *Going Negative: How Political Advertisements Shrink and Polarize the Electorate* (New York: The Free Press, 1995). Acrimonious political dialogue feeds public cynicism, which in turn invites further acrimony because political leaders invariably craft messages that build on the public's predispositions.

42. Quoted in Alison Mitchell, "Battle Shifts to Character Issue as Clinton and Dole Ads Duel over Drug Abuse," *New York Times*, September 21, 1996, 8.

43. Key, *Public Opinion and American Democracy*, 391–96 (italics mine).

44. Over the past thirty years, newspaper readership has declined one-third, while the average American household now watches television more than seven hours a day. According to a recent Media Studies Center/Roper Survey, television remains the main source of news about the presidential campaign for 56 percent of Americans (only 17 percent get most of their information from newspapers, and 11 percent from radio). For a discussion of how the media, especially television,

have appropriated tasks once the exclusive preserve of political professionals, see Gary R. Orren and William G. Mayer, "The Press, Political Parties, and Public-Private Balance in Elections," in *The Parties Respond: Changes in the American Party System,* ed. L. Sandy Maisel (Boulder, Colo.: Westview Press, 1990), 204–24.

45. Lionel Trilling, *Beyond Culture: Essays on Literature and Learning* (New York: Viking Press, 1965), especially the preface.

46. Daniel C. Hallin, *The Uncensored War: The Media and Vietnam* (New York: Oxford University Press, 1986).

47. Thomas E. Patterson, *Out of Order* (New York: Alfred A. Knopf, 1993), 16–25, 201–204. Also, Thomas E. Patterson, "Bad News, Bad Governance," *The Annals of the American Academy of Political and Social Science* 546 (July 1996):97–108; Michael J. Robinson and Margaret Sheehan, *Over the Wire and on TV: CBS and UPI in Campaign '80* (New York: Russell Sage, 1983), 91–116.

48. For example, the length of an average sound bite of a presidential candidate's own words on television shrank from more than forty seconds in 1968 to less than ten seconds in 1988. Quotes or paraphrases of the candidates' own words also have been squeezed out of newspaper coverage, falling from an average of fourteen lines in 1960 to six lines in 1992. Daniel C. Hallin, "Sound-Bite News: Television Coverage of Elections, 1968–1988," *Journal of Communications* 42 (Spring 1992):5–24; Patterson, *Out of Order,* 75–77.

49. Robinson and Sheehan, *Over the Wire and on TV,* 3–9, 207–16, 222; Patterson, "Bad News, Bad Governance," 100–02; Patterson, *Out of Order,* 80–82; Paul Weaver, "Is Television News Biased?," *Public Interest* 27 (Winter 1972):57–74.

50. Quoted in Joanna Vecchiarelli Scott, "Hannah Arendt, Campaign Pundit," *New York Times,* July 27, 1996, sec. 1, p. 23 (italics mine).

51. Paul Weaver, "Captives of Melodrama," *New York Times Magazine,* August 29, 1976, 6–7.

52. From a letter dated August 13, 1728, in Charlotte Elisabeth Aisse, *Lettres de Mlle Aisse a Madame Calandrini* (Paris: Gerdes, 1846), 161.

53. Craig, *Broken Contract,* 27–43.

54. Robert J. Samuelson, *The Good Life and Its Discontents: The American Dream in the Age of Entitlement, 1945–1995* (New York: Times Books, 1995); Mary Ann Glendon, *Rights Talk: The Impoverishment of Political Discourse* (New York: The Free Press, 1991); and Jean Bethke Elshtain, *Democracy on Trial* (New York: Basic Books, 1995).

55. Michel J. Crozier, Samuel P. Huntington, and Joji Watanuki, *The Crisis of Democracy: Report on the Governability of Democracies to the Trilateral Commission* (New York: New York University Press, 1975).

56. From a speech at Lakeland Community College near Cleveland quoted in the *New York Times,* October 2, 1996, 16.

57. Quoted in Craig, *Broken Contract,* 15 (italics mine). Alan Ehrenhalt arrived at a similar conclusion in his analysis of the 1996 presidential election. The word that best described the mood of the 1996 electorate, in his view, was "sober." The public's expectations, in the sense of wants, remained high, and so they opposed the idea of shutting down or dismantling the government. Yet their expectations as anticipations were equally sober: they were "disinclined to listen to a lot of easy answers from either party's candidate." Alan Ehrenhalt, "The Voters Sober Up," *New York Times,* October 20, 1996, E15.

58. Quoted in Robin Toner, "Democrats' New Goal in Congress: Modesty," *New York Times,* June 28, 1996, A26.

59. David Rosenbaum, "Past Is No Guide to Stands Taken by Candidates," *New York Times,* September 8, 1996, 30; Robert Kuttner, "Clinton's Gutting of Government," *The Boston Globe,* September 9, 1996, A19; and "Mr. Clinton's Bridge," *New York Times,* August 31, 1996, 20.

60. From a speech at Boston's Pioneer Institute, quoted in *The Boston Globe,* August 4, 1995, 22.

61. Citrin and Green, esp. 438–50; Miller and Borrelli, esp. 166–68. The rise in citizen confidence during Ronald Reagan's first term is a particularly interesting anomaly as, contrary to popular memory, Reagan's popularity was quite low at the time. In fact, Reagan registered lower poll ratings than any postwar president in their first two years in office. Reagan's popularity improved between 1984 and 1986, yet the public's trust in government plummeted. This lack of harmony between presidential popularity and trust in government is not confined to the Reagan years. Since 1964, the correlation between presidential popularity and public trust has been surprisingly low and inconsistent. Political trust, it appears, reflects a more complex set of attitudes toward government than simply an evaluation of incumbent presidents. See Miller and Borrelli, 157–59.

62. On the partisan and ideological polarization of political elites that is out of synch with the views of most Americans see E.J. Dionne, Jr., *Why Americans Hate Politics* (New York: Simon and Schuster, 1991) and David King's Chapter 6 in this volume.

63. CNN/*USA Today*/Gallup polls, January 12–15, May 9–12, 1996; NBC/*Wall Street Journal* poll, June 20–25, 1996; and CBS/*New York Times* polls, May 31–June 3, October 27–29, 1996.

Chapter 4, Is It Really the Economy, Stupid?
I have benefitted considerably from discussion at the Bretton Woods conference on the Visions of Governance in the Twenty-First Century, July 29–August 2, 1996.

In addition I received very helpful comments from George Borjas, Jack Donahue, Richard Parker, Dani Rodrik, Raymond Vernon and Shirley Williams.

1. Michael K. Brown, "Remaking the Welfare State: A Comparative Perspective," in *Remaking the Welfare State,* ed. Michael K. Brown (Philadelphia: Temple University Press, 1988), 9.

2. Because of slow employment growth, between 1980 and 1995, output per working-age person in Europe has actually grown more slowly than in the United States. See *OECD Economic Outlook,* June 1996, 22.

3. George Borjas, "Economic Slowdown and Attitudes towards Government," paper prepared for the Visions of Governance in the Twenty-first Century conference, Bretton Woods, New Hampshire, July 29–August 2, 1996.

4. It appears that in the 1990s, however, this source of inequality has not continued. Indeed, the share of white-collar workers being laid off has increased.

5. Absent faster productivity growth, an economy can exceed its potential growth pace only by reducing unemployment. By 1996, however, according to most observers, (and, more importantly, the Federal Reserve Board), U.S. growth is constrained by a sluggishly expanding potential. Even if the economy actually has scope to reduce unemployment by another percentage point before inflation accelerates, this one-time gain leaves the long-run growth rate unaffected.

6. *OECD Economic Outlook,* December 1994, 27.

7. *OECD Economic Outlook,* December 1994, 27.

8. For a more complete analysis, see Robert Z. Lawrence, *Single World: Divided Nations? The Impact of International Trade on OECD Labor Market* (Washington, D.C.: OECD Development Center and Brookings Institution, 1996).

9. James Goldsmith, *The Trap* (New York: Carroll & Graf, 1993).

10. For further discussion, see Dani Rodrik, *Has International Integration Gone Too Far?* (Washington, D.C.: Institute for International Economics, 1997).

11. See Raymond Vernon, "International Economic Dimensions in the 'Declining Trust' Phenomenon," paper prepared for the Visions of Governance in the Twenty-first Century conference, Bretton Woods, New Hampshire, July 29–August 2, 1996.

12. Researchers generally assign a larger role to technology than to trade, but precise explanations are difficult because institutional factors (for instance, the decline in union power and deregulation), demographic factors (for example, changes in labor supply), and shifts in product demands add to the complexity of disentangling these effects.

13. According to Griliches, the share of "hard to measure" sectors increased from 51 percent of the economy in 1947 to 69 percent in 1990. See Zvi Griliches,

"Productivity, R&D and the Data Constraint," *American Economic Review* 84, no. 1 (1994): 1–23.

14. Robert Gordon, "Problems in the Measurement and Performance of Service-Sector Productivity in the United States," *NBER Working Paper,* no. 5519, 1996.

15. See the projections of growth in the Economic Report of the President over the 1980s.

16. Robert J. Samuelson, *The Good Life and Its Discontents* (New York: Times Books, 1995).

17. Fredrick Hu, "What Is Competition?" *Worldlink* (July–August 1996): 14–33.

18. Joel Slemrod, "What Do Cross-Country Studies Teach about Government Involvement, Prosperity, and Economic Growth?" *Brookings Papers on Economic Activity* 2 (1995):373–415.

19. See, for example, Douglas A. Hibbs, Jr., *The American Political Economy: Macroeconomics and Electoral Politics* (Cambridge, Mass.: Harvard University Press, 1987); Michael S. Lewis-Beck, *Economics and Elections: The Major Western Democracies* (Ann Arbor: University of Michigan Press, 1990).

20. See Peter Taylor-Gooby, "The Role of the State," in *British Social Attitudes: Special International Report,* ed. Roger Jowell, Sharon Witherspoon, and Brook Lindsay (England: Gower, 1989).

21. "Since . . . the 1930s, most Americans have said they favor a number of policies that fit together into a substantial, though bounded, welfare state: Social Security; certain kinds of help with jobs, education, income support, medical care and urban problems. . . . This configuration reflects a fundamental individualism . . . yet it also reflects a sense of social obligation, a strong commitment to government action in order to smooth capitalism's rough edges, to regulate its excesses, protect the helpless, and to provide a substantial degree of equal opportunity for all" (Benjamin I. Page and Robert Y. Shapiro, *The Rational Public: Fifty Years of Trends in Americans' Policy Preferences* [Chicago: University of Chicago Press, 1992] 118). Although differences do exist, these attitudes are shared in other advanced Western countries. According to Taylor-Gooby, "Public opinion . . . criticizes the failure of the system to provide more generously for some of its most vulnerable groups . . . [b]ut does not necessarily support the equalization of incomes or higher levels of benefits. Rather it wants more equal access to jobs and universal benefits" (51).

Chapter 5, Social and Cultural Causes of Dissatisfaction with U.S. Government

1. Tables 5-1 through 5-3 and Figure 5-1 prepared by Christopher Jencks for the Visions of Governance for the Twenty-first Century conference, Bretton Woods, New Hampshire, July 29–August 2, 1996.

2. Figure 3-1 in Chapter 3, "Trust in the Federal Government to do the Right Thing," shows the greatest drop in trust from 1964 to 1980, followed by a stable level of low trust, broken only by a small surge in the "Reagan years," 1984 to 1988. Similarly, Figure 8-1 in Chapter 8, "Public Confidence in Leaders of the Executive Branch and Congress," shows a drop in confidence from 1966 to 1978, with stability at a low level after that except for a small surge from 1982 to 1986.

3. Barbara Ehrenreich, *The Hearts of Men* (Garden City, N.Y.: Anchor Press, 1983).

4. Susan Thistle, "Women's Poverty and the Inadequacies of Current Social Welfare Policy: Consequences of Women's Move from Household to Waged Work," Working Paper #93–15, Institute for Policy Research, Northwestern University.

5. Christopher Jencks, "Who Gives to What?," in *The Nonprofit Sector: A Research Handbook,* ed. Walter Powell (New Haven, Conn.: Yale University Press, 1987).

6. Alan Altshuler, "The Decline of Family and Other Intense Communal Ties," paper prepared for the Visions of Governance for the Twenty-first Century conference, Bretton Woods, New Hampshire, July 29–August 2, 1996.

7. Altshuler, "The Decline of Family."

8. Herbert Jacob, *Silent Revolution: The Transformation of Divorce Law in the United States* (Chicago: University of Chicago Press, 1988).

9. Otis Dudley Duncan, David L. Featherman, and Beverly Duncan, *Socioeconomic Background and Achievement* (New York: Seminar Press, 1972); William H. Sewell, Robert M. Hauser, and Wendy C. Wolf, "Sex, Schooling, and Occupational Status," *American Journal of Sociology* 86, no. 3, (1980), 551–83.

10. It is useful not to describe this problem with statistics on the "percentage (or number) of children in poverty," because, at least in the United States, the increases these numbers suggest may be an artifact of faulty price indices (Jencks and Meyer, 1996).

11. Donald R. Kinder and D. Roderick Kiewiet, "Sociotropic Politics: The American Case," *British Journal of Political Science* 11 (1981):129–61.

12. Theodore R. Marmor, "The Politics of Medical Care Re-Form in Mature Welfare States: Fact, Fiction and Faction," paper prepared for the Visions of Governance for the Twenty-first Century conference, Bretton Woods, New Hampshire, July 29–August 2, 1996.

13. Rudolf Klein and Michael O'Higgins, "Defusing the Crisis of the Welfare State: A New Interpretation," in *Social Security: Beyond the Rhetoric of Crisis,* eds.

Theodore R. Marmor and Jerry L. Marshaw (Princeton, N.J.: Princeton University Press, 1988).

14. Robert J. Samuelson, *The Good Life and Its Discontents: The American Dream in the Age of Entitlement* (New York: Times Books, 1995).

15. Mary Ann Glendon, *Rights Talk: The Impoverishment of Political Discourse* (New York: The Free Press; Toronto: Collier MacMillan; New York: Maxwell MacMillan, 1991); Michael J. Sandel, *Liberalism and the Limits of Justice* (Cambridge: Cambridge University Press, 1996).

16. For the argument that supportive government policies reduce individual responsibility, see Alan Wolfe, *Whose Keeper? Social Science and Moral Obligation* (Berkeley, Calif.: University of California Press 1989). For a critique, see Jane Mansbridge, review of Wolfe, *Social Justice Research* 4 (1990):265–69.

17. Frederick Schauer, "Allocating the Cost of Rights," paper prepared for the Visions of Governance for the Twenty-first Century conference, Bretton Woods, New Hampshire, July 29–August 2, 1996.

18. Elinor Ostrom, Roger B. Parks, and Gordon P. Whitaker, *Patterns of Metropolitan Policing* (Cambridge, Mass.: Ballinger Publishing Co., 1978).

19. Altshuler, "The Decline of Family."

20. Robert D. Putnam, "Tuning In, Tuning Out: The Strange Disappearance of Social Capital in America," *PS: Political Science and Politics* 28, no. 4 (December 1995).

21. Theda Skocpol, "Unraveling from Above," *The American Prospect* 25 March–April 1996):24.

22. Putnam, "Tuning In, Tuning Out."

23. Skocpol, "Unraveling from Above," 22.

24. Everett C. Ladd, "The Data Just Don't Show Erosion of America's 'Social Capital,'" *The Public Perspective* (June–July 1996):5.

25. Sidney Verba, Kay Lehman Schlozman, and Henry E. Brady, *Voice and Equality: Civic Voluntarism in American Politics* (Cambridge, Mass.: Harvard University Press, 1995), 76 and 83.

26. Michael Schudson, "What if Civic Life Didn't Die?" *The American Prospect* 25 (March–April 1996):18.

27. Skocpol, "Unraveling from Above."

28. Steven J. Rosenstone and John Mark Hansen, *Mobilization, Participation, and Democracy in America* (New York: Macmillan, 1993).

29. Richard M. Valelly, "Couch-Potato Democracy," *The American Prospect* 25 (March–April 1996):26.

30. Pippa Norris, "Does Television Erode Social Capital? A Reply to Putnam," *PS: Political Science & Politics* 29, no. 3 (September 1996):3.

31. Paul Peterson, "Some Political Consequences of the End of the Cold War," paper prepared for the Visions of Governance for the Twenty-first Century conference, Bretton Woods, New Hampshire, July 29–August 2, 1996.

32. Eric M. Uslamer, "Democracy and Social Capital," in *Democracy and Trust,* ed. Mark E. Warren (forthcoming).

33. Tom Patterson, "News Professionals, Journalism, and Democracy," paper prepared for the Visions of Governance for the Twenty-first Century conference, Bretton Woods, New Hampshire, July 29–August 2, 1996.

34. Theda Skocpol, "Successful Policies in American Democracies," paper prepared for the Visions of Governance for the Twenty-first Century conference, Bretton Woods, New Hampshire, July 29–August 2, 1996.

35. Suzanne Garment, *Scandal: The Crisis of Mistrust in American Politics* (New York: Times Books, 1991).

36. Joseph P. Kalt, "Declining Social Capital or Decaying Social Contract?," paper prepared for the Visions of Governance for the Twenty-first Century Conference, Bretton Woods, New Hampshire, July 29–August 2, 1996.

37. Marmor, "The Politics of Medical Care Re-Form."

38. Jennifer Hochschild, *Facing Up to the American Dream: Race, Class, and the Soul of the Nation* (Princeton, N.J.: Princeton University Press, 1995).

39. Tom R. Tyler, *Why People Obey the Law* (New Haven, Conn.: Yale University Press, 1990); Margaret Levi, *Of Rule and Revenue* (Berkeley: University of California Press, 1988); and Margaret Levi, *Consent, Dissent and Patriotism,* (Cambridge: Cambridge University Press, 1997).

Chapter 6, The Polarization of American Parties and Mistrust of Government

1. "Clinton Promises to Govern from the Center," Reuter Wire Service, December 11, 1996.

2. Anthony Downs, *An Economic Theory of Democracy* (New York: Harper & Row, 1957).

3. Richard Darman, *Who's in Control: Polar Politics and the Sensible Center* (New York: Simon & Schuster, 1996). E. J. Dionne, Jr., *Why Americans Hate Politics* (New York: Simon & Schuster, 1991), chapter 13.

4. Beginning with their 1972 survey, the NES staff has asked Americans to place themselves on a seven-point ideological scale ranging from extremely liberal to extremely conservative (NES Cumulative Dataset, variable #803). Question: "We hear a lot of talk these days about liberals and conservatives. Here is [1972, 1974: "I'm going to show you"] a 7-point scale on which the political views that people might hold are arranged from extremely liberal to extremely conservative. Where would you place yourself on this scale, or haven't you thought much about this?" (seven-point scale shown to respondents.)

5. Another way of viewing Table 6-1 is by examining the ratio of self-identified conservatives to liberals, which stood at 1.44 in 1972, increased gradually over the next twenty years, and peaked at 2.57 in 1994. In 1972, with most of the Great Society initiatives in full operation and with President Nixon proposing liberal-sounding social programs, three out of five Americans leaned more to the conservative side than to the liberal side. By 1984, the ratio had grown to 1.61, and it was at 1.63 in 1990. This is *gradual* change in the ratio of self-identifying conservatives, but an upward trend is unmistakable, culminating in the 1994 figure. Ratios of self-identifying conservatives to liberals: 1972, 1.44; 1974, 1.24; 1976, 1.56; 1978, 1.35; 1980, 1.65; 1982, 1.80; 1984, 1.61; 1986, 1.67; 1988, 1.88; 1990, 1.63; 1992, 1.55; 1994, 2.57.

6. Hans-Dieter Klingemann, "Party Positions and Voter Orientations," in *Citizens and the State,* eds. Hans-Dieter Klingemann and Dieter Fuchs (New York: Oxford University Press, 1995), table 6.4.

7. Angus Campbell, Philip E. Converse, Warren E. Miller, and Donald E. Stokes, *The American Voter* (New York: John Wiley & Sons, 1960), chapter 9; Hans-Dieter Klingemann, "Measuring Ideological Conceptualizations," in *Political Action,* eds. Samuel H. Barnes, Max Kaase, et al. (Beverly Hills, Calif.: Sage, 1979).

8. The proposition that most Americans might hold stable issue positions (as opposed to stable partisan and ideological positions) was once hotly debated but has now been largely reserved in the favor of stability. In other words, it is unlikely that respondents are making up different answers year after year, and their opinions are likely based on assessments of relatively stable underlying preferences. John E. Jackson, "The Systematic Beliefs of the Mass Public: Estimating Policy Preferences with Survey Data," *Journal of Politics* 45 (1983):840–65; Jon Krosnick, "The Stability of Political Preferences," *American Journal of Political Science* 35 (1991):547–76. For an assessment of the apparent stability of opinions within a framework that allows voters to have few stable preferences, see John R. Zaller, *The Nature and Origins of Mass Opinion* (New York: Cambridge University Press, 1992).

9. As usual, respondents placed their opinions on a seven-point scale, with the three highest categories indicating a more conservative position.

10. Not all of the questions were asked in each of the years. For missing years, response estimates were made by a two-year moving average. For example, the abortion question was not asked in 1974. The 1972 and 1976 responses were both 11 percent, so for the purpose of establishing a trend line, the figure 11 percent was assumed for 1974 as well.

11. NES Cumulative Dataset, variable #829. Question: "Some people are afraid the government in Washington is getting too powerful for the good of the country and the individual person. Others feel that the government in Washington is not getting too strong. Do you have an opinion on this or not? [IF YES:] What is your feeling, do you think the government is getting too powerful or do you think the government is not getting too strong?"

12. The ratio of "too strong" to "not too strong" increased markedly in 1976 because of a change in the filtering question, which made it more acceptable for respondents to say that they do not have an opinion on the subject.

13. John E. Jackson and David C. King, "Public Goods, Private Interests, and Representation," *American Political Science Review* 83 (1989):1143–64.

14. "There is much concern about the rapid rise in medical and hospital costs. Some feel there should be a government insurance plan which would cover all medical and hospital expenses. Others feel that medical expenses should be paid by individuals, and through private insurance companies like Blue Cross. Where would you place yourself on this scale, or haven't you though much about this?" (NES Cumulative Dataset, variable #806). There was a minor 1984 change in question wording, which should not have affected the results.

15. NES Cumulative Dataset, variable #837. Question: "There has been some discussion about abortion during recent years. Which one of the opinions on this page best agrees with your view? You can just tell me the number of the opinion you choose. (1) Abortion should never be permitted [after 1980: "By law, abortion should never be permitted"]." Three other response options were given, and those options changed in 1982, so they are not comparable. Response option 1, however, was unchanged, giving us data to 1972.

16. NES Cumulative Dataset, variable #830.

17. M. Kent Jennings and Richard G. Niemi, *Generations and Politics: A Panel Study of Young Adults and Their Parents* (Princeton, N.J.: Princeton University Press, 1981); William Claggett, "Partisan Acquisition Versus Partisan Intensity," *American Journal of Political Science* 25 (1981):193–214.

18. Only the "pure independent" category is used in Table 6-2, and with good reason. Independent-leaning Democrats and independent-leaning Republicans are partisans, and there is good evidence that they behave like partisans. While

the percentage of independent leaners has grown over this period, I do not consider this to be good evidence of greatly weakening party loyalties. See William G. Mayer, "Changes in Mass Partisanship, 1946–1996," Annual Meeting of the American Political Science Association, September 1, 1996; Bruce E. Keith, David G. Magleby, Candice J. Nelson, Elizabeth Orr, Mark C. Westlye, and Raymond E. Wolfinger, *The Myth of the Independent Voter* (Berkeley: University of California Press, 1992).

19. V. O. Key, Jr., *Politics, Parties, and Pressure Groups* (New York: Thomas Y. Crowell, 1942). For an excellent overview of parties, organized in this tradition, see Paul Allen Beck, *Party Politics in America,* 8th ed. (New York: Longman, 1997).

20. James L. Gibson, Cornelius P. Cotter, John F. Bibby, and Robert J. Huckshorn, "Whither the Local Parties?" *American Journal of Political Science* 29 (1985):139–60; John F. Bibby, "Partisan Organizations," Annual Meeting of the American Political Science Association, September 1, 1996; David W. Rohde, "Electoral Forces, Political Agendas, and Partisanship in the House and Senate," in *The Postreform Congress,* ed. Roger H. Davidson (New York: St. Martin's Press, 1992).

21. All figures are derived from William Mayer, "Changes in Mass Partisanship, 1946–1996," table 6. Notice that the decreases described in the text are differences in percentages, not percentage changes. For example, presidential-congressional straight ticket voting decreased from 86 percent to 71 percent, a 15 point decline, or a decline of more than 17 percent.

22. The NES records whether respondents claim to have done any of the following six political activities: talk to others and try to influence them how to vote, attend political meetings, work for a party or candidate, wear a campaign button or use a bumper sticker, donate money, or write letters. Among the set of respondents who do five of these activities, 5.19 percent are political independents and 56.29 percent strong partisans. In the full sample, 11.12 percent are independents and 30.69 percent are strong partisans. So strong partisans are about twice as likely to be activists.

23. Sidney Verba, Kay Lehman Schlozman, and Henry E. Brady, *Voice and Equality: Civic Voluntarism in American Politics* (Cambridge, Mass.: Harvard University Press, 1995); Dalton, chapter 3.

24. John H. Aldrich, "A Downsian Spatial Model with Party Activism," *American Political Science Review* 77 (1983):974–90; John H. Aldrich, *Why Parties? The Origin and Transformation of Party Politics in America* (Chicago: University of Chicago Press, 1995), chapter 6; Robert S. Erikson, Gerald C. Wright, and John P. McIver, *Statehouse Democracy: Public Opinion and Policy in the American States* (New York: Cambridge University Press, 1993), chapter 5; Austin Ranney, "Rep-

resentativeness of Primary Electorates," *Midwest Journal of Political Science* 12 (1972):224–38.

25. James A. McCann, "Presidential Nomination Activists and Political Representation: A View from the Active Minority Studies," in *In Pursuit of the White House: How We Choose Our Presidential Nominees,* ed. William G. Mayer (Chatham, N.J.: Chatham House, 1996), 79, 80.

26. Herbert McClosky, "Consensus and Ideology in American Politics," *American Political Science Review* 58 (1964):361–82; Jeane J. Kirkpatrick, *The New Presidential Elite* (New York: Russell Sage, 1976); Nelson W. Polsby, *Consequences of Party Reform* (New York: Oxford University Press, 1983); Walter J. Stone and Alan I. Abromowitz, "Winning May Not Be Everything, but It's More Than We Thought," *American Political Science Review* 77 (1983):945–56; Warren E. Miller and Kent Jennings, *Parties in Transition* (New York: Russell Sage, 1986).

27. David W. Brady, Joseph Cooper, and Patricia A. Hurley, "The Decline of Party in the U.S. House of Representatives, 1887–1968," *Legislative Studies Quarterly* 4 (1979):381–407; Melissa P. Collie, "Electoral Patterns and Voting Alignments in the U.S. House, 1886–1986," *Legislative Studies Quarterly* 14 (1989):107–28.

28. Gary W. Cox and Mathew D. McCubbins, *Legislative Leviathan: Party Government in the House* (Berkeley: University of California Press, 1993); David W. Rohde, *Parties and Leaders in the Postreform House* (Chicago: University of Chicago Press, 1991).

29. For a similar observation, see Jon Bond and Richard Fleisher, "Why Has Party Conflict among Elites Increased if the Electorate Is Dealigning?" Annual Meeting of the Midwest Political Science Association, April 1996.

30. V. O. Key, Jr., *Southern Politics in States and Nation* (New York: Alfred A. Knopf, 1949); Nicol C. Rae, *Southern Democrats* (New York: Oxford University Press, 1994).

31. Edward G. Carmines and James A. Stimson, *Issue Evolution: Race and the Transformation of American Politics* (Princeton, N.J.: Princeton University Press, 1989), chapter 2.

32. Nicol C. Rae, "Intra-Party Conflict in an Evolving Electoral Order: American Party Factionalism, 1946–52 and 1990–96," Annual Meeting of the American Political Science Association, September 1, 1996.

33. Harold W. Stanley and Richard G. Niemi, "The Demise of the New Deal Coalition: Partisanship and Group Support, 1952–92," in *Democracy's Feast: Elections in America,* ed. Herbert F. Weisberg (Chatham, N.J.: Chatham House, 1995). Additional demographic data that are included in their analysis but are not present in Figure 6-3 include Catholic, Jewish, Female, Union Household, White Protestant Fundamentalist, Hispanic (non-Cuban), Born 1959–70, and Born 1943–58.

34. Dionne, *Why Americans Hate Politics,* 116.

35. William G. Mayer, *The Divided Democrats: Ideological Unity, Party Reform, and Presidential Elections* (Boulder, Colo.: Westview Press, 1996), chapter 4.

36. Nicol C. Rae, *The Decline and Fall of the Liberal Republicans: From 1952 to the Present* (New York: Oxford University Press, 1989); Mary C. Brennan, *Turning Right in the Sixties: The Conservative Capture of the GOP* (Chapel Hill: University of North Carolina Press, 1995).

37. Ironically, increased party competition in the South may have made the parties more extreme. When the Democratic party dominated the South, congressional and state-office primaries were essentially equivalent to general elections, and the position of the median *primary* voter was likely to be close to that of the media *general election* voter. This is because the primary electorate was more likely to draw participants from across the ideological and policy landscapes. Competitive two-party primaries may have changed this completely. Conservatives are less likely to vote in the Democratic primary than they used to be, so the expected difference between the median positions of primary and general-election voters have almost certainly increased over time. If this is true, then competitive two-party primaries are not unambiguously good institutions, although I am not comfortable calling for a return to one-party dominance.

38. Anthony Downs, *An Economic Theory of Democracy* (New York: Harper & Row, 1957).

39. NES Cumulative File, variable #801. This index is constructed from the thermometer score for liberals (V211) and the thermometer score for conservatives (V212). First, the value of V211 is subtracted from 97, and that difference is added to the value of V212. This sum is then divided by 2, and 0.5 is added to the result. Finally, the solution is truncated to obtain an integer value. These questions were not asked in 1978.

40. The "average Americans" category includes all respondents *including* strong partisans.

41. I have replicated the analysis for campaign activists, and the results are even more striking. To maximize the number of observations available for estimating the model later in this chapter, however, I am using the more modest figures from strong partisans.

42. It is interesting that the party positions are not equidistant from the average respondent. The Democrats are closer. Perhaps this is one of the reasons that the Democratic party has remained a majority in the electorate even though the average American is slightly more conservative than liberal.

43. Aldrich and McGinnis analyze an equilibrium with party activists in two parties and across multiple-issue dimensions. The equilibrium amounts to a "stopping

point" in polarization. See John H. Aldrich and Michael McGinnis, "A Model of Party Constraints on Optimal Candidate Positions," *Mathematical and Computer Modeling* 12 (1989):437–50.

44. Eric Uslaner makes an interesting argument that the decline in bipartisanship and civility in Congress reflects growing intemperance and activism society. Eric M. Uslaner, *The Decline of Comity in Congress* (Ann Arbor: University of Michigan Press, 1993).

45. It is well known that voters like their own Congress members better than they like the institution of Congress. Among scholars, this is usually attributed to incumbency advantages and self-promotion by reelection-oriented legislators. That must certainly be part of the story, but a natural inference from my thesis is that citizens show more respect for their own legislators because those politicians are, on average, going to be closer to the survey respondent's policy positions than to the median position in Congress. Thomas E. Mann, *Unsafe at Any Margin: Interpreting Congressional Elections* (Washington, D.C.: American Enterprise Institute, 1978).

46. The dependent variable is bimodal, with "0" corresponding to the two survey response categories associated with trust and "1" corresponding to the two categories associated with mistrust.

47. Warren E. Miller and J. Merrill Shanks, *The New American Voter* (Cambridge, Mass.: Harvard University Press, 1996), chapter 8; Morris P. Fiorina, *Retrospective Voting in American National Elections* (New Haven, Conn.: Yale University Press, 1981).

48. Morris Fiorina, *Divided Government,* 2d ed. (Boston: Allyn & Bacon, 1996), 77.

49. I ran a probit estimate of a model with the same independent variables shown in Table 6-3 and with an independent variable of self-professed ticket-splitting from the NES (n = 9,214). The critical independent variable was distance to the closest strong partisans, which was statistically significant at $p > 0.000$ with the expected sign. The propensity to split tickets was also related to partisan strength (strong partisans are much less likely to split tickets), race (whites are more likely to split tickets), and region (southern Democrats are much more likely to vote Republican than non–southern Democrats). I do not have a sense yet for how substantively significant the polarization findings are, but in this first form, these results are consistent with a story that split-ticket voting has increases *because* the parties have polarized.

50. Michael Alvarez and Matthew Schousen, "Policy Moderation or Conflicting Expectations: Testing the Intentional Models of Split Ticket Voting," *American Politics Quarterly* 21 (1993):410–38; Richard Born, "Split Ticket Voters, Divided

Government, and Fiorina's Policy-Balancing Model," *Legislative Studies Quarterly* 19 (1994):95–115.

Chapter 7, *The Politics of Mistrust*

1. Frederick Jackson Turner, "United States (History, 1890–1910)," *Encyclopaedia Britannica,* 11th ed., vol. 37 (New York, 1911), 735.

2. See the Harris Poll (No. 10), released February 12, 1996. "Confidence" may not mean quite the same thing as "trust" to questioners, respondents, or compilers of these data, or to readers of this note. Polls reek with subjectivity in such respects. But every measurement I find that sounds at all like "trust," at least to me, shows the precipitous decline to which I refer. Agreement that "You can trust government in Washington to do what is right" plunged from a high of 77 percent in 1964 to 19 percent in 1994. Agreement that "Government is run for the benefit of all people" fell from 64 percent in 1964 to 19 percent 30 years later. And disagreement that "Public officials don't care what people like me think" dropped from a high of 70 percent in Eisenhower's time and Kennedy's to 22 percent in Clinton's second year. These figures were yielded by Michigan Survey Research Center polls from National Election Study (Ann Arbor: University of Michigan, Center for Political Studies, indicated years).

3. This is an assertion, not a demonstrated fact, but it is widely shared among political observers with whom I have compared notes, except with respect to the West Coast. There, in California especially, with no comparable historical referent since World War II, the recession came later than elsewhere and was experienced as a consequence, primarily, of military base closings combined with downsizing at defense plants in the aftermath of the cold war—a reminder that our regions defy national generalizations, even a century after the close of the frontier and still more since the Civil War. However that may be, I can offer one suggestive shred of polling evidence, but only on a national basis. One election study from the Michigan Survey Research Center has asked in alternate years from 1984 through 1994 (omitting 1990), "Have economic policies of Federal Government made things better/worse?" Under "Made worse," responses for the five sequential years are: 22, 23, 23, 44, and 16 percent. Incidentally, for what it is worth, compare with note 18, regarding 1938.

4. For example, in July 1995, 62 percent of Americans favored a constitutional amendment to make flag burning illegal. See Gallup Poll No. 104456, July 1995.

5. See Hugh Heclo, "Presidential Power and Public Prestige," in *Presidential Power Revisited,* ed. Roger Porter (forthcoming).

6. See Gary C. Jacobson, *The Politics of Congressional Elections,* 3d ed. (New York: Harper Collins, 1992).

7. See, among others, James Fallows, *Breaking the News* (New York: Pantheon, 1996); Austen Ranney, "Broadcasting, Narrowcasting, and Politics," in *The New American Political System,* ed. Anthony King, 2d ed. (Washington, D.C.: American Enterprise Institute, 1990).

8. See, among others, Nelson Polsby, *Presidential Elections* (Chatham, N.J.: Chatham House, 1996); Ronald Radosh, *Divided They Fall: The Demise of the Democratic Party, 1964–1996* (New York: The Free Press, 1996).

9. The reference is to the Supreme Court holding in *Buckley et al.* v. *Valeo,* 424 US 1 (1976). Thereafter, any candidate could spend as much of his or her own money on his or her own campaign as desired, unless the candidate took public funds with an explicit limitation on private additions. Even the limitation leaves open the back door of the candidate's own "soft money"—a door that seems to widen with every judicial decision.

10. The Employment Act of 1946 did not commit the government to "full" employment, nor the president to a "Nation's Economic Budget," spelling out means and measures, as the Senate version had done, but only to "maximum employment, production, and purchasing power," and to an annual Economic Report, which was supposed to reconcile the three in an advisory way for Congress. See Stephen K. Bailey, *Congress Makes a Law* (New York: Columbia University Press, 1950). In the first generation after enactment, the distance between those two positions was not thought to be as great as practice has since made it.

11. In 1946–47 I was serving as staff assistant to the budget director, across the street from the White House. By 1950–51 I had crossed the street to serve as assistant to the special counsel to the president. In 1938–39, by contrast, I was merely in college on the West Coast, where the chief "movement," Townsend's aside, and an open-shop drive in Los Angeles, was the "Okie" migration to the Central Valley from the Dust Bowl of the southern Midwest. But I had lived in Washington during FDR's first term, when my father, a New Dealer, was at work there. He continued from the coast to visit his old friends there, among them Harry Hopkins, and passed his impressions on to me. Besides, after the war I spent much time with James H. Rowe, Jr., who took it upon himself to attend to my practical education. Tales from 1938–39 figured in Jim's curriculum. (He then had been a Roosevelt aide.)

12. In the spring of 1939, the closest Roosevelt came to open interventionism was to plead with Senate leaders for repeal of the Neutrality Act, so the British and the French could buy (and pay for) munitions from us when war broke out in Europe, as the administration thought almost inevitable after Hitler's seizure of Prague that March. This led to the famous rejoinder of Senator Borah of Idaho, a leading isolationist: "There's not going to be any war in Europe this year. . . . I have my own sources of information, which I regard as superior to the State

Department's." James MacGregor Burns, *Roosevelt: The Lion and the Fox* (New York: Harcourt Brace, 1956), 392. Borah won that round. There was no repeal until after war had actually commenced, and Poland had been destroyed, in September.

13. These are retrospective judgments. At the time, the president and his associates refused to take it tragically, with defense, not domestic measures, being already much in mind; southerners were likely to be helpful. Roosevelt's secretary of the interior, Harold Ickes, the Chicago Progressive, unabashedly liberal and interventionist, wrote in his diary under date of November 15, 1938, "The Republicans made very substantial gains, November 8, but I could not read in the results any conclusive repudiation of the President or of his policies. . . . When I saw him after he had come back from Hyde Park, he seemed not only well physically but cheerful in spirits. . . . Of course I hope that the President will more than ever follow the liberal course." Harold L. Ickes, *The Secret Diary* (New York: Simon & Schuster, 1954), 2:500. For an antidote, see Rexford Guy Tugwell's *The Democratic Roosevelt* (New York: Doubleday, 1957), 476–77.

While polls in this period are distinctly unreliable, FDR's Gallup approval rating just after the election was split three ways, in answer to the question, used for the first time, "In general, do you approve or disapprove of Franklin Roosevelt as President today?" Responses are reported as "Yes, a lot" 41 percent; "Yes, a little," 26 percent; and "No," 33 percent. (Interviewing dates November 16–21, 1938, Survey No. 138, Question 6c.) Compare this, if you can, with 60.4 percent "For" in August 1937 before the recession's onset (but after the court-packing fight). The Gallup question then was "Are you for Franklin Roosevelt or against him?" (Interviewing dates August 4–9, 1937, Survey No. 94, Question 10.) See also Note 18.

14. Estimates of unemployment varied widely. See Frances Fox Piven and Richard A. Cloward, *Regulating the Poor: The Functions of Public Welfare* (New York: Vintage Books, 1993), 109–110.

15. Dr. Francis E. Townsend, of Long Beach, California, began a campaign in early 1934 to give every person over age sixty some $200 a month of federal funds, provided that he or she would spend it, thus ending abject poverty among the aged and boosting national consumption (hence production) both at once. The Townsend movement swept California, and its national appeal was such as to encourage congressional action on the old-age insurance provisions of the Social Security Act passed in April 1935. Those provisions, which have since assumed the name of the whole act, proved immensely popular (although by Townsend's standard they were very conservative) and helped to take the political wind out of his sails in the course of the next years.

16. As a vehicle for isolationist sentiment and its promotion, America First was launched in the summer of 1940. The Japanese attack on Pearl Harbor fatally affected it after December 1941.

17. Landon, the Progressive Republican Governor of Kansas, ran an increasingly traditional campaign, in 1936, the more so as the difficulty of his situation grew more evident. (Roosevelt was to win a two-thirds vote, the largest popular majority known up to that time, carrying all states but Maine and Vermont.) Landon's attacks came to be Simon-pure, amateur, classical economics, on the order of Coolidge administration strictures, such as "The business of government is business." A threat was made to repeal the Social Security Act, lest "grass grow in the streets" with impairment of the work ethic. Whether the Kansan ever actually formulated Reagan's later slogan, "Government's the problem," I do not know, but the tenor of his campaign was consistent with it. Poor Landon. How else to attack Roosevelt that year as a necessarily partisan Republican?

18. Nothing in Gallup Polls for 1938 and 1939 resembles the polling questions and answers we have identified with "trust," or its lack, since the late 1950s. Interestingly, in 1938, at the height of the recession, answering the question "What is your explanation of the cause of the present recession?," 70 percent of respondents answered, "Business, natural economic trends, bad distribution of wealth, lingering effects of the [first] World War." Only 30 percent answered "Roosevelt and New Deal policies." How President Bush would love to have governed then! How much less had expectations changed since Herbert Hoover's time than we tend to recall from the 1990s, smushing the 1940s and 1930s together! By income, even "upper" only blamed Roosevelt by 42 percent, and "middle" by 31 percent, while "lower" blamed business by only 16 percent and other causes by 63 percent, leaving 21 percent for the New Deal. (Interviewing dates May 29–June 4, 1938, Survey No. 124B, Question 8.)

19. From the late 1930s to now, the Gallup Poll has periodically asked this question of a sample of Americans: "Do you approve or disapprove of the way the President is carrying out his duties (or doing his job)." Although sampling techniques and procedures were revised considerably after the debacle of 1948 (when Gallup stopped polling in October, being certain of a Dewey landslide), this long-conducted series by the same organization, perpetuating the same biases, if any, has the virtue of relative consistency. These and subsequent references to Truman's approval ratings are drawn from my *Presidential Power and the Modern Presidents* (New York: The Free Press, 1990), where the entire Gallup series on Truman is reproduced, pp. 327–28.

20. For more detail, see, among others, my aforementioned book, pp. 40–46.

21. For details on the two sessions of the 81st Congress, see my "Congress and the Fair Deal: A Legislative Balance Sheet," in *Public Policy* (Harvard University: Graduate School of Public Administration, 1954), 5:366–72.

22. See Stanley Kelley, *Professional Public Relations and Political Power* (Baltimore: Johns Hopkins University Press, 1966).

23. See, among others, Alonzo Hamby, *Man of the People: A Life of Harry S Truman* (New York: Oxford University Press, 1995).

24. Hamby, esp. 542–98. Regarding "trust" as distinct from a president's "approval," assuming the distinction can be drawn, a month after the 1950 congressional election and a week after the Chinese intervention in Korea, the Gallup Poll found that only half the respondents thought "Our government is doing a poor job of handling foreign policy in Asia." Twelve percent had no opinion. This was while American forces were in full retreat. In another question, 73 percent agreed that the defense budget should be doubled in the year ahead. There is, of course, a rally-'round-the-flag effect, with General MacArthur's forces in flight. Even so, however, compare with contemporary attitudes toward government and spending. (See Interviewing dates December 3–8, 1950, Survey No. 467K, Questions 17a and 11a.) In a third question, the same survey asked about "pet peeves": "What annoys you the most?" (Question 12). Thirteen percent answered "Government practices, policies, and personalities," as against 7 percent for the "war situation"; 20 percent for "inconsiderate, disagreeable persons"; and 13 percent again for "no particular peeves." At the start of the new year, incidentally, Mr. Truman's approval rating was 36 percent.

25. This is to flag, in one inadequate sentence, an immensely complex set of crisscrossing differences.

26. As indicated earlier and in notes 18, 19, and 24, the venting of anger on public objects, insofar as it occurred, seems to have been directed in 1937–38 mainly against the economy, with Roosevelt but a secondary target, whereas in my second and third winters Truman got almost all of it (together with certain associates whom I haven't mentioned for the sake of brevity). Partly, the difference is accounted for by the postwar assimilation, in effect, of the economy into expectations about government. Partly, the difference has to do with personalities and their holds on public affection. Truman was no Roosevelt in the public mind (if one can write of such a thing). Besides, in 1948, Truman had done unforgivable injury to Southern Democrats and Northern Republicans alike, having embraced the findings of his Civil Rights Commission and then gone on to win the presidential election, which the Republicans had thought was theirs by right. He then had gone to war on his own motion. Why mistrust the government with such a target handy? Anyway, our contemporary sort of mistrust seems not to have been in fashion, not anyway outside the South. For one thing Truman had not done, not in national terms: he had not appeared disingenuous. He had opened no credibility gap. He was called corrupt, abrupt, unthinking, little, petty, stupid, hip-shooting, too soft on Communists, too hard, and a traitor to the South and even to the nation. But so far as I can make out, he was never called a liar to the nation. The particular corrosive element that Johnson introduced with Vietnam and Nixon with Watergate—both for good reason as each man saw it,

but with dreadful side effects—entered neither Truman's campaign nor, I think, his mind.

27. The worrying changes include a lengthening of the average work week, as well as growing disparities of wages between skilled and unskilled workers, and also between workers and top managers. There are growing disparities, as well, of real income between the top two-fifths in income and all others, and the same with wealth, two-thirds of which is held in the wealthiest 10 percent of the population. Average real family income virtually ceased to increase after the abrupt decline of productivity in 1973, although it was sustained for a time by two-income households, with wives increasingly at work. Since 1979, however, household real income has stagnated for some two-thirds of families, despite working wives, lengthened hours, and other improvisations. Savings rates are minuscule by historical standards. See Economic Report of the President, February 1996. See also Lawrence's Chapter 4.

As for downsizing, it seems to be the neighborhood effect—somebody knowing someone—together with extensive television reportage and commentary that give job cuts their widespread impact, almost regardless of actual numbers.

28. The Reagan reductions in income tax, achieved with fanfare during the summer of 1981, were offset in a minor way by subsequent upward adjustments, and then in a very major way by the bipartisan Social Security reform of 1983. This raised payroll taxes on employees to the point of canceling out income tax reductions for middle-income taxpayers, while actually increasing the tax burden for those in lower brackets. Each state or federal increase in consumption taxes since has marginally increased their burden (although the Clinton income tax rise did not, falling almost all on higher incomes, while his extension of the Earned Income Tax Credit partly compensated at the bottom).

29. In his candid, vivid memoir, Richard Darman, Reagan's aide and Bush's budget director, spells out dilemmas, conflicts, and misreadings that beset President Bush in economic policy. See Richard Darman, *Who's in Control?* (New York: Simon & Schuster, 1996), esp. 191–298.

30. The reasons for this shift of policy are set forth in an extensive piece of investigative reporting by Elizabeth Drew, *On the Edge* (New York: Simon & Schuster, 1994), 57–87, 114–22, 261–72.

31. FDR actually made that brag in the course of the 1936 campaign, although he had cheerfully presided in his first term over rampant experimentation, programmatic contradictions, and shifting ideological thrusts. Rex Tugwell, the chief advocate of "planning" in the early Roosevelt "Brains Trust," writes about the actualities with affectionate irony. See Tugwell, esp. 293–341, 364–83.

32. See Anthony King, *Running Scared* (New York: The Free Press, 1997).

33. For an introduction to the historical and philosophical roots of mistrust for government in the English colonies on the east coast of North America, dating from the seventeenth and early eighteenth centuries, one cannot do better than begin with Don K. Price, *America's Unwritten Constitution* (Cambridge, Mass.: Harvard University Press, 1985). For subsequent developments see, among others, James S. Young, *The Washington Community, 1800–1828* (New York: Columbia University Press, 1966); Seymour Martin Lipset, *American Exceptionalism* (New York: W. W. Norton, 1996); Michael Sandel, *Democracy's Discontents* (Cambridge, Mass.: Harvard University Press, 1996); Jacob Weisberg, *In Defense of Government* (New York: Scribners, 1996); and, of course, two classics: Bryce's *American Commonwealth* (1888) and De Tocqueville's *Democracy in America* (1842).

34. See, among others, E. J. Dionne, Jr., *They Only Look Dead: Why Progressives Will Dominate the Next Political Era* (New York: Simon & Schuster, 1996).

Chapter 8, Changing Attitudes in America

1. *Washington Post*/Henry J. Kaiser Family Foundation/Harvard University Poll (Storrs, Conn.: Roper Center for Public Opinion Research, 1995).

2. The survey is one in a series to be conducted as part of the *Washington Post*/Kaiser Family Foundation/Harvard University Survey Project. The purpose of this initiative is to examine public knowledge, values, and beliefs on major issues and challenges facing our country—issues such as race, poverty, reducing the deficit, the role of government in our society, and our nation's obligations in the world.

3. Center for Political Studies, *American National Election Studies* (Ann Arbor, Mich.: Inter-University Consortium for Political and Social Research, 1958–90); Gallup Poll (Storrs, Conn.: Roper Center for Public Opinion Research, 1993).

4. Harris Poll (New York: Louis Harris and Associates, 1996).

5. *Washington Post*/Kaiser/Harvard, 1995.

6. *Washington Post*/Kaiser/Harvard, 1995. The survey also asked Americans how much confidence they had that a problem would actually be solved when the government in Washington decides to solve it. Fewer than four in ten said they had a lot (4 percent) or some (35 percent) confidence. Trust in the federal government to solve problems is highest among Jewish Americans (56 percent) and Democrats (49 percent). Trust on this measure is again quite low among Republicans (33 percent) and Limbaugh listeners (22 percent). Other groups who have little trust are Perot voters (29 percent) and those with household incomes of $50,000 to $75,000.

7. Gallup Poll (Storrs, Conn.: Roper Center for Public Opinion Research, 1936).

8. Roper/*Fortune* Poll (Storrs, Conn.: Roper Center for Public Opinion Research, 1939).

9. Respondents could select multiple reasons. "Is more likely to have effective solutions to problems" was chosen by 51 percent; "wastes less money because it is better managed" was also chosen by 51 percent, and "better reflects your own beliefs and values" was chosen by 49 percent of the respondents.

10. NBC News/*Wall Street Journal* Poll (Storrs, Conn.: Roper Center for Public Opinion Research, 1994, 1995).

11. CBS News/*New York Times* Poll (Storrs, Conn.: Roper Center for Public Opinion Research, 1996).

12. Harris Poll (New York: Louis Harris and Associates, 1996).

13. Seymour Martin Lipset and William G. Schneider, *The Confidence Gap: Business, Labor, and Government in the Political Mind* (New York: The Free Press, 1983).

14. Harris Poll (New York: Louis Harris and Associates, 1996).

15. Patterson, *Out of Order* (New York: Knopf, 1993), 246.

16. John Brehm and Wendy Rahn, "An Audit of the Deficit in Social Capital," unpublished paper, 1995.

17. Center for Political Studies, 1964, 1968. For results from the intervening years, see James Allan Davis and Tom W. Smith, *General Social Surveys, 1972–1996: Cumulative Codebook* (Chicago: National Opinion Research Center, 1996).

Chapter 9, Post Materialism Values and the Erosion of Institutional Authority

1. A similar trend appears in response to the question "Would you say that the government is pretty much run by a few big interests looking out for themselves, or that it is run for the benefit of all the people?" In 1964, only 29 percent said that the government was run by a few big interests. This figure rose sharply until 1980, declined during the 1980s and then reached an all-time high of 76 percent in 1994.

2. See Ronald Inglehart, *Culture Shift in Advanced Industrial Society* (Princeton, N.J.: Princeton University Press, 1990); Ronald Inglehart, *Modernization and Postmodernization: Cultural, Economic and Political Change in 43 Societies* (Princeton, N.J.: Princeton University Press, 1997).

3. Robert Rohrschneider, "Citizens' Attitudes toward Environmental Issues: Selfish or Selfless?" *Comparative Political Studies* 21 (1988):347–67.

4. Inglehart, 1990 and 1997; Sidney Verba, *Voice and Equality: Civic Voluntarism*

in American Politics (Cambridge, Mass.: Harvard University Press, 1995); Hans-Dieter Klingemann and Dieter Fuchs, eds., *Citizens and the State* (Oxford: Oxford University Press, 1995).

5. Seymour Martin Lipset, *Political Man* (New York: Doubleday, 1990); Ross E. Burkhart and Michael S. Lewis-Beck, "Comparative Democracy: The Economic Development Thesis," *American Political Science Review* 88, no. 4 (1994):903–10.

6. Inglehart 1990.

7. For a more detailed discussion of how to estimate the effects of population replacement on mass attitudes, see Paul R. Abramson and Ronald Inglehart, *Value Change in Global Perspective* (Ann Arbor: University of Michigan Press, 1995).

8. Inglehart 1997.

9. Confidence in many other national institutions also showed a similar pattern of (1) being correlated with materialist values and (2) declining over time. We do not analyze these attitudes here, however, as their correlation with postmaterialist values was relatively weak.

10. NORC surveys reported in *The American Enterprise* (November–December 1993):94–95.

11. Samuel Barnes et al., *Political Action* (Beverly Hills, Calif.: Sage, 1979), 548–49; Inglehart 1997.

12. See Barnes et al. 1979.

13. Inglehart 1990, 357–58.

14. Nie, Verba, and Petrocik 1979; Abramson 1979.

15. Inglehart 1997.

Chapter 10, Public Trust and Democracy in Japan

Portions of this chapter appeared in "Japanese Videocracy," *Press/Politics,* (2(1) 1997). I would like to thank Brad Richardson, Ikuo Kabashima, Ellis Krauss, Ron Inglehart, Dennis Patterson, Robert Putnam, and Shinji Asanuma for their help with data or for their comments; Paul Talcott for his able research assistance; Keiko Higuchi of the International House Library for assistance in securing Diet Library materials; and Yoshio Murakami, Mikinori Yoshida, and Koji Mori for providing access to *Asahi Shimbun*'s Data Archives.

1. Bradley M. Richardson, *The Political Culture of Japan* (Berkeley: University of California Press, 1974), 232.

2. Scott C. Flanagan, "The Genesis of Variant Political Cultures: Contemporary

Citizen Orientations in Japan, America, Britain and Italy," in *The Citizen and Politics: A Comparative Perspective* (Stamford, Conn.: Greylock, 1978), 156.

3. *Asahi*/Harris survey reported in *Asahi Shimbun,* May 11, 1989.

4. The new system has 300 single-member seats and 11 multimember constituencies returning 200 members to the lower house.

5. Tōru Hayano, Yasunori Sone, and Kenzō Uchida, *Dai seihen* [The Big Political Change] (Tokyo: Tōyō Keizai Shinpōsha, 1994), 152–68; "Japan's New Political Order," *Economist,* February 5–11, 1994, 27.

6. *Nihon Keizai Shimbun* [Japan Economic Journal], December 19, 1995, 1.

7. *Nihon Keizai Shimbun,* December 19, 1995, 1.

8. Junnosuke Masumi, *Contemporary Politics in Japan* (Berkeley: University of California Press, 1995), 255.

9. *Asahi Shimbun,* March 28, 1996, 3.

10. *Nihon Keizai Shimbun,* December 19, 1995, 1.

11. Joji Watanuki, *Politics in Postwar Japanese Society* (Tokyo: University of Tokyo Press, 1977), 69–72.

12. Bruce Cain, John Ferejohn, and Morris Fiorina, *The Vote: Constituency Service and Electoral Independence* (Cambridge, Mass.: Harvard University Press, 1987).

13. Bradley M. Richardson, *Japanese Democracy: Power, Coordination, and Performance* (New Haven, Conn.: Yale University Press, 1997).

14. *Japan Times Weekly,* June 10–16, 1996, 4.

15. Shinichi Yamamoto, *Akarui Senkyo Suishin no Tebiki* (Guide to Clean Elections) (Tokyo: Gyōsei, March 1995), 93. Data are from Akarui Senkyo Suishin Kyōkai (Clean Election League) national survey conducted in March 1987.

16. Michel Crozier, Samuel Huntington, and Joji Watanuki, *The Crisis of Democracy* (New York: New York University Press, 1975).

17. Karel van Wolferen, *The Enigma of Japanese Power* (New York: Alfred A. Knopf, 1989); James Fallows, *Looking at the Sun: The Rise of the New East Asian Economic and Political System* (New York: Pantheon Books, 1994).

18. Ikuo Kabashima, "Kiken no kenkyū" [Research on Rights], *Zashi Senkyo,* November 1987.

19. *A Bilingual Guide to the Japanese Economy* (Tokyo: NHK Overseas Broadcasting Department Economic Project and Daiwa Institute of Research, 1995), 229–33.

20. *A Bilingual Guide to the Japanese Economy,* 233.

21. The Asian countries included, other than Japan, were India, Taiwan, and Thailand; in the latter three, the optimistic responses exceeded the pessimistic ones. The remaining countries (other than those shown in Table 10-5), with the percentage of the public who said they thought the next generation would be worse off, were Spain (39 percent), Chile (50 percent), Dominican Republic (60 percent), Hungary (48 percent), Iceland (31 percent), Mexico (59 percent), Costa Rica (64 percent), and Venezuela (78 percent). International Gallup Poll conducted in April 1995.

22. International Gallup Poll, April 1995. France was 56 percent.

23. See, for example, Robert D. Putnam, "The Strange Disappearance of Civic America," in *The American Prospect,* no. 24 (Winter 1996); James Fallows, *Breaking the News: How the Media Undermine American Democracy* (New York: Pantheon Books, 1996).

24. The numbers are 587 per 1,000 vs. 249 per 1,000. See Everett C. Ladd, "Japan and America: The Two Nations Draw Closer," *The Public Perspective* 6, no. 5 (August–September 1995):21.

25. In the cross-national study conducted in Japan in 1966, 81 percent of the Japanese sample reported watching television or listening to the radio once a week or more, compared with 59 percent of the American sample, 36 percent of the U.K. sample, and 19 percent of the Italian sample. For newspapers, the figures were 64 percent (Japan), 50 percent (United States), 43 percent (United Kingdom), and 16 percent (Italy). For magazines, the figures were 29 percent (Japan), 24 percent (United States), 6 percent (United Kingdom), and 12 percent (Italy). Flanagan 1978, 147.

26. These figures are from a 1996 study by Ronald Inglehart, cited in Susan J. Pharr, "Japanese Videocracy," *Press/Politics* 2(1) 1997, 134. Heavy viewers (those who watch over three hours daily) are more numerous in the United States, however. See Note 34.

27. Susan J. Pharr, "Media and Politics in Japan," in *Media and Politics in Japan,* eds. Susan J. Pharr and Ellis S. Krauss (Honolulu: University Press of Hawaii, 1996), 3–17. The mini media consist of the books, magazines, newsletters, brochures, and so on of various nongovernmental organizations, including citizens' groups and movements.

28. Scott C. Flanagan, "Media Exposure and the Quality of Political Participation," in *Media and Politics in Japan,* 304.

29. Kristin Kyoko Altman, "Television and Political Turmoil: Japan's Summer of 1993," in *Media and Politics in Japan,* 165–86.

30. Ellis S. Krauss, "Portraying the State: NHK Television News and Politics," in *Media and Politics in Japan,* 116–21.

31. Krauss, 117.

32. Laurie Anne Freeman, "Ties That Bind: Press, State and Society in Contemporary Japan." Ph.D. diss., University of California Berkeley, 1995.

33. Helen Hardacre, "Aum Shinrikyo and the Japanese Media: The Pied Piper Meets the Lamb of God," Institute Report, East Asian Institute, Columbia University, November 1995, 4.

34. The data are from a study by Ronald Inglehart, cited in Susan J. Pharr, "Japanese Videocracy," *Press/Politics* 2(1) 1997, 134. According to the 1996 study, 26 percent of Americans watched more than three hours daily; the figure for Japanese was 24 percent.

35. Articles and papers by Ikuo Kabashima, Yoshiaki Kobayashi, Yasunori Sone, Aiji Tanaka, and Joji Watanuki are recent examples. A seven-wave Japan Election Study and other major surveys currently under way or in the planning stages, and involving all of these and other political scientists, social psychologists, and sociologists, are creating rich new data sources for scholars worldwide who are exploring sources of disaffection in comparative perspective.

Chapter 11, Reflections, Conjectures, and Puzzles

1. Quoted in Morton Keller, *Regulating a New Society: Public Policy and Social Change in America, 1900–1933* (Cambridge, Mass.: Harvard University Press, 1994), 8.

2. Keller, *Regulating a New Society,* 4.

3. In March 1993 49 percent of Americans polled by Gallup thought government should do more and 45 percent thought it was doing too much. In January 1996 the proportion had shifted, though, to 35 percent in the "do more" camp and 58 percent saying "too much." Michael Golay and Carl Rollyson, *Where America Stands 1996* (New York: John Wiley & Sons, 1996), 42.

4. General Social Survey, Spring 1994, National Opinion Research Center, Chicago. Congress received 58 percent and the executive branch received 63 percent. The survey prepared by Survey Research Consultants International is reprinted in *Index to International Public Opinion, 1994–1995,* eds. Elizabeth Hann Hastings and Philip K. Hastings (Westport, Conn.: Greenwood Press, 1996). Surveys about trust or confidence in other major institutions are subject to similar caveats. And questions most frequently asked in Europe refer to "satisfaction with the way democracy is working in your country," which creates a more positive context for responses than the way most poll questions have been phrased in the United

States. When Gallup asked the same question in the United States in 1995, 64 percent said that they were very or somewhat satisfied. Gallup Poll of eighteen countries, "Satisfaction Index," June 21, 1995, Survey No. 22-50001-018 in *The Gallup Poll, Public Opinion 1995* (Wilmington, Del.: Scholarly Research, 1996), 96. Differences in questions and context make us wary of international comparisons of absolute levels of confidence.

5. See, for example, *Citizens and Politics: A View from Main Street America* (Dayton, Ohio: Kettering Foundation, 1991).

6. After reflecting on the various outputs and outcomes of government labors, James Q. Wilson usefully distinguished between production, procedural, craft, and coping organizations; he also noted the unique constraints and sets of goals that thwart ready comparability between work in the private and public sectors. See Wilson's *Bureaucracy: What Government Agencies Do and Why They Do It* (New York: Basic Books, 1989), 158–75, 113–36.

7. To understand why, see, for instance, the dispassionate but detailed accounts in Junnosuke Masumi, *Contemporary Politics in Japan,* trans. Lonny Carlisle (Berkeley: University of California Press, 1995).

8. Inglehart often refers to World Values surveys that ask different questions in a different context from the surveys relied on in other chapters. So the absolute numbers he cites may not be directly comparable.

9. Asked whether they feel they can rely on their national government, 45 percent of the EU citizens polled say then can; 43 percent say they cannot; 12 percent do not know. These numbers are not alarming, but they are also not especially reassuring. The survey methodologies and reporting formats for the satisfaction question have changed twice in the last four years, but the results since 1994 have been reasonably consistent, and current sample sizes are the largest to date (about 800 in each member state), with monthly tracking surveys. On the question of general satisfaction, see European Commission, Europinion No. 1, *Monthly Monitor,* January–April 1994, April 1995. On the current numbers, see Europinion No. 8. The Eurobarometer now also asks whether people feel that they can rely on their national parliaments or national government. The numbers in the text are from the European Commission, Eurobarometer No. 44, April 1996 (surveys done during the last quarter of 1995).

10. Calculated from Table 10.1 in Ola Listhaug and Matti Wiberg, "Confidence in Political and Private Institutions," in *Citizens and the State,* eds. Hans-Dieter Klingemann and Dieter Fuchs (Oxford: Oxford University Press, 1995), 304, 305. Note that the questions asked were similar to the questions used in American surveys. Contrary to these data (and Inglehart's argument), some authors, including Listhaug and Wiberg (303), see no general trends.

11. Brian Balogh, "Introduction," *Journal of Policy History* 8 (1996):25.

12. Seymour Martin Lipset and William Schneider, *The Confidence Gap* (Baltimore: Johns Hopkins University Press, 1987), 32.

13. Tom Loveless, "The Structure of Public Confidence in Education," *American Journal of Education* 105, no. 112, (February 1997) p. 127.

14. Daniel Katz et al., *Bureaucratic Encounters: A Pilot Study in the Evaluation of Government Services* (Ann Arbor: Survey Research Center, University of Michigan, 1975), 178.

15. Lipset and Schneider, *The Confidence Gap,* 402.

16. Thomas Patterson, "News Professionals, Journalism, and Democracy," paper prepared for the Visions of Governance for the Twenty-first Century conference, Bretton Woods, New Hampshire, July 29–August 2, 1996. See also James Fallows, *Breaking the News* (New York: Pantheon Books, 1996).

17. See Dennis F. Thompson, *Ethics in Congress: From Individual to Institutional Corruption* (Washington, D.C.: Brookings Institution, 1995); Suzanne Garment, *Scandal: The Crisis of Mistrust in American Politics* (New York: Times Books, 1991).

18. Other anomalies exist, such as the continuing high status of science in the United States. Lipset and Schneider suggest that altruistic institutions may do better in holding public confidence, but this would not explain the experience of the churches or universities. The Supreme Court shows considerable oscillation but no marked decline in public opinion polls since the early 1970s. Business in Europe, but not in the United States, shows a rise since the 1970s, perhaps reflecting the impact of the end of communism in Europe.

19. Balogh, "Introduction," 14, 17.

20. Hugh Heclo, "The Sixties' False Dawn: Awakenings, Movements, and Postmodern Policy-Making," *Journal of Policy History* 8 (1996):50, 58.

21. Americans polled by the *Washington Post* in the summer of 1996 said that they were most worried about crime, the quality and cost of education, and various linked social maladies (AIDS, drug use, welfare dependency). Mario Brossard and Richard Morin, "What About Us?," *Washington Post National Weekly Edition,* September 23–29, 1996, 8–9.

22. Robert Kuttner, "Thinking Small," *Washington Post National Weekly Edition,* September 23–29, 1996, 5.

23. Neil MacFarquhar, "In New Jersey, Meeting the Voters Is a Luxury," *New York Times* (November 6), 1996, 1.

24. On this point, see especially Larry Sabato and Glenn Simpson, *Dirty Little Secrets: The Persistence of Corruption in American Politics* (New York: Times Books, 1996).

25. Kenneth Newton, "The Mass Media and Modern Government," Discussion Paper FS III 96–301, Wissenschaftszentrum Berlin.

26. Joseph N. Cappella and Kathleen Hall Jamieson, "News Frames, Political Cynicism, and Media Cynicism," *Annals* 546 (July 1996):84.

27. Stephen Ansolabehere and Shanto Iyengar, *Going Negative: How Political Advertisements Shrink and Polarize the Electorate* (New York: The Free Press, 1995).

28. For example, Michel Crozier, Samuel Huntington, and Joji Watanuki, *The Crisis of Democracy* (New York: New York University Press, 1975). In July 1979 President Jimmy Carter delivered a television address to the American people warning that their lack of confidence in governing institutions was a "fundamental threat to American democracy."

29. Sidney Verba, Kay Lehman Schlozman, and Henry E. Brady, *Voice and Equality: Voluntarism in American Politics* (Cambridge, Mass.: Harvard University Press, 1995).

30. David Easton distinguished between support for particular political authorities, for the institutions of a political regime, and for the political community or system as a whole. He called attention to the more serious implications of pervasive, persistent discontent that transcended any particular office-holder. David Easton, "A Reassessment of the Concept of Political Support," *British Journal of Political Science* 5 (1975): 435–57.

31. See also the interesting ideas about moral deliberation, grounded in practice, of Amy Gutmann and Dennis Thompson, *Democracy and Disagreement* (Cambridge, Mass.: Harvard University Press, 1996); Avishai Margalit, *The Decent Society,* trans. Naomi Goldblum (Cambridge, Mass.: Harvard University Press, 1995); Michael Sandel, *Democracy's Discontent: America in Search of a Public Philosophy* (Cambridge, Mass.: Harvard University Press, 1995); and Amartya Sen, *Inequality Reexamined* (Cambridge, Mass.: Harvard University Press, 1995).

Contributors

Robert J. Blendon is a professor of health policy and political analysis at the John F. Kennedy School of Government and the director of the Harvard Program on Public Opinion in Health/Social Policy. Other contributors to his chapter include John M. Benson (deputy director of the Harvard Program on Public Opinion in Health/Social Policy); Richard Morin (director of Polling) and Mario Brossard (assistant director of Polling) of the *Washington Post;* Drew E. Altman (president and CEO), Mollyann Brodie (senior researcher/director of Special Projects), and Matt James (vice president, Communications and Media Programs) for The Henry J. Kaiser Family Foundation.

Derek Bok is Harvard's 300th Anniversary University Professor. He has been a lawyer, professor of law, dean of the Harvard Law School, and president of Harvard University. His current research interest includes the state of higher education and the adequacy of U.S. government to cope with the nation's domestic problems.

Ronald Inglehart is a professor of political science at the University of Michigan and a program director at the Center for Political Studies. His ongoing research focuses on the consequences of cultural change through analysis of worldwide mass values and attitudes reflected in the World Values and Euro-Barometer surveys.

David C. King is an associate professor of public policy at the John F. Kennedy School of Government and the assistant director of the Visions of Governance for the Twenty-first Century Project. His first book, *Turf Wars,* explores how congressional committee jurisdictions adapt, or fail, to embrace emerging social problems.

Robert Z. Lawrence is the Albert L. Williams Professor of International Trade Investment at the John F. Kennedy School of Government. A research associate at the National Bureau of Economic Research, and a nonresident scholar at the Brookings Institution, his current research on trade policy focuses on America's role in the international market.

Jane Mansbridge is a professor of public policy at the John F. Kennedy School of Government. She is the author of *Beyond Adversary Democracy* and *Why We Lost the ERA,* and is currently researching the relationship between coercion and deliberation in democracy, and the public understanding of collective action problems.

Ernest R. May is the Charles Warren Professor of History at Harvard. He has been dean of Harvard College, director of the Institute of Politics, and chair of the Department of History. At the Kennedy School, he teaches courses on reasoning from history and he directs a research and teaching program on intelligence and policy.

Richard E. Neustadt is the Douglas Dillon Professor of Government, Emeritus, at Harvard. He was the first director of the Institute of Politics. Having served Presidents Truman, Kennedy, and Johnson in various roles, he is also the author of the classic *Presidential Power.*

Joseph S. Nye, Jr., is the Don K. Price Professor of Public Policy and dean at the John F. Kennedy School of Government. He returned to Harvard in 1995, after serving as assistant secretary of defense for international security affairs, and launched the Visions of Governance for the Twenty-first Century Project.

Gary R. Orren is a professor of public policy at the John F. Kennedy School of Government. A former political advisor, pollster, and opinion analyst, he currently teaches and writes on public opinion, electoral politics, the media, and the rights and duties of democratic citizenship.

Susan J. Pharr is the Edwin O. Reischauer Professor of Japanese Politics, director of the U.S.-Japan Relations Program, and the associate dean of the Faculty of Arts and Sciences. Her current work is a comparative study of political ethics and public trust in advanced industrial democracies.

Philip Zelikow is an associate professor of public policy at the John F. Kennedy School of Government and director of the Visions of Governance for the Twenty-first Century Project. His most recent book is the award-winning *Germany Unified and Europe Transformed: A Study in Statecraft.*

Index